W9-DBC-865

27049

F
1465.1
.P36
H56

DATE DUE

NOV 26 76			
NOV 22 1982			
OCT 24 '94			
NOV 14 '94			

DEMCO 38-297

PITT LATIN AMERICAN SERIES

PITT LATIN AMERICAN SERIES

Cole Blasier, Editor

Argentina in the Twentieth Century
David Rock, Editor

Barrios in Arms: Revolution in Santo Domingo
Jośe A. Moreno

Beyond the Revolution: Bolivia Since 1952
James M. Malloy and Richard S. Thorn, Editors

Bolivia: The Uncompleted Revolution
James M. Malloy

Constructive Change in Latin America
Cole Blasier, Editor

Cuba, Castro, and the United States
Philip W. Bonsal

Female and Male in Latin America: Essays
Ann Pescatello, Editor

Panajachel: A Guatemalan Town in Thirty-Year Perspective
Robert E. Hinshaw

Puerto Rico and the United States, 1917-1933
Truman R. Clark

Revolutionary Change in Cuba
Carmelo Mesa-Lago, Editor

San Bernardino Contla: Marriage and Family Structure in a Tlaxcalan Municipio
Hugo G. Nutini

Selected Latin American One-Act Plays
Francesca Colecchia and Julio Matas, Editors and Translators

Society and Education in Brazil
Robert J. Havighurst and J. Roberto Moreira

Panajachel

Robert E. Hinshaw

Foreword by Sol Tax

PANAJACHEL
A Guatemalan Town in Thirty-Year Perspective

University of Pittsburgh Press

F
/465./
P36
H56

Copyright © University of Pittsburgh Press, 1975
All rights reserved
Feffer and Simons, Inc., London
Manufactured in the United States of America

Library of Congress Cataloging in Publication Data

Hinshaw, Robert E   birth date
    Panajachel: a Guatemalan town in thirty-year
perspective.

    (Pitt Latin American series)
    Bibliography: p. 199
    Includes index.
    1. Panajachel, Guatemala. 2. Indians of Central
America—Guatemala—Atitlán, Lake.
F1465.1.P36H56   301.35'1'097281   74-17838
ISBN 0-8229-3296-2

Part of chapter 9 first appeared, in a slightly different form, in "Environmental Effects on Child-Spacing and Population Increase in Highland Guatemala," by Robert Hinshaw, Patrick Pyeatt, and Jean-Pierre Habicht, *Current Anthropology,* vol. 13, no. 2 (April 1972), p. 218.

27049

To Ardith, Julia, Ken, and Chris

About the Author

R O B E R T H I N S H A W received his B.A. from Haverford College and his M.A. and Ph.D. in Anthropology from the University of Chicago. He has served on the faculty of the University of Kansas and currently is president of Wilmington College in Ohio.

In addition to devoting two years with his family to the field research in Guatemala which produced this book, he was a visiting professor in 1968-69 at the Universidad de San Carlos in Guatemala City.

Contents

Maps and Illustrations

Tables

Foreword

T H I S book marks a new phase in the maturing of social anthropology. Not long ago, it was a mark of pride for an anthropologist to break new ground in a previously unstudied tribe. Indeed, this seemed more rational in our profession than it is for a gold miner to stake his claim in a new field; cultures exist wherever people live, and a new one easily finds a welcome place in the literature. But even forty years ago, we began to regret that all of us were taking this easy way to fame. We were neglecting problems of method and historical continuity which could only be understood by repeat studies in the same place, preferably by a new anthropologist. In the 1950s there were finally some notable restudies, which taught us much.

The present work is much more than a restudy, however. Oscar Lewis returned to Margaret and Robert Redfield's Tepoztlán with new problems, new tools, and new people to do new things. The Lewis team saw the Tepoztlán of two generations through the filter of their own eyes, data, problems, and personalities. Of course Lewis had with him the Redfields' published work, but not the primary data on which they were based. The Hinshaws began rather by thoroughly internalizing every item that my wife and I, and Juan Rosales, had written into our notebooks from 1935 to 1941. In anthropology, published works represent conclusions which use data relevant to particular problems; these data are often a minuscule percentage of the total collected. In my own case, I doubt that *Penny Capitalism* and all of the articles I published, and even summaries in unpublished lectures, represent more than 5 to 10 percent of the total in our notebooks. The painstaking maps, genealogies, and household censuses which are essential to careful ethnography do not appear in the pages of published work. The thousands of incidents and items of observation and conversation recorded in diaries are left for the archives, or destroyed when the anthropologist dies.

Panajachel is a "continuation study" which incorporates a restudy. Just as in a relay race, the second runner picks up speed alongside his teammate before he takes the baton, so the Hinshaws caught up with the Taxes before they went to Panajachel. By the time the Hinshaws went to Panajachel, all of the material in our notes—which they carried with them—was as fresh in their minds as it was vague in my memory.

By this time I was secure in my professional position; and far from fearing the mistakes that would be discovered in my original data and the interpretations I had made, I eagerly looked forward to what these would teach us of methodological significance. I am nevertheless not displeased that my errors turn out to have been too few and unimportant to provide us with such opportunities.

Although Hinshaw's work is especially important to me, its own importance is independent of anything I have done. Every anthropologist bases his study on whatever historical background is available; and it can be considered an accident that Hinshaw had a special historical source in the notebooks of thirty years before. I need only testify that he has used his literary sources well and wisely; and then the present book stands on its own merits. However it will be at least interesting for the record for me to provide a chronology of the earlier study of Panajachel.

My wife and I began field work in Guatemala in October 1934. We based ourselves first in Chichicastenango, undertaking from there a survey of the northwestern highlands. On the way back to Chichicastenango, we first saw Lake Atitlán, spending a night at the Hotel Tzanjuyú on the edge of Panajachel. In April 1935, after some days at the lake, we decided to select several towns on its shore for comparative study during our next field season. We purchased a launch, therefore, and from October 1935 to June 1936 undertook a survey of the lake towns and of course included Panajachel itself. Here we found Juan de Dios Rosales, an educated native Panajacheleño who was willing and able to become our fulltime field assistant. The survey completed, it became evident to us that Panajachel was as good a town as any around the lake for concentrated field work during the next field season; and we employed Rosales to continue to collect data for us even in our between-seasons absences. Until December 1937 (when he moved across the lake to San Pedro to undertake an independent study), Rosales steadily filled notebooks of data on Panajachel conceptions of the world which his friends, neighbors, and relatives supplied in the Cakchiquel language. Between times, I was busy simultaneously preparing two volumes on Panajachel—one on the world view, the other on the economy—when in autumn of 1938 the Redfields (living in Agua Escondida, near the lake) and we (living again in Chichicastenango) began systematically to compare notes on beliefs in their village with those we had recorded for Panajachel. And we returned to Panajachel for a last field season in 1940-41 both to collect material needed for the book on the economy (which became *Penny Capitalism)* and to get deeper into the distribution of beliefs in Panajachel by means of sampling. The sample of persons questioned then about a sample of beliefs became eventually a specific tool for the Hinshaws' comparison of the Panajacheleño community at two intervals thirty years apart.

Although I visited Panajachel briefly in 1944 and again in 1956 and had some impression of the changes which had occurred—which piqued but could not satisfy curiosity—it was not until the Hinshaws completed their work that anything became clear. Then at once the importance of their conclusions became evident. Panajachel happens to be a type-case of theory in economic development (see especially T. W. Schultz, *Transforming Traditional Agriculture*) showing that peasant peoples behave not only rationally but efficiently. The Hinshaws now show concretely how these same people have adjusted to a doubling of their population without increase in their land base or improvement in their agricultural technology, and how in this process the economic, educational, social, and religious changes interacted.

Anthropologists often see the cream skimmed off their work and used (or misused) comparatively in somebody's theory, to be itself thereafter forgotten even before the new theory is outdated. In the present case—to continue a difficult metaphor—the whole milk is mightily enriched and so made especially useful to theory. The before and the after are causally tied together; one plus one becomes considerably more than two. Sir Charles Darwin (the astronomer's grandson) once wrote an essay showing the limitations placed on scientific advance by the limited life span of the individual scientist. The people of Panajachel, and Robert and Ardith Hinshaw, have shown in this book how the Darwin limitation can be circumvented; and I am grateful to be a guinea pig who has been given a tail!

SOL TAX
January 1975

Preface

T H E first term paper I wrote as a philosophy major in college was about Saint Francis of Assisi. I learned much from this man and was pleased to find that he was the patron saint of the Indian community in Guatemala whose people are the subject of this book. I learned much from these people, much more than I can now attribute to them or than is shared in these pages. I learned that very little of what I had learned in college about Saint Francis was known by Panajacheleños,[1] and that very little of what they had learned about Saint Francis from their ancestors was known by me. The little knowledge, or the few meanings, we did share hardly suggested the same man. Indeed, the Saint Francis worshiped by Panajacheleños is not the Italian I studied; he is not even the Saint Francis worshiped by other Mayan communities that have this patron saint. Panajacheleños believe that the patron saints of the dozens of communities of Guatemala bearing the name Saint Francis are brothers, and in this way they insure that the spiritual forces on which their crops and health depend are distinctively their own.

Panajacheleños depend on some shared understandings about Saint Francis I neither need nor can accept . . . but then they can say the same about me and all the books about Saint Francis I have read. Of all that Panajacheleños taught me, this was perhaps the most important: different meanings for the common referents of humankind are the very means by which humankind survives.

What people the world over have learned about Saint Francis, and hence his meaning, I suppose has no confines. Possibly there are limits to what people have learned or can learn about making cloth, planting corn, and bathing; yet Panajacheleños have taught me things about even these I had not learned before. These latter things I learned quickly, in the course of a few days or weeks of observing and participating in the daily round of activities in Panajachel. Other things I am learning now as I write this book, or will only come to understand later as I integrate experiences in Panajachel with those which preceded and have followed. So it is that the Saint Francis of my books and the children of Saint Francis in Panajachel are clarifying for me a simple truth: poverty is easier for those who have chosen it than for those whom it has chosen.

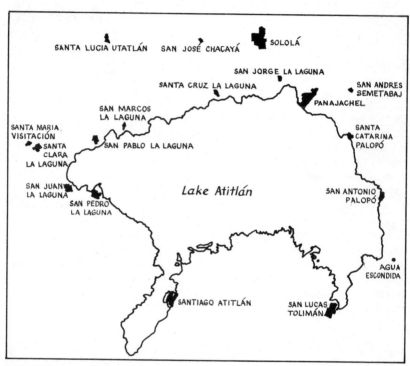

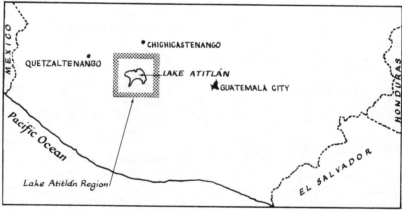

Map 1. Lake Atitlán and Environs

Introduction

T H E work of staying alive in Panajachel virtually demanded that the initial study of this Mayan community by Sol and Gertrude Tax focus on its economic organization. *Penny Capitalism* (1953) is the one published book-length product of their field work in Panajachel during 1936-41. Sol Tax is preparing a companion volume, an ethnography of beliefs and social organization, from data available on microfilm (Tax 1950). My investigations in Panajachel during 1963-65, 1968-69, and 1974 build upon those data.

A number of articles resulted from the Tax research (1937; 1941). In his 1941 article, Tax presented hypotheses concerning the effect of social relations on belief patterns in Panajachel, and together we have examined the bearing of my 1963-65 data on those hypotheses (Tax and Hinshaw 1970). The categories of data on community income and expenditures and on distribution of wealth which Tax presented in *Penny Capitalism* were duplicated wherever possible in 1963-65. These comparisons constitute the initial chapters of this book and lay the groundwork for integrating four sets of data: (1) sources of income and distribution and functions of wealth; (2) social networks influencing communication and bases of community identity; (3) structure and continuity of mental culture; and (4) population dynamics in the face of growing pressure of people on available resources.

Tax's research anticipated most of my own inquiry, and even where it did not (for example, analysis of different rates of natural increase in population), his data were adequate for the thirty-year comparisons which have proven so useful. His detailed census of households and belongings, permitting reconstruction of complete genealogies and wealth histories over forty years, enabled me to monitor the responses of the 780 Indians present in 1936 to expanding resources and the doubling of their numbers by 1964. This population increase is typical of the region, but the history of growth in resources is not. Thus, the documentation of responses among Panajacheleños to the developments of the past quarter century sets the stage for the comparisons of highly variable responses among the dozen other Indian communities bordering Lake Atitlán. Yet even the comparisons among communities benefit from data Tax collected in the 1930s. The scope and procedures of his data collection are exemplary.

Given the lapse of time between my initial research in 1963-65 and the book's appearance in print, I have yielded to the temptation to add an epilogue describing Panajachel in 1974. The breadth, as well as depth, of perspective I attempt to provide is perhaps too ambitious an undertaking for one volume. I have been greatly tempted to include as many interrelated responses to environmental pressures on the people as those of us observing the lake region have been able to monitor. The reader may find more detail of population and economic trends than is readily digestible. Particularly in the initial chapters, the detailed comparisons with 1936 data may appear unnecessary. As the book unfolds, however, the utility of the comparisons will become evident. Even an endeavor as seemingly inconsequential as documenting which Panajachel Indians are descendants of Panajacheleños and which have ancestry in other communities becomes important in measuring erosion of traditional beliefs and the effect of basic psychological responses to environmental changes on spacing of children.

The thesis which emerges from the data is that for the past quarter century a hierarchy of values has permitted enough flexibility among competing values in Panajachel to accommodate shifts in income base and allocation of resources. The visibility of acceptable economic motives for changes in social relations has permitted experimentation with new networks of communication with non-Indians. Such experimentation has in turn influenced the transmission and acceptability of traditional belief patterns identified as distinctively Indian. The visibility of shifts in mental culture has been low, however, due largely to the communication network within Indian society, resulting in acculturation in mental culture as well as in economic pursuits without strong sanctions being applied. The result is a high degree of flexibility in responding to environmental changes without community disintegration or individual disorientation, and with surprisingly few shifts in ethnic identity.

On a larger canvas, the response to environmental changes includes the option of using acculturation as a springboard for leaving the community. Brief research in Panajachel since 1965 reveals increasing choice of this option, not from the desperation which forces the very poorest to migrate or emigrate to the coast, but from contacts with Guatemala City employers made initially in Panajachel. My data are too sparse to explore in detail this demographic response to the changing Panajachel scene. The comparative data that are available on migration and emigration from lake towns to the coast and to Guatemala City (as of 1965) are presented in chapter 9. Yet another demographic response to environmental changes is altered patterning of reproduction. Fortunately data from Panajachel and the two lake towns with highest and lowest birth rates since 1950 are sufficiently complete to correlate economic vicissitudes and institutional changes with family planning as evidenced by spacing of births.

The measurement of change and continuity among these many variables necessitates comparisons over time. Studies of culture change frequently are handicapped by insufficient historical perspective to assess adequately the continuities persisting through and influencing the change. Panajachel in 1963 had changed in some highly visible respects since 1941. The population had doubled; half the population was supported by nonagricultural service occupations (in contrast to 95 percent reliance on agriculture in 1936); the *cofradías* (confraternities)[1] were approaching their demise; Protestant sects claimed adherents in one-sixth of the households; and virtually all Panajacheleños were using the services of a resident doctor and health clinic, most to the exclusion of Indian curers. Particularly in dress and language, the Indians appeared acculturated.

Had I gone to Panajachel without the benefit of Tax's data, the natives' perceptions of having emerged into the "civilized" world would have biased unduly my interpretations of the significance and implications of the acculturative changes. These changes had been too numerous and had occurred too rapidly for Panajacheleños not to feel that their way of life was significantly altered from the life style of parents and grandparents. Even equipped with the perspective afforded by Tax's study, my interpretations of the changes since 1941 reflect a certain bias. In describing and analyzing these dramatic changes, I have tended to see shifts in values, belief patterns, and bases of identity resulting from changes in social relations precipitated by an expanding occupational base. A causal relationship is indeed demonstrable, but by limiting myself to these factors I may have underestimated the importance of events before the period of recent history bracketed by anthropological observation.

It is possible that the events most causally significant in the shifts in world view and social relations were the abolition in the 1920s of the *mandamientos* (a system of enforced labor whereby employers were given quotas of laborers) and in 1934 of debt peonage in Guatemala. Since then Panajacheleños no longer have been forced to spend portions of many years on coastal *fincas* (plantations), at the mercy of laws which limited the little autonomy they possessed as members of an Indian community. The subservience of Indians, their withdrawal and insulation, were reactions and adjustments to such conditions. With the greater freedom since 1935 it is probable that the boundary-maintaining mechanisms of endogamy, occupational specialization, and the cult of the saints would have weakened even in the absence of Protestantism, Catholic Action, schooling, and other institutional innovations since 1936. Recent changes in social relations and belief patterns have their more immediate cause in these latter innovations, but in analyzing this history, we will do well to bear in mind the psychological impact upon Panajacheleños of earlier changes.

One means of examining the impact of earlier events is to compare post-1940 developments in Panajachel with post-1940 developments in other lake towns differentially experiencing the recent changes in religious, educational, economic, and other community institutions. Fortunately, enough data on lake communities are available to permit some such comparisons in the final chapter. However, the definitive comparative study of the lake towns must await publication of detailed data other researchers have been gathering in several of the lake towns over the past quarter century.

If a strength of this book is its detailed comparisons of selected data over several decades in one community, a resultant weakness is its lack of attention to many other ethnographic data which would round out the reader's understanding of this community. I talk about a changing occupational base without describing either the pre-1940 or the post-1960 occupations in any detail. Belief awareness and acceptance are measured before the beliefs are described, and even when described the resultant world view is fragmentary and stripped of the myth which enlivens Tax's yet unpublished ethnography. For the reader with no prior acquaintance with Guatemalan Indian cultures, the book will seem lacking in description of basic technology, institutions, and life history material. Such descriptions for culturally similar communities have been written by a number of other anthropologists, however (Reina 1966; Nash 1958; Wagley 1949). For a brief introduction to the culture area of the midwestern highlands of Guatemala as a whole, see the *Handbook of Middle American Indians* (Tax and Hinshaw 1969).

I describe data-gathering procedures in considerable detail, in part because the comparability of 1936-41 and 1963-65 data is so important for meaningful discussion. To my knowledge, Tax was the first to include in his investigation of world view the data on informant variations in awareness and acceptance of beliefs which permit measurement of changes in belief-patterning. Tax's voluminous 1936-41 data enabled me to resume study in Panajachel with enough of an insider's view to probe into awareness and acceptance of belief patterns without betraying the extent to which my own world view differs from that of the Panajacheleños. From the outset of our eighteen months' sojourn in Panajachel my wife, Ardith, and I were able to converse about the mundane and the intimate with a knowledge of genealogies, history, folklore, and world view which immeasurably enhanced the rapport essential for the extensive interviewing that followed. The resumption of study of Panajachel also was enhanced by the informed assistance of Juan de Dios Rosales, a Panajacheleño trained in data-gathering by Tax during the 1935-41 research and in anthropological theory through subsequent study in Mexico. Moreover, Sol Tax journeyed to Panajachel to introduce my family to former informants, insuring a degree of rapport from the outset which otherwise would have taken months to nurture.

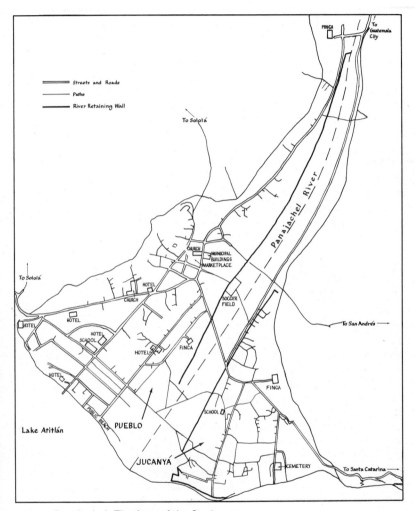

Legend:
═══ Streets and Roads
─── Paths
━━━ River Retaining Wall

To Solalá

FINCA

To Guatemala City

Panajachel River

CHURCH
MUNICIPAL BUILDINGS
MARKETPLACE

To Solalá

HOTEL
CHURCH

SOCCER FIELD

HOTEL
HOTEL
HOTEL
SCHOOL
HOTEL
FINCA

To San Andrés

HOTEL

FINCA

PUBLIC BEACH

Lake Atitlán

PUEBLO

SCHOOL

JUCANYÁ

CEMETERY

To Santa Catarina

Map 2. Panajachel: The Area of the Study

Over the course of their six years of association with the community, the Taxes were asked to become *compadres* (sponsors, or parents of those sponsored, in baptism, confirmation, or marriage) of numerous Indian couples and godparents of their children. Some of these children, adults with families of their own by 1963, in turn asked Ardith and me to become their *compadres* and to oversee the baptism, confirmation, or marriage of their children. That the Taxes are Jews and the Hinshaws are Quakers is unimportant, if even understood, to our *compadres,* and this says something about the meaning of Catholicism to Panajacheleños. But that the officiating Spanish priests also knew we are not Catholic and yet consented to this ritual kinship is equally significant, and it says something about the priests' appreciation of the importance of such relationships for gaining acceptance by the Catholic sector of the Indian community. In my case, the freedom to enter into *compadre* relationships was very important, for had Ardith and I been identified with Protestantism during that period of religious competition in the community, our continuity with the Taxes and our rapport with the conservative majority of Panajacheleños would have been much more difficult to develop and maintain.

Our indebtedness to others is therefore unusually great. To the Taxes and to Juan de Dios Rosales in particular, but also to Father Augustine and the many Panajacheleños who shared in this research, Ardith and I are deeply grateful. Special thanks go also to José Rosales, Laura, and Cecilia.

Such continuity in data-gathering and community perception of the purposes of the research over thirty years is unusual in the history of our young discipline of anthropology. The data permit comparisons over several generations in one community and among several towns bordering Lake Atitlán whose cultures are basically very similar yet whose histories over the past thirty years have been measurably different with respect to economic fortunes and socioreligious contacts with other Indians and non-Indians. The latter non-Indians have included North American Protestant and Catholic missionaries, community development volunteers, tourists, and researchers, as well as Guatemalan Ladinos. The latter share Guatemala with Indians in about equal numbers, but they control fully 80 percent of the country's tangible wealth and share a national political identity much more fully than do most Indians.

This book shares the bias typical of anthropological research in Guatemala: the main object of investigation is Indian society. Comparisons are drawn with Ladino patterns of belief and social organization to understand Indian cultures better, not to describe Ladino cultural patterning in any systematic way. Since conducting the research of 1963-65 in Panajachel, I have taught for one year in the Universidad de San Carlos in Guatemala City. Had I embarked on research in Panajachel with the understanding of

Ladino society in the capital city, my observations of Ladinos in Panajachel would have benefited considerably. I would have been interested at least as much in the understandings shared by Ladinos and Indians as in their differences.

Panajachel

◦ I ◦

The People

C H A N G E S in environment produce human responses which help clarify for the observer the distinguishing cultural characteristics of a society. When one of the environmental changes is rapid increase in human population, the social scientist observing the situation notes both the changes in relations among the people themselves and the resultant changes in people's relationships to the physical environment. Changes in relationships among people are usually more difficult to detect and measure than are changes in numbers of people and their relationships to the physical environment. And yet the social interaction often is the primary interest of the social scientist. Counting and measuring all that is readily observable are the necessary first steps of ethnological research, and accordingly this and the following two chapters provide the basic demographic and economic data on which the subsequent analyses of social relations, attitudes, and beliefs are based. The ordering of the material in the book reflects the order of its gathering, and accordingly the syntheses and analyses of most interest to author and reader necessarily come toward the end.

All but the final chapter deal with the 1,800 Indians in Panajachel, drawing comparisons between these people and 780 of their ancestors who inhabited the community in the 1930s. The final chapter compares the changes in Panajachel since 1936 with changes elsewhere around Lake Atitlán, placing in more adequate perspective one distinguishing attribute of Panajachel: its accessibility by paved highway and its consequent popularity among tourists.

To the Guatemalans and foreign tourists responsible for Panajachel's rapid growth since 1936, the community has had little of the Indian charm characteristic of highland communities to recommend it. Its attractiveness lies in the natural setting, the incomparable Lake Atitlán. Aldous Huxley, in the early 1930s, found Panajachel "to be a squalid, uninteresting place, with a large low-class Mestizo population and an abundance of dram shops." Regarding the lake, however, which "touches the limits of the permissibly picturesque . . . it is really too much of a good thing" (1934: 128). In 1964 the Indians were no more in evidence to visitors than they were to Huxley, despite the fact that they always have outnumbered Ladino residents by at least two to one. For local color, tourists still take the launch across the lake to Santiago Atitlán or attend the Sunday market in Chichicastenango (see map 1).

Huxley erred in referring to the population as *mestizo.* The term does not apply in Guatemala as it does in Mexico to a distinctive culture carried by persons of mixed Indian, African, and European ancestry. And since there

The eastern end of Lake Atitlán and San Antonio.

is no culture in Guatemala characteristic of persons of mixed ancestry, the term *mestizo* is not used. In tact many and probably most Indians in Panajachel have mixed ancestry. Yet the proportion will be little if any larger than in neighboring towns, despite the impression the town has given for several decades of being less Indian. This impression is due in part to the many Panajacheleños wearing Ladino dress (a majority of the men in 1964) and in part to the river which divides the delta. It is to the east of the river, in Jucanyá, that the native Indians always have predominated, yet even in Jucanyá the homes are not readily observable amidst the coffee groves and cane and thicket fences. It was here that the Taxes lived during two of their field seasons and also where I settled with my family from December 1963 to June 1965.[1] To Indians, Jucanyá is no more than the name implies, the other side of the river; it is not to them "the Indian *barrio*" of the community which it tends to be in the minds of Ladino authorities.

For the purposes of my study of Panajachel, differences between Indians and Ladinos were no more important than differences between native Panajacheleños and Indians born outside the community who have immigrated to Panajachel (hereafter designated as "foreign"). The Indians residing in Panajachel in 1936 had slightly less than doubled the native Indian population by 1964, to 1,418, but the influx of foreign Indians had

A family sorting onions among their garden beds and irrigation ditches.

greatly increased the total Indian population, which rose to 1,806 by 1964. The resident Ladino population similarly had almost tripled, to 973, and on weekends the arrival from Guatemala City of seventy families owning second homes in Panajachel swelled the Ladino population conspicuously.[2] It is these latter, affluent families plus the tourists who frequent the seven hotels and two public beaches who account in large part for the diversification of employment since 1936.

Before describing the effects of such rapid population increase, from 1,180 to 2,779 in twenty-eight years, on employment and emigration, I need to describe the composition of the Indian households. Within the 297 Indian households present in 1964 there were 351 unions (that is, couples considered married, including 2 polygynous unions involving 4 households) and 53 widows and widowers. Obviously many households contained more than 1 union; and where there were 2 or more, the family heads in most instances were a father and his sons.

In 41 of the 351 unions, both spouses were foreign. Of the widows and widowers, 12 were foreign. Adding to these the foreigners marrying into native households, I conclude that 27 percent of the unions and 37 percent of the households in 1964 contained at least one foreign spouse. These foreign Indians represented 30 *municipios* (townships), the majority being from the neighboring *municipios* of Sololá, San Jorge, Concepción, Santa Catarina, and San Andrés.

The desirability of residence in Panajachel is reflected not only in the influx of foreign Indians and Ladinos, but also in the relatively few Panajacheleños who have married or sought employment elsewhere since 1936. Of the 18 persons who left Panajachel to marry elsewhere, only 3 were native Panajacheleños; the other 15 were children of foreign Indians. Panajacheleños living elsewhere in 1964 but still considered members of Panajachel households totaled 54, of whom 40 were Panajacheleños by birth. Of these 40, 27 were men, most of whom were working on the coast or in Guatemala City. Several were in prison or military service. Many of these persons doubtless have been lost to the community, as have approximately a dozen others who moved away earlier in the 1936-64 interim and are no longer considered members of Panajachel households.

The major conclusion to be drawn from these data on emigration is that as of 1964 the native Indians of Panajachel continued to identify deeply with Panajachel. Despite strong competition from Ladinos and foreign Indians for farm land and employment, a doubled native population was supported by the local economy and evidenced little interest in seeking fortunes elsewhere. This situation would soon change, however. In chapter 9 I discuss the upswing in emigration observed from 1964-69. Those emigrating tended to be young and acculturated, in many instances able to assimilate within Ladino society if they so chose. By 1964, however, Panajacheleños still gave to insider and observer alike the impression of considerable continuity in shared beliefs, values, and expectations of one another.

Since the mid-1960s appear to mark a turning point in Panajacheleños' dependency on local resources and community identity, closer documentation of population increase will be useful in assessing the number of years and the degree of pressure of people on resources the community had experienced through 1964.

In the fourteen years from 1950 to 1964, the Indian population increased by 60 percent, compared with a 44 percent increase from 1936 to 1950. The acceleration since 1950 is due to two factors: most of the foreigners have arrived or been born since 1950; and the death rate has declined steadily since the early 1950s, when the public health clinic was established.[3] The annual population increase through births over deaths among native Indians averaged 2.6 percent from 1951 to 1964, in contrast to the 1.5 percent increase averaged the preceding fourteen years.

Of course, the short-term effects of these two sources of increase are different. Immigrants enter the labor force immediately, whereas reduced mortality initially means a barely noticeable growth in family size.[4] The longer-term effect of reduced mortality becomes very significant, however, once the additional children surviving to adulthood begin producing their own offspring. Children under fourteen years of age constituted 33 percent of the population in both 1921 and 1936; in 1964 this age group constituted 42 percent of the Indian population.[5] This means that the 1964 population contained approximately 170 more children under fifteen than would have been the case had the 1936 rate for this age group not been altered. As this generation marries, the crude birth rate will increase sharply, and pressure of people on resources will build accordingly. The increase in emigration since 1965 is one predictable response, and it probably will continue through the 1970s.

Between the censuses taken by Tax in 1936 and by me in 1964, a national census was taken in 1950. The Indian population in 1950 was 1,125, excluding the community of Patanatic.[6] No more than 1,000 of those persons relied on the farm lands of the *municipio* for their livelihood. To the best of my knowledge, the farming population previously had not exceeded that number but apparently had equaled this figure back in 1921, when a national census reported 1,150 Indians in Panajachel.[7] There is unfortunately no way of assessing how adequately the 1921 population was supported by the landholdings in Panajachel. It is known from Tax's 1936 data that the land base supported 780 Indians adequately by local standards, with a comfortable margin of savings registered for the year. From comparisons of 1936 and 1964, I judge the "carrying capacity" of the land owned or rentable by Indians (approximately 140 delta and 92 *milpa* [cornfield] acres) to have been around 1,000 persons for many years. This capacity may have been reached at various times in the past; it was reached again around 1950, when for the first time in the experience of Panajacheleños the infant mortality rate also began to decline. By 1950 at least some of the poorer households would have been forced either to overtax their land or to seek nonagricultural employment. In fact, both alternatives were followed but, significantly, not by the same households. In most cases the innovators in experimentation with new sources of income were among the wealthier households,[8] and the innovation, especially in construction work, occurred early in the 1940s. It would appear that the expansion into service occupations was prompted less by economic necessity than by the economic opportunity presented by the expanding Ladino and tourist populations. The population pressure was then effectively eased by those new employment opportunities through the 1950s. The data suggest that the economic base would have broadened without the population pressure on the agricultural subsistence base. Once broadened, the local economy for two decades permitted the population to increase through immigration and a lowered death rate without threatening the bases of community integration and identity. In the next chapter I examine how adequately the broadened economic base has met the material needs of the expanded population.

° 2 °

Economic Comparisons

*

T H E principal objectives guiding Tax's research in 1936 with regard to the Panajachel economy were: (1) a careful estimate of local community income and expenditures for one year; (2) determination of the cost of living to permit comparisons of living standards and allocation of resources; and (3) determination of the wealth of each Indian household, permitting the ranking of families to analyze functions of wealth. My research interests in 1964 focused more on the last two objectives than on the first, although I gathered sufficient data on community income and expenditures to permit rough comparisons with 1936. Since these comparisons reveal only slight shifts in land use (away from farming through sale of land to Ladinos for chalets, and away from labor-intensive truck farming to permit part-time nonagricultural employment), it seems safe to assume that values surrounding agriculture have not significantly altered. This assumption is examined in later chapters. At the same time, psychological dependency on agriculture would appear not to have been so great as to lead Panajacheleños to choose continued reliance on farming over new service occupations at the expense of a perceptible decline in standard of living. This assumption is examined in this chapter. The procedure followed is calculation of total household income and expenditures, examination of standard of living, and comparisons with the equivalent data from 1936.

The Land and Its Use

To the casual observer passing through Panajachel, the community appears to be largely a Ladino *pueblo* (town), the business district incorporating the majority of the Ladino homes and only a few Indian households. Moreover, the area stretching south from the business district to the lake, which in 1936 was largely farm plots interspersed with Indian homes, has now been filled with two-thirds of the seventy chalets of the community and other Ladino homes and shops which hide the few Indian homes and garden plots occupying the central region of each "city block" created by the network of roads added since 1936. It is north of the business district and across the river in Jucanyá that the majority of the Indians dwell. No new roads have been added in Jucanyá since 1936, and the chalets are limited largely to the shoreline, stretching from the river to the neighboring *municipio* of Santa Catarina and on as far as San Antonio Palopó, four miles east of Panajachel. Indeed, the twenty-two chalets situated in Jucanyá are as difficult to imagine and locate as are the 160 Indian families residing in the western half of the delta (see map 2).

Given the increase in residences, it comes as a surprise to discover that the total acreage of Indian-owned tillable land in the delta has remained nearly constant since 1936. Hill land, suitable for the growing of corn and beans, owned by Panajacheleños within the *municipio* has increased by four acres since 1936, while *milpa* land (used for corn, beans, and squash) owned by Panajacheleños in other *municipios* has almost tripled. If delta land rented from Ladinos is added to the Indian land base, the 1936-64 delta acreage farmed by Panajacheleños remains exactly the same as the 1936 total of 142 acres. This apparent lack of change, however, disguises a great deal of buying and selling. At least 19 of the 129 acres owned by Indians in 1936 have since been sold to Ladinos, who have purchased an additional 10 acres from nonresident Indians. Panajacheleños, in turn, have purchased at least 6 acres from Ladinos and nonresident Indians. But the main source of new Indian-owned tillable land has been the 14 acres reclaimed through the construction of retaining walls to limit the meandering of the river.

Apart from the greater proportion of land used for house sites, the use of Indian-owned delta land had not changed appreciably since 1936. Twenty-

The main street of Panajachel.

six of the 130 delta acres were house plots, an estimated 5 to 10 acres more than in 1936. The remaining 104 acres, plus limited tillable land in house environs, were planted either in coffee or in other cash crops, irrigated by the intricate network of ditches which had grown even more complex over the intervening years.

I lack data on the specific quantities of truck crops grown on the many hundreds of parcels of land comprising those 104 acres.[1] The subdivision of landholdings since 1936 had resulted in nearly a thousand owners and at least twice this number of individual plots. The effort involved in determining the specific use of each plot of land would have been prohibitive. I do have data on the proportion of tillable land used for truck gardening in general compared to land planted in coffee, however, thanks to a national land census conducted in 1964.[2] Of the 104 delta acres, 30 percent were designated as coffee and the other 70 percent as truck. These percentages were 28.6 and 71.4 in 1936. I suspect the shift toward coffee has been somewhat greater than these figures indicate, however, since in house environs I estimate twice as much coffee as other crops are grown. Estimating these latter acreages to total 8 acres of coffee and 4 of truck, the adjusted total percentages are 33.7 and 66.3.

Hill land continued to be planted almost entirely in corn and beans. The exception is four acres of hill land in Panajachel and an estimated two acres in Santa Catarina owned by one Panajachel family that are fed by springs and hence usable for truck crops.

Truck gardening on land reclaimed from the riverbed. A coffee grove is in the background.

Income from Agriculture

Given the fact that agricultural income accounted for less than half the total income of Panajacheleños in 1964, I did not gather as comprehensive data on acreages and yields for various crops as did Tax in 1936, when agriculture accounted for over 90 percent of the Indian income. Readers interested in a detailed description of agricultural practices and agricultural accounting are referred to *Penny Capitalism*. In the several pages that follow, I summarize my 1964 data on agricultural earnings and compare community reliance on agriculture with the reliance in 1936. Readers not interested in the procedures followed in gathering this information are invited to peruse table 1 and proceed to page 15.

Lacking data on specific acreages planted in each truck crop, but knowing the number of total truck acres planted in 1964, I asked a dozen farmers to estimate their earnings from a *cuerda* (0.178 acre) of onions (the only truck crop warranting a full *cuerda* of any farmer's land) and from a *cuerda* of mixed crops. The estimates varied considerably for onions but averaged slightly more than $100 per *cuerda*.[3] For the other truck crops, profits ranged from $75 to $100 per *cuerda*. In the absence of more exact data I have placed the average net return for all truck crops at $100 per *cuerda* or $570 per acre. Table 1 gives the estimated truck income in relationship to other agricultural income.

TABLE 1
Value of Agricultural Products

	1936[a]	1964
Milpa (corn, beans, squash)	$ 2,546	$ 6,000
Truck crops	18,452	51,300
Coffee	1,052	6,156
Fruit	1,239	4,956
Total	$23,289	$68,412

a. Sol Tax, *Penny Capitalism*, p. 116.

Coffee yields per *cuerda*, taking into consideration the age of the trees, had not changed since 1936, but coffee profits had increased disproportionately to truck by virtue of international trade agreements boosting the price of coffee. Whereas 1964 prices of corn, beans, and onions were three to four times higher than in 1936, just keeping pace with the declining purchasing power of the *quetzal* ($1.00 U.S.), coffee prices were up five times the 1936 market value. On the basis of many data gathered from the land census as well as from coffee growers, the profits from coffee were averaged at $168 per acre. Since only 56 man-days of labor are required per acre of coffee per year, compared with an average of 600 man-days per acre of truck, the daily earnings were $3.00 from coffee compared with

$0.95 from truck. A family was ahead in 1964 to put its land in coffee and seek supplementary employment if the wage earners could average at least $0.75 per day the remaining 544 man-days truck gardening would require per acre. Even at a lower daily wage, service employment would be a tempting choice, since coffee and service employment earnings involve less risk than truck gardening. Since 1964 was a reasonably good year for truck farming, a truck gardener could not expect to average daily earnings of $0.95 over several years. That the shift toward coffee since 1936 has not been greater is the surprising finding. Possible explanations are the initial costs of converting land to coffee, the loss of income from such land for the first two years of the young trees' growth, limited nonagricultural employment in Panajachel, and cultural restraints until recent years on acceptance of such employment. If opportunities for employment in service occupations and associated wages continue to increase, it seems reasonable to expect a continuing shift away from truck gardening and into coffee production. In this regard, it is significant that the youngest son of the wealthiest and most landed Panajacheleño in 1936, with seven *cuerdas* in truck crops, has found his margin of profit decreasing in recent years to the point where he is seriously contemplating placing all of his land in coffee and embarking upon service employment at the age of 35.

Data on corn yields were obtained from a dozen owners of *milpa* land, only two or three of whom own or rent enough *milpa* land to supply their family's annual corn needs. Only one *milpa* owner interviewed averaged substantially more than the ten bushels per acre reported by the great majority of Panajacheleños as well as the *milpa* owners queried in four other *municipios* around the lake. This compares with the average of twenty bushels per acre reported in 1936. The explanation lies in soil exhaustion due to the more intensive use of hill lands necessitated by the expanding population and failure of most *milpa* holdings to meet the needs of the respective households. One informant reporting yields as high or higher than the 1936 averages attributes his success to a policy of not burning off the underbrush. Another informant has experimented with commercial fertilizer with fair results, achieving the 1936 twenty-bushel average. Possibly because of the effort involved in transporting the fertilizer up the steep hillsides to the Panajachel fields and the limited reliance upon locally grown corn, the use of fertilizer has not been considered worth the cost or effort by most *milpa* growers. This is in sharp contrast to *milpa* owners of San Antonio, who rely heavily upon corn yields for sale as well as for their own use. The two Indians selling fertilizer in Panajachel reported substantial sales of fertilizer to Antoñeros and somewhat less to Catarinecos. Proper use of fertilizer, combined with hybrid strains of corn, can significantly increase yields; experimental plots in the *municipio* of San José Chacayá northwest of the lake produced forty bushels per acre.

The price of corn fluctuated considerably but averaged four cents per pound during 1964, and the total *milpa* income from corn is estimated at two and one-half times that of 1936. This increase was achieved only with the acquisition of some fifty additional acres of *milpa* land, however. Lacking more specific data, I have assumed that bean and squash yields from *milpa* land provided the same proportion of total hill profits as in 1936. In the absence of data on fruit tree yields or numbers of trees owned in 1964, I merely multiplied the 1936 fruit income by four, the average percentage increase in market prices for all fruits grown in Panajachel.

Reliance Upon Agriculture in 1964

The income from agriculture constituted 46 percent of the Indian community's total receipts in 1964. If one assumes that agriculture supported a comparable percentage of the population, it would appear that at least as many Panajacheleños were supported by the land base as in 1936. In fact a considerably smaller percentage of the 1964 population was supported solely by agriculture, while a considerably larger total number of households derived a portion of their income from farming or marketing produce. In 1964 as well as in 1936, 10 percent of the Indian households owned 40 percent of the land. These 30 households in 1964 owned an average of ten *cuerdas* of land and were among the 40 households able to maintain themselves solely through farming their own land. An additional 38 households were supported by hiring out as farm laborers to Indians and Ladinos, supplementing these wages in some cases with income from limited landholdings of their own. From these data I conclude that one-fourth of the 1964 population, or one-third of the native Indian population, had remained dependent solely upon agriculture. Of these 78 households, 46 resided in Jucanyá, pointing up the more traditional orientation of this sector of the community toward the economic base.

Ascertaining the percentage of native households relying partially upon agriculture but supplementing their income with service employment was more difficult. A rough estimate can be obtained from the observation that 58 percent of native households owned more than one *cuerda* of land in 1964. Since the average house site (that is, buildings and yard) is one-half *cuerda*, it can be assumed that the great majority of households owning a *cuerda* or more would derive some income from at least coffee or fruit trees. To this 58 percent would be added the poorest Panajacheleños, owning or renting only a house site and hiring out as farm laborers. These households would include the dozen men who sought employment on the coast during the cotton harvest in 1964. Altogether, I estimate that two-thirds of native Panajachel households derived at least some of their income in 1964 from agriculture. By contrast, only 22 percent of the foreign Indian households owned in excess of one *cuerda* and hence relied in part upon income from farming. Seven foreign houses relied solely upon agriculture, owning most of the 13 acres of delta land in foreign Indian possession in 1964. In 1936, foreign Indian holdings were only .2 acres. Forty percent of the foreign households were renting their homes in 1964, and 38 percent owned house sites no larger than one-half *cuerda*. Native Panajacheleños owning only house sites were a comparable 37 percent, but only 5 percent of native households were reduced to renting their homes. This was the same percentage as in 1936.

Income from Service Occupations

Estimating nonagricultural income involved determining the occupational histories of all households and the wage scales for the various kinds of employment. For businesses owned by Indians, calculations of earnings were obtained from the owners themselves wherever possible and otherwise from estimates of other informants. In table 2, the total income from each category of employment was estimated by multiplying the average wage by 300 workdays and by the number of men over fifteen years of age thus employed. I do not have such complete data on women, such as the few domestic servants in Ladino homes and those employed part-time as laundresses, weavers of *huipiles* (blouses, usually sleeveless) and carrying cloths for sale to Panajacheleñas, and venders of food from house to house or along the highway. As their wages are low and I know of only forty-six such women, I doubt that the total income from such endeavors can be much greater than indicated. A few women are employed in hotels and have been included with the men in that category. As a check on these calculations, I made an independent estimate of the earnings for each household on the basis of specific salary data and months of work in 1963, arriving at a total of $91,880—$6,500 less than the first estimate. The actual figure probably lies between the two. Not included in either estimate are earnings of Panajacheleños working in Guatemala City and elsewhere, a small portion of which find their way back to households in Panajachel.

TABLE 2
Income from Nonagricultural Employment, 1964

Type of employment	Average daily wage	Number of workers	Total annual wage
Domestic service, laundry	$ .25	46	$ 3,450
Finca, road labor	.50	40	6,000
Unskilled construction labor	.50	38	5,700
Carpentry, masonry	2.00	39	23,400
Marketing produce	.75	10	2,250
Store and other business ownership	.75—3.00	17	7,300
Business employment	.75	30	6,750
Chalet-keeping	.75	73	16,400
Hotel labor	1.50	63	27,000
Total		356	$98,250

Cost of Living

The purchasing power of the *quetzal* has dropped to at least one-third that of 1936, judging by minimum wage and market price comparisons. The daily wage for farm and other unskilled labor had increased from 16 2/3 cents in 1936 to 50 cents in 1964. Comprehensive surveys of market prices in Panajachel in 1936, and again in December 1963 and June 1965, provided the comparisons of costs of food, clothing, and building supplies. The total expenditures of the Indian population in 1964 were estimated on the basis of these data to provide comparisons on the balance of payments and standard of living in 1936 and 1964.

In the case of food, comprising roughly 70 percent of the community's expenditures, the diet of Indians has altered but minimally since 1936,[4] and an estimate of food costs which cannot be far off was obtained by determining the average rise in cost of a representative list of foods and multiplying this by the total expenditures of 1936. This sum was then increased in proportion to the increase in numbers of adults and children. Percentage increases since 1936 in costs of sixteen food staples ranged from 500 percent (beans, coffee, and meat) to 200 percent (sugar, *panela,* [brown noncrystallized sugar] , and chocolate), with corn averaging a 400 percent increase. The proportions of these staples consumed by Indians vary considerably, however, and this rather casual estimate of a 370 percent increase in the cost of food was checked against the actual food costs of one family to determine the difference in cost of the same weekly diet in 1936 and 1964. These data also revealed a 370 percent increase in food expenditures for one family, which I accept as reasonably accurate for the community as a whole. Of course wealth differences among families are reflected in varying quantities of foods consumed (that is, the wealthier the family, generally the more meat consumed), but the proportions of staples averaging the 370 percent increase are assumed to differ very little from family to family. On the basis of Tax's calculations of quantities of food consumed by 780 Panajacheleños in 1936, and allowing for the doubled population plus 170 additional children under fifteen, the extrapolated value of food consumed by Indians in 1964 was $117,628.

While I indicated above that any dietary changes since 1936 have been too minimal to affect measurably the above estimates of community expenditures for food, the few changes which have occurred warrant description. I listed meat above as a staple with hesitation; certainly not all households consume meat on a regular basis, but it is my impression that proportionately more is consumed than previously. I am referring to increased beef and pork consumption, because chicken has always constituted an important ingredient in ceremonial dishes such as *pulique.* Traditionally Indians have rationalized ethnic differences in diet in terms of the greater physical strength and hotter, stronger blood needed by Indians to do their heavy manual labor. A diet of vegetables in contrast to a diet strong in meat and fats is believed to be the cause of blood differences between Indians and Ladinos, and a folk tale from Huehuetenango tells of the first time the gods of the two races sat down to eat together, when the Indian god took only vegetables out of respect for the Ladino god. The assumption is pervasive that vegetables, especially beans, build strong blood, and that meat in large quantities is an unnecessary if not detrimental luxury for people destined to physical labor. That this attitude is changing is attributable largely to information disseminated by the health clinic and the greater local availability of meat to cater to the growing Ladino market. A number of Indian informants now believe that proteins found in meat and dairy products are essential to good health.

Meat prices remain high, however, having increased 500 percent since 1936, and for this reason the Indian community's consumption has not altered appreciably. The situation is different with regard to milk, available at no cost in powdered form from the health clinic. More Ladinos than Indians take advantage of this service, and nurses expressed discouragement over the number of Indians obtaining the CARE milk merely to sell it to venders of ice cream. Many Indian families are too proud to accept this handout, and while little milk is produced locally, a Ladino-owned dairy in neighboring San Andrés and Indians owning cows in Concepción bring milk to Panajachel on a regular basis. Again, far more Ladinos than Indians purchase from these sources, but Indian milk consumption definitely is increasing. The school lunch program provides milk daily for children, and a number of my informants volunteered that they drink milk with some regularity in their homes.

Estimating community expenditures for clothing in 1964 was complicated by the wide range of attire worn by Panajacheleños. Costs of each kind of garment, estimates of quantity purchased per individual, and data on dress patterns of all households were required. To simplify my task, I adopted Tax's 1936 estimates of the amounts of each kind of attire the average adult and child purchase in a year (1953: 158-62). I was amazed to learn how knowledgeable Panajacheleños are concerning the dress patterns of their fellows. José Rosales, an Indian of thirty-two years of age and my chief assistant in data collection, was able to tell me the clothing patterns and footwear of virtually every adult Panajacheleño, and in very few cases did subsequent checking of my own prove him wrong. These clothing preferences are given in table 3.

There has been since 1936 a marked shift away from the distinctively Panajachel attire toward Ladino dress for men and a generalized Indian costume for women. This latter is distinctively Indian, using the wrap-around skirt and traditional *huipil,* but the tie-dyed skirt fabric and richly colored *huipil* material are woven on foot looms in the department of Totonicapán and widely marketed throughout western Guatemala. The attire is termed "generalized" since the provenance of its wearer cannot be determined, except possibly by waist sash or carrying cloth, which in many instances are home-woven on backstrap looms in the distinctive patterns associated with particular communities.

Whether man or woman, to keep oneself outfitted in distinctively Panajachel Indian attire costs slightly less than three times as much per year as in 1936, while the Ladino shirt, belt, and trousers, and the generalized woman's attire cost slightly more than three times as much. This does not mean, however, that outfitting oneself in the modern attire costs more initially than outfitting oneself in traditional costume. Particularly if a woman purchases the cheaper, noncolorfast *huipil* and skirt material, a modern outfit can be obtained considerably more cheaply than the home-woven *huipil* and embroidered skirt. The latter, however, far outwear the former. Paradoxically, therefore, the poorest Panajacheleños may wear the attire which is the most costly in the long run, simply because it is the cheapest on a per garment basis. Given the range in quality and hence cost of Ladino and generalized dress, the estimated community expenditures for these categories of attire probably are less accurate than are the calculations for Panajachel garments. The total clothing expenditures for 1964 are estimated to have been $25,585.

The third largest category of expenditures in 1936 was that of ceremonies and fiestas. Only if one includes all liquor consumption in this category does it retain much importance in 1964. The community religious fiestas remained virtually the same in number in 1964, but the total financial outlay for these fiestas sponsored by the *cofradías* had been substantially reduced. The reasons for the demise of *cofradías* and hence the reduction in associated expenses will be examined in chapter 4; at this point it is sufficient to report that expenditures associated with the four *cofradías* could not have totaled more than $500 in 1964. The most important and costly of the community fiestas continues to be the October 4 fiesta honoring the patron saint, Saint Francis. In 1964 a committee, largely consisting of Ladinos, was appointed to collect funds for fireworks, a marimba, and municipal decorations, and while I have no data on Indian

TABLE 3
Dress Patterns

Style	Men 1936[a]	Men 1964	Women 1936[a]	Women 1964
Ladino	17%	67%	1%	3%
Modern Panajachel[b]	59	26	8	57
Traditional Panajachel	15	3	75	27
Foreign	9	4	16	13

a. Sol Tax, *Penny Capitalism*, p. 159.
b. Women's dress in this category is the Totonicapán, generalized Indian costume.

contributions to these expenses, I doubt that anyone other than a few of the wealthy Indian business owners contributed a few dollars apiece. Other voluntary religious associations have become institutionalized in Panajachel since 1936, such as Protestantism and Catholic Action;[5] and, Catholic Action sponsors seasonal activities such as the *Posadas* at Christmas and pilgrimages to Esquipulas by bus. Only membership in the Protestant sects involve a financial outlay significant enough to warrant measurement. The three sects tithe, but few if any attenders actually give one-tenth of their earnings. Of the forty-nine Protestant households, averaging $1,360 annual income, I doubt that more than half the families tithe at all. Of those who do, I estimate the average annual contributions to approach one-twentieth of the income, or roughly $1,500. To this sum I add an additional $500 to cover all other non-*cofradía* ceremonial expenditures of Panajacheleños in 1964, apart from liquor consumption.

Estimates of liquor expenditures were arrived at in two ways, the resultant estimates differing by only $100 and suggesting $5,000 total Indian consumption in 1964. Three informants were asked independently to assign all men over eighteen to one of four categories: nondrinkers, drinkers in obligatory ceremonial contexts only, occasional tavern drinkers (at least once a month), and regular tavern drinkers (every week or

A Panajacheleño family with women in traditional (center) and generalized (left) dress.

two). Annual expenditures were estimated to average $10, $25, and $50 per individual for the three categories of drinkers. To check the resultant total of $5,000, I obtained records of liquor sales over an eighteen-month period from the one Indian-owned store-tavern in Jucanyá, where the residents of Jucanyá do most of their drinking. Estimating that the $1,300 spent annually at this tavern represents two-thirds of Jucanyá's expenditures (with the remaining third spent in the town center or on clandestinely brewed liquor), and adding proportionate expenditures for the half again as many Indians living on the west side of the river, the estimated total community expenditures again are $5,000.

For the other expenditures included in the 1936 study (supplies, furnishings, markets, travel, personal, and legal), I have assumed an increase of three times the 1936 totals multiplied by the doubled adult population. This procedure is not justified for estimating 1964 expenditures on housing, however, because the distribution of types of construction and the rate of replacement have altered significantly since 1936. The increase in homes of adobe brick with metal roofs (from one in 1936 to 134 in 1964) makes it difficult to determine housing expenditures in 1964. I am certain the figure was at least $2,000, but it could have been higher.

The resultant totals for all known expenditures and receipts are compared with the 1936 data in table 4. The difference between expenditures

TABLE 4
Balance of Payments

	1936 [a]		1964	
Receipts				
Agricultural [b]	$23,730		$ 71,062	
Nonagricultural	1,897		98,250	
Total		$25,627		$169,312
Payments				
Food	$15,220		$117,628	
Clothing	4,066		25,585	
Ceremonial, liquor	1,901		7,100	
Supplies [c]	1,395		14,448	
Personal, legal	691			
Markets, travel	323			
Housing	80		2,000	
Total		$23,676		$166,761
Balance		$ 1,951		$ 2,551

a. Sol Tax, *Penny Capitalism*, p.184.
b. The 1936 income from agriculture includes $441 realized through animal husbandry, fishing, hunting, and plant-gathering. For lack of comparable data on these sources of income in 1964, I have increased the 1936 sum sixfold, allowing for the inflation of the *quetzal* and the nearly doubled number of households.
c. The 1964 sum for supplies includes personal, legal, market, and travel expenditures; in each of these categories the 1936 sum has been increased sixfold to provide an approximation of 1964 expenditures in these areas.

and receipts in 1964 is not significant; as indicated, receipts from services could well be several thousand dollars less and outlay for housing could be more, reducing net savings to nothing. Of course income from agriculture fluctuates from year to year, but with such a diversified cash crop base, it is not likely that the total income would differ appreciably from one year to the next, barring drought or sudden change in the value of coffee. In these respects, 1964 was apparently an average year for agriculture. Assuming, therefore, that agricultural income for 1964 was typical of recent years, it appears that income from the expanded economic base is providing less margin of savings than the basically agricultural base provided in 1936. This does not jibe with the appearance of prosperity give by the many new homes, consumer goods such as radios and bicycles, and the acquisition of fifty acres of land in other *municipios,* however. The apparent anomaly is removed when income from sale of land is considered, for this factor must figure significantly in any attempt to measure the community's wealth relative to 1936.

In 1964 Indians paid from $200 to $300 per *cuerda,* or $1,568 per acre, for the few small farming plots which changed hands. This in itself represented a tenfold increase in land values since 1936 but hardly compares with the prices ranging to $1,000 per *cuerda* received by Indians fortunate enough to own some of the few remaining farm plots suitable for chalets close to the lake. To determine accurately the receipts since 1936 from sale of land to Ladinos would require data on dates of sale and rates of increase in land values. The partial data on these points I did obtain reveal that sizes of plots sold in the 1940s (six cases known) averaged 5 *cuerdas* or roughly one acre, and since 1950 have averaged just 1.5 *cuerdas* (eighteen cases known). This change appears to have reflected a gradual increase in land value until 1955 and a quickening upward spiral since then which led to the doubling of values between 1960 and 1964. My data on land sales to Ladinos for chalets account for 37 *cuerdas* sold before 1960 and 26 since then. In addition I accounted for 20 *cuerdas* sold to nonresident Indians and Ladinos for farming. Estimating the average income to have been $100 per *cuerda* from 1936-49, $150 from 1950-54, $200 from 1955-59, and $400 from 1960-64, the total realized from these sales was roughly $21,300. I do not know the dates of sale for the additional 21 *cuerdas* which have passed out of Indian possession since 1936. Estimating an average of $200 per *cuerda,* $4,200 was realized from these lands. This total of $25,500 received from sale of land should be reduced by the estimated cost of the 36 *cuerdas* known to have been purchased from Ladinos in the same period. I estimated these cost an average of $150 per *cuerda* on the assumption that these were plots useful for farming but not for chalets. This results in a net gain from sale of land conservatively estimated at $20,000. In several instances during my sojourn in Panajachel, receipts from the sale of a *cuerda* or less of land suitable for a chalet covered not only the purchase of a larger plot of land deeper within the delta but also the construction of a new home complete with metal roof. I assume this has occurred numerous times since 1936, explaining many of the 133 adobe and metal-roofed dwellings constructed since then. In other cases the sale of land has provided the capital needed for purchasing tools for construction work, for establishing a store, and for purchasing motorized launches. In yet other cases, sudden wealth led to celebration and prolonged drinking, reducing previous landowners to paupers.

On the strength of these comparisons, it seems fair to conclude that Indians in Panajachel enjoy a higher standard of living only by virtue of a spectacular inflation in land values. The new employment opportunities in themselves do not enable the Indians to live much if any more comfortably than a predominately agricultural economic base permitted in 1936, and if no more land were to be sold the prospects would be for declining prosperity or emigration, given the narrow margin of earnings over expenditures. Of course, land values may, and in all likelihood will, continue to increase disproportionately to other costs, enabling the community to hold its youth and absorb the natural population growth through gradual sale of land and increased dependence upon services to non-Indians.

° 3 °

Wealth and Innovation

Household Distribution of Wealth

P E N N Y   C A P I T A L I S M concludes with an analysis of the distribution of wealth among Panajachel households, the differences in standards
of living attributable to wealth differences, and the factors mitigating
against the formation of classes within Panajachel society on the basis of
wealth. It is instructive to examine how the altered economic base has
influenced the distribution of wealth and the allocation of resources, and
to ascertain the functions of wealth differences in the responses Panajacheleños have made to the changing social environment since 1936.

Requisite to any comparisons of functions of wealth in 1936 and 1964 is a
determination of the wealth-ordering of all households. Land was so
largely the basis of income in 1936 that a comparison of acreages owned
and controlled in itself provided a reasonably accurate ranking of households by wealth. This was much less true in 1964, given the sole or partial
reliance upon income from service occupations by 75 percent of the
households. Moreover, any appraisal of wealth in 1964 had to take into
account the uneven inflation of land values, depending upon location with
regard to the lake, paths, and streets. Finally, the altered expectations of
Panajacheleños toward allocating periodically some of their accumulated
savings to care of the saints had resulted in more consumer goods and, I
assume, proportionately more accumulated cash in 1964.

With the data described in the previous chapter, plus additional data on
composition of each household, I estimated household wealth on the
bases of property, difference between earnings and expenditures in 1964,
and accumulated savings.[1] The wealth of households ranged from nothing
to $14,000, the latter household owning three motorized launches which in
themselves represented a $7,500 investment over the years since 1936,
when the owner had begun with just a dugout canoe. The second wealthiest household was worth only half as much, and the average for all
households (foreign included) was $1,290. The average for native Pan-
ajacheleños was $1,360 and for foreign, $958. The averages are mislead-
ing, however, for the wealthiest 25 percent of the households controlled 64
percent of the wealth, whereas the poorest quartile owned just 2 percent of
the wealth (table 5). To sharpen the contrast even further, the wealthiest 10

percent of households owned almost 40 percent of the wealth, and the poorest 10 percent were landless, with no balance of income over expenditures and no accumulated savings. In view of this uneven distribution of community resources, the median wealth of $750 ($850 if only native households are considered) is more indicative of the resources of the average household. As the average per capita income was roughly $90 in 1964, this means that the average family of six persons had assets of approximately one and one-half times its annual income.

In 1936, the most productive lands lay near the river and the lake, and accordingly the households owning and living upon these lands tended to control a disproportionate share of the community's wealth. This continued to be the case in 1964. Of the 70 families in the upper quartile of the wealth order, 48 live in the southern sectors of the Pueblo and Jucanyá, 16 live in the northern half of the delta, and 6 live in the business district. The concentration of wealthier families near the lake on both sides of the river has produced no more consciousness of this fact in the minds of Panajacheleños than Tax found in 1936. Many of the poor also live in the southern sector; in fact the proportion has increased since 1936 for the simple reason that many employees of the hotels and chalets live on the premises of the Ladino properties in the southern sector.

Influence of Wealth on Housing and Dress

In 1936, Tax was able to find few differences in standards of living and occupation that resulted from differences in wealth. Panajacheleños employed part-time as merchants (market middlemen), builders of Indian homes, curers, midwives, etc., were evenly distributed throughout the wealth order of households in 1936. House construction differed little from family to family. The few homes with openings left for windows were limited to some of the adobe brick houses, but the great majority of households had uniform dwellings of *bajareque* (cane and mud) construction without windows and with dirt floors. House furnishings were more numerous in the wealthier households, but since they remain within the houses, these are not public indicators of wealth differences. Only in the matter of dress did Tax find any suggestion of the material symbolization of wealth. The 1964 variations among Panajacheleños in these above respects were greater than in 1936, and I examined in detail the degree to which the differences correlate with differences in household wealth. Dress continues to reflect wealth more than does housing, especially if footwear is taken into consideration. These latter correlations are presented in table 7 for readers with limited interest in the detail of the intervening pages.

Most Panajachel households consist of at least two dwellings, one housing sleeping quarters and the other containing the cooking hearth.

TABLE 5
Distribution of Wealth

	First Quartile		Second Quartile		Third Quartile		Fourth Quartile	
	Range	%age of total	Range	%age of total	Range	%age of total	Range	%age of total
1936[a]	$ 225-950	56	$110-225	28	$ 50-110	13	$0-50	3
1964	1,500-14,000	64	725-1,500	22	300-725	12	0-300	2

a. Sol Tax, *Penny Capitalism*, p. 192.

Often the kitchen is attached to the main living quarters. A breakdown of the main living quarters of the 315 domiciles for which data were obtained reveals that 247 are of adobe brick construction, 40 are of *bajareque,* and 28 are of makeshift cane walls. The *bajareque* and cane structures invariably are topped with thatched roofs, whereas 35 of the adobe structures have tile roofs and the balance are about equally divided between thatch and metal roofs. Seventy percent of the dwellings are of adobe brick, compared with 20 percent in 1936; and 30 percent have metal roofs, compared with just one home in 1936. Three homes have two stories, with the second floor constructed of lumber, and a half-dozen single-floor structures are of wood construction. With the great increase in adobe brick homes there has been a comparable increase in the popularity of windows. In *bajareque* construction windows are difficult to make, whereas in adobe brick construction they are comparatively simple; I suspect the greater prevalence is therefore attributable more to the type of wall construction than to any marked change in attitudes toward windows. There is one other noteworthy comparison with 1936 data: the number of households owning sweat baths has dropped from 85 percent to 52 percent. Lake bathing is more popular than in 1936, and use of the sweat bath has been discouraged by the health center.

To examine the effect differential wealth has upon house construction, I have compiled the following comparisons of households within the upper quartile and the balance of the population. The seventy wealthiest households own one-third of the adobe dwellings, and only two of these house-

New adobe brick houses with metal roofs built on land reclaimed from the river.

holds retain *bajareque* construction for their principal living quarters. This means, however, that a majority of Panajacheleños in the middle half of the wealth order also own adobe structures. Adobe construction together with a metal roof is a slightly more reliable indicator of wealth status, the upper quartile owning 40 percent of the metal roofs. This quartile also owns 40 percent of the sweat baths. In summary, roughly 70 percent of the wealthiest quartile own sweat baths and homes roofed with metal, but enough

A Panajacheleño couple in front of a *bajareque* house with a straw roof. To the right is an adobe brick house.

others scattered throughout the middle half of the wealth order own comparable dwellings to limit the reliability of these factors as criteria of wealth status.

Seventeen of the seventy wealthiest households have tile or cement floors in at least one building, and to my knowledge no households lower in the wealth order have afforded this luxury. Several also have indoor plumbing, toilets, and electricity, although no one in Jucanyá has these amenities. Several households on both sides of the river have installed outdoor faucets in their patios to take advantage of piped water (installed in the late 1950s to supply public fountains at numerous locations on both sides of the river), and this appears to be a luxury also afforded only by the well-to-do. I believe that proportionately fewer Panajacheleños sleep on the floor than in 1936, and that proportionately more women cook on raised hearths. I made no house-to-house tabulation, however, to permit comparison of the wealth status of families with such furnishings.

Table 3 compared the proportions of Panajacheleños preferring the various alternatives in dress available in 1936 and 1964. In 1936, 8 percent of the women wore the Totonicapán or generalized Indian skirt and *huipil*. The remainder wore one of a number of variations of distinctively Panajachel attire. Few women wore any footwear, and only five men wore Ladino-style shoes. By 1964, 67 percent of the men were wearing Ladino dress and 60 percent of the women were wearing the generalized Totonicapán costume or Ladina dresses. Moreover, the range of locally woven *huipiles* had narrowed: only one elderly woman retained the red-and-white-striped *huipil* common among women in 1936, and no one to my knowledge used the San Andrés white *huipil* preferred by some for everyday use in 1936. The Panajachel *huipil* in 1964 was basically red, with at least purple and usually multicolor designs woven into the front and back, plus in some instances embroidered designs on the sleeves copying *huipiles* of Concepción and Sololá. For men preferring Indian dress, the choices were between white cotton pants and a *rodillera* (small blanket) of wool around the waist (the modern dress) or a knee-length *rodillera* in place of the pants (the traditional dress). The shirts were the same for either attire, but hand-woven and distinctively Indian. Only two men still wore the wool *gabán* (cloak) in 1964; in 1936 twenty-one men wore the *gabán* in place of a shirt.

Occupational factors largely explain the shift to Ladino dress by men. Virtually all men and boys in construction work and other services have adopted western-style dress (see p. 59). Since many in such occupations are Protestants, it is difficult to isolate the influence of Protestantism upon men's dress preferences. That there is an influence is suggested by the fact that the great majority of women adopting Ladina dress are Protestants. With women, as well as with men, there is a tendency for the young to adopt Totonicapán and in the case of boys Ladino attire, while the older

Panajacheleños retain stronger preferences for the more traditional garb. Accordingly, I suspect that wealth is less a factor influencing dress preferences than are age and occupational and religious affiliations with Ladinos.

To examine the correlation of wealth with dress preferences, table 6 compares the percentages of persons wearing each category of attire

A father, wearing traditional *gabán* and *rodillera* skirt, and his son, wearing abbreviated *rodillera,* contemporary shirt, and white trousers.

within the wealthiest and the poorest quartiles of the wealth order. It is readily apparent that among men the kind of attire gives little clue to wealth status. Quality, quantity, and condition are of course considerations, but as far as style itself is concerned, comparable proportions of the wealthy and the poor dress in each kind of attire. Among women, almost as many of the wealthy retain the home-woven Panajachel *huipil* and embroidered skirt as have adopted the generalized dress, whereas among the poor only a third as many afford the traditional costume. This is not surprising, given the considerably greater cost of the home-woven costume over at least the average quality Totonicapán dress.

TABLE 6
Influence of Wealth Upon Dress, 1964

	Men		Women	
Style	Wealthiest Quartile	Poorest Quartile	Wealthiest Quartile	Poorest Quartile
Ladino	64%	57%	5%	—
Modern Panajachel[a]	30	36	42	70%
Traditional Panajachel	5	3	40	23
Foreign	1	4	13	7

a. Women's dress in this category is the Totonicapán, generalized Indian costume.

The choice of footwear proves to be a more reliable indicator of wealth status, especially for men. Table 7 compares the percentages of persons within each category of clothing owning shoes, leather sandals (open-toed shoes, or "half-shoes" as they are designated locally), *caites* (sandals) of tire rubber, or no footwear. Among women a greater preference for going barefoot among those retaining the home-woven costume (regardless of wealth) makes the wearing of plastic sandals or shoes a fair indicator of wealth only among women wearing the generalized or Ladina attire. Among men, however, shoes are decidedly more prevalent among the rich than among the poor, while going barefoot is the choice of relatively few among the wealthy. The few exceptions are full-time farmers. Since no man wearing the Panajachel costume also wears shoes (see p. 61), the sandals or half-shoes are much more indicative of wealth within this category of attire than they are among men wearing Ladino dress. Finally, the median wealth position of all men wearing shoes, sandals, *caites,* and going barefoot are 110, 154, 182, and 205 respectively, further suggesting that among men, dress is a fairly reliable indicator of wealth position when footwear also is taken into consideration.

Wealth and Innovation

For those households in 1964 whose heads (or whose parents) had been ranked by wealth in 1936, it is possible to assess the effect wealth differences have had upon experimentation with new occupations and in turn the effect such experimentation has had upon subsequent distribution of wealth. Such an assessment is made by comparing the proportions of the 1964 labor force in each category of employment supplied by the wealth quartiles, and then comparing wealth standing in 1964 and 1936 of those households first experimenting with the new occupations.

The foreign households not present in 1936 have been excluded from table 8, and since a disproportionate number of foreign Indians fall within the poorest half of the population, the numbers of workers within each quartile are not proportional. Were the total work force included, the poorest quartile would have considerably higher percentages of unskilled laborers, business employees, and chalet caretakers. Even with foreign households included, the poorest quartile has the smallest labor force, since twenty of the poorest households consist of widows.

TABLE 7
Influence of Wealth Upon Footwear, 1964

	Wealthiest Quartile	Poorest Quartile
Men		
Ladino attire and		
Shoes	53%	18%
Half-shoes	20	23
Caites	10	12
Barefoot	17	47
Panajachel attire and		
Shoes	—	—
Half-shoes	42	18
Caites	30	41
Barefoot	28	41
Women		
Ladina attire and		
Shoes	100	—
Plastic sandals	—	—
Barefoot	—	—
Generalized attire and		
Shoes	35	8
Plastic sandals	23	22
Barefoot	42	70
Traditional attire and		
Shoes	3	8
Plastic sandals	20	23
Barefoot	77	69

The wealthiest quartile has a disproportionate share of the labor force in all categories of employment where the minumum daily wage of $.50 is exceeded: hotel, restaurant, and service station employment; building contracting; business ownership; and farming on one's own land. This trend continues down through the second and third quartiles with the exception of building contractors, 29 percent of whom fall within the third quartile. Indian contractors are of two kinds: those specializing in construction of Ladino chalets (with the carpentry, plumbing, and masonry skills entailed), and those possessing only the tools and skills for building Indian homes. The latter builders not uncommonly are hired by contractors for work on chalets but are not themselves contractors for such tasks. With few exceptions, builders serving the Ladino community fall within the upper half of the wealth order and builders serving the Indian community fall within the lower half, thus accounting for the percentages of table 8.

TABLE 8
Distribution of Labor Force, 1964

	First Quartile	Second Quartile	Third Quartile	Fourth Quartile
Business ownership	64%	27%	9%	—
Farming	54	37	7	2%
Hotel, gas, restaurant service	50	32	14	4
Construction	37	18	29	16
Other business service	23	23	23	31
Unskilled labor	13	25	38	24
Chalet-keeping	20	32	31	17

A more detailed examination of the wealthiest 25 percent of the labor force is instructive in a number of respects. These 70 households (58 native and 12 foreign) account for 65 percent of all farmers living off their own land, 70 percent of the business owners (apart from construction work), and almost half of the contractors of Ladino chalets. Forty-six of the households are wholly self-employed, another 8 supplement farming with a little farm work for others, and the remaining 18 have one or more household members employed by Ladinos or by Indian building contractors. In only 10 of the latter 18 households is the head of the household so employed. The combined assets of these 70 households represent 64 percent of the community total, and the comparisons of Table 5 indicate that this quartile controls an even greater proportion of the community's wealth than did the wealthiest 25 percent of the households in 1936. Obviously the expanded economic base has benefited some Panajacheleños more than others, and the rich have become comparatively richer. I pursue the implications of this after examining the role wealth differences played in the experimentation with new occupations and the effect of the expanded economic base upon the wealth standing of the innovating families.

The acquisition of new building skills was the first major innovation, and for the nineteen contractors over forty years of age in 1964 who were engaged in construction work by at least 1950, the 1936 wealth ranking provides a reasonably accurate assessment of their families' wealth status prior to the building boom. Since experimentation with hotel, restaurant, and other tourist-oriented services by Panajacheleños did not begin until after 1950, the 1936 wealth assessments are less reliable indicators of wealth positions of Panajacheleños at the time of their expansion into these services. The development of new Indian-owned businesses has spanned the entire interim of twenty-eight years, and as the capital for such investments was obtained in some instances from sale of land, I will be able to offer little in the way of generalization about the dozen Panajacheleños with their own businesses. Finally, data on farmers purchasing commercial fertilizers since the latter became available locally in 1959 permit examination of the effect differential wealth among farmers has had upon willingness to experiment in agriculture.

I have compared the financial fortunes since 1936 of construction contractors serving the Ladino community on the one hand and the Indian community on the other for at least the fifteen years prior to 1964. In several cases the 1936 and 1964 wealth standing (by quartile) used was of the same individual, but more often the 1964 heads of household were sons of the heads of household ranked in 1936. With the exception of two 1936 masons, all 1964 builders had acquired their skills and tools since Tax's study. It is noteworthy that none of the masons in 1936, nor their relatives who subsequently have entered construction work, have acquired the skills requisite for building chalets. Those who innovated in this regard came entirely from farming backgrounds, but from families that for one reason or another were the first to show interest in the Protestant sects. For example, relationships with foreign Indians and Ladinos within Protestantism, several of whom were builders, led the sons of Bonifacio Cululen to become apprentice builders. From the outset they specialized in constructing chalets, and in turn tended to hire and thus train fellow Protestants. Of the eight innovators in chalet construction by 1950, all but one were from rather well-to-do families, and in general they have improved their economic position in the community. By contrast, the eleven restricting themselves to traditional construction skills have come from the lower half of the wealth order and with only one exception have not improved their status. In fact, four have lost ground relative to their own or their parents' standing in 1936.

While the native masons in 1936 have shown little interest in expanding into the Ladino market, it is noteworthy that sons of two of these masons were among the first to experiment with hotel employment. In addition to these two men, three other families present in 1936 had entered hotel employment by 1955. Of these five households, three were in the second quartile in 1936 and two were in the third. In each case, the wealth position of the household in 1964 was one quartile higher than previously. I do not know who innovated as chalet guardians and gardeners; expansion into such employment began early, and in some cases relatives of Indian building contractors obtained the jobs. Unlike hotel and restaurant work, however, chalet care pays little if any more than hiring out as a farm hand or unskilled construction laborer and to my knowledge has not enabled many households to raise their financial status significantly relative to others in the community.

All foreign Indian business enterprises except one are owned by persons not included in Tax's study, precluding the possibility of assessing their assets prior to building the businesses and hence the success of the enterprises. The Panajacheleño-owned businesses differ greatly in scope, in capital investment, and in the influence of the businesses upon subsequent wealth status. There are, for example, a cobbler in the poorest quartile; a tailor about midway in the wealth order; two venders of clandestinely distilled and imported liquor, one in the upper and the other in the second quartile; and two venders of ice cream and cold drinks, one of whom is in the upper quartile and another in the third. None of these enterprises involved much initial outlay, and without sizable infusions of capital none is likely to develop into full-time employment or in itself significantly improve wealth position.

By contrast, several entrepreneurs have stores representing considerable investments, and in all instances but one the households were high in the wealth order in 1936. The exception is an enigma. Emelio Matzar and his brother, Juan, were orphans and virtual paupers in 1936. Their father had sold his land to a Ladino, embarked upon a drinking spree, and died as a result, leaving his sons little or no inheritance. By 1964 Emelio was tenth in the wealth order, owning his own grocery store and butcher shop in the town center. His family opened a tourist novelty shop in 1964, under the management of a son and daughter. The daughter had attended a Catholic vocational school in Antigua for a total of eleven years of formal education. The son was a collector of antiquities, registered with the National Museum of Guatemala. Gossip has it that Emelio uncovered a relic in his field, which supplied the capital for beginning a store, but this may be only an envious community's rationalization for an enterprising member's success.[2] Emelio's brother, Juan, also has tried various business ventures, including cabinet-making and more recently the sale of refreshments on the beach and during fiestas. He shows little evidence of improving his wealth standing thereby, but the persistence of Juan and of several other poorer households in modest business enterprises suggests that small investments plus patience and perseverance have in at least a few instances paid off.

Examples are to be found among foreign Indians as well as native Panajacheleños. One foreigner, Felipe Ajcojom, whose arrival in 1937 precluded assessing his wealth relative to others in 1936, embarked upon wholesale marketing of produce in Guatemala City and thereby had climbed to seventh place in the 1964 wealth order. Another foreigner, Jesus Queché, initiated a market restaurant catering to Indians. In 1936 the market activity was limited largely to Sundays, when an average of 80 Panajacheleños and 160 foreign merchants sold produce in the course of the morning. By 1964 the market was active every day; on Thursdays it was as large as Sunday markets formerly had been; and on Sundays it was attended by 200 Panajacheleños and 500 foreign Indians selling to several thousand Indians and Ladinos. Jesus' restaurant business flourished, and from the lower half of the wealth order in 1936 he had climbed to midway in the wealthiest quartile.

I have mentioned the wealthiest Panajacheleño, José Rosales, who began with a single dugout canoe in the 1930s and since then has virtually monopolized the freight transportation on the lake and has competed successfully with hotel launches for transportation of Indians and occasionally even tourists. Although José was midway in the upper quartile in 1936, comparison with the only other canoe owner in 1936 suggests that the size of the initial investment was less a factor in José's subsequent success than his perseverance and frugality. A brother-in-law, Mariano Yach, was high in the second wealth quartile in 1936 and like José had hopes of making a business of transportation on the lake. He also had experimented with weaving nets, baking bread, and owning a marimba. Since 1936 he has tried the sale of refreshments in addition to working his own fields. He would appear to be as entrepreneurial as any Panajache-

Yachts and motor boats belonging to the Rosales family.

leño, and yet with all his enterprises he has managed to improve his wealth standing only slightly. A major factor explaining the varying fortunes of the two brothers-in-law is Mariano's enjoyment of the esteem deriving from community service, sponsorship of fiesta dances, and playing in a marimba band. He has realized some substantial profits from sale of land to Ladinos; but these assets, adequate for launching a large-scale business enterprise, have been liquidated through community service and rather free spending.

Two half-brothers monopolize the sale of commerical fertilizers, seeds, etc. Samuel Xingo is employed by the government agricultural extension office, and Lucas Xingo operates independently. Lucas is of the household thirteenth in the 1936 wealth order, compared with Samuel, who was in the third quartile in 1936. This financial advantage appears to have made the difference in enabling Lucas to embark upon business independently, and with this beginning he was prepared to expand his business in 1964 with the construction of a large storage warehouse. In his case, sale of land to Ladinos was being used in further business investment, which I anticipate will place him among the wealthiest Panajacheleños within a few years. Samuel, by contrast, does not have land to sell to realize quick profits for investment, and while he has increased his standing in the community relative to 1936, he is not likely to alter his present status significantly. This is in part because of his willingness to contribute his limited savings to *cofradía* service; in 1964 he was *cofrade* of San Francisco, the foremost *cofradia* in Panajachel. Lucas, by contrast, is a Catequista, or member of Catholic Action, opposed to the maintenance of the *cofradías,* and this is another factor explaining the financial success of one relative compared to a kinsman of similar entrepreneurial bent and occupational involvement.

These examples account for all of the native Indian business owners whose business endeavors approach full-time employment. They suggest that risk-taking in business experiments has been restricted to a few families, and that most were in the upper quartile prior to such investments. Not all Panajacheleños presented with the possibility of improving financial security through business investments have chosen such security above the social esteem deriving from continued participation in wealth-leveling *cofradía* service. Those who have chosen financial security have in some instances greatly accelerated the rate of business expansion through judicious sale of land and use of the capital in their business. The success of most business owners in maintaining or strengthening their wealth position relative to others has encouraged a number of poorer Panajacheleños to venture into small-scale enterprises, but with the exception of Emelio Matzar, no Panajacheleño has managed to build a successful business career without having a substantial land base from which to begin.

The preceding data on occupational specialization suggest that where capital investment has been needed to move into new occupational ventures (construction of chalets, private businesses), the upper quartile has supplied the great majority of innovators. Where capital was not a requisite (hotel employment) but the labor involved working directly for Ladinos, the innovation came more slowly and by persons in the middle wealth range. In no instance, however, have the wealthiest families been the innovators, and in agricultural experimentation this also proves to have been the case.

Chemical fertilizers were introduced by Servicio Fomento Economía Indígena (SFEI) in 1959, and the 12 Panajacheleños purchasing fertilizer for experimentation that year ranged from 9th to 186th in the wealth order. The median and average wealth position of the households using these fertilizers for the first time in 1959, compared with the subsequent years, are presented in table 9. The average for the first year falls in the second quartile, while those waiting until the second and third years to experiment were noticeably wealthier and averaged in the first quartile. By 1962, still only 9 of the 35 households most dependent upon agriculture in the upper quartile had tried the new fertilizers, whereas by 1965, 27 of the 35 were purchasing the fertilizer, and the average wealth rank of persons trying it for the first time had dropped to 130. In summary, the data suggest that: (1) only households within the upper half of the wealth order have sufficient margin to warrant taking even minimal risks; and (2) the wealthiest are more cautious than those in the second quartile, preferring to let others take the initial risks and absorb the gossip and envy that inevitably accompany innovation. While these findings are similar to those of Frank Cancian in his more exhaustive analysis of wealth and innovation correlations in Zinacantan (1972), the Panajachel innovators tend to be slightly higher in the wealth order than do the innovators in Zinacantan. Of course the fact that I was ranking innovators several years after the experimentation with chemical fertilizer began could mean the wealth positions of innovators had improved in the interim by virtue of the increased yields and income the fertilizer produced.

TABLE 9
Wealth Status of Innovators in the Use of Chemical Fertilizer

	1959	1960-61	1962	1963-64
Number of first-time purchasers	12	10	19	25
Median wealth position in 1964	60	44	62	124
Average wealth position in 1964	77	53	84	130

Wealth and Class Consciousness

In the concluding pages of *Penny Capitalism,* Tax discussed the factors mitigating against the aggregation of wealth in the same families over successive generations. Bilateral inheritance, marriage across wealth lines, and *cofradía* service were among the wealth-leveling mechanisms offered in explanation of the ups and downs of family fortunes in successive generations. While this situation has not reduced the accuracy of Tax's description of Panajacheleños as classless in terms of wealth, there are indications that the wealthy are proportionately wealthier than in 1936, that wealth is redistributed less effectively than formerly, that conspicuous consumption has increased the visibility of wealth differences, and that Protestants are tending to control a disproportionate share of the community's wealth. These trends are due in part to an expanded economic base and in part to a shift in value orientations reducing the effectiveness of wealth-leveling mechanisms. Why they are less effective is the subject of chapter 4; the effects of this change upon the distribution of wealth are my present concern.

The classlessness of closed, corporate Indian communities of this region has been maintained in part by reducing wealth differences and in part by reducing the visibility of those differences which do exist. *Cofradía* service, through considerable expenditures for food, liquor, fireworks, and other entertainment, functioned as a wealth-leveling mechanism by consuming accumulated capital. Bilateral inheritance and marriages across wealth lines redistributed any remaining resources of the wealthy. Tax's comparisons of the households in 1936 make abundantly clear, however, that marked differences in household resources existed despite such mechanisms (1953:192). The factors producing these differences are examined in detail in *Penny Capitalism:* on the one hand, entrepreneurial initiative and hard work are highly valued; on the other, household fortunes vary because the household is the only unit of production, exchange, and consumption. Size of family, vicissitudes of illness, death, and drinking, and the narrow margin of profit in the subsistence-based economy alter family fortunes rapidly. Wealthy families of more than one or two generations' depth are rare, but at any given point in time, household wealth varies considerably.

The 1936 data also make clear that these differences were not highly visible; they did not constitute the bases for conspicuous consumption or for predictable differences in consumption patterns except possibly in clothing. The reasons for maintaining low visibility of wealth differences have been examined exhaustively in other contexts. Cognitive orientations regarding the nature and cause of illness and psychological orientations regarding the bases of identity produce a fear of envy which might jeopardize health, happiness, and security. Eric Wolf has labeled this syndrome the "cult of poverty" (1955), and George Foster has placed these orientations within the context of an image of "limited good," postulated as typical of peasant societies relying on subsistence economies (1967).

Although these cognitive and psychological orientations were still operative in 1964, they had become less effective in restraining conspicuous consumption. This trend, together with the declining interest in liquidating assets through *cofradía* service, is the most noticeable effect of the shift in values analyzed in chapter 4. The diminishing effectiveness of *cofradía* service in liquidating savings together with the expanded economic base accounts in large part for the aggregation of 64 percent of the community's resources within the wealthiest 25 percent of the 1964 population. As pointed out above, those benefiting the most from the new sources of income tended to have been among the wealthiest to begin with. They saw alternative uses for their savings and found *cofradía* service an obstacle to possibly attaining a goodly measure of individual financial security. This change in attitude toward the autonomy of individuals in allocation of resources accounts in large part as well for the increase in conspicuous consumption (bicycles, radios, watches, etc.). These results of an expanded economic base and altered bases of security and prestige are by no means unique to Panajachel; comparable changes have been documented and analyzed in detail in numerous other Latin American communities. The Panajachel data merely permit documentation of the shift in distribution of wealth which such changes have been assumed to produce.

The greater proportion of resources controlled by the wealthiest 25 percent of the population (table 5) has yet additional implications which the 1936 data enable us to explore. Knowing that wealth-liquidating mechanisms have diminished in importance, is there evidence that wealth-redistributing mechanisms also have been affected by the expanded economic base? Bilateral inheritance continues to be the norm, but the tendency noted by Tax for marriages to scramble wealth appears to have altered measurably since 1936.

From 1936 to 1941, there were 36 unions of Panajacheleños whose parents' wealth status had been assessed in 1936. Only 13 of the unions were between households of comparable wealth status. The 66 unions occurring during the decade prior to 1964 are compared with the 1936-41 unions in table 10.

One factor in the greater tendency to marry persons of comparable wealth is the decreasing economic importance of women in many Panajachel households. With the increase in population and number of households sharing the delta acreage, landholdings average less per household than previously, even among those households relying on agriculture. As a result, wives of farming families are less often needed for farm work, and where wives are needed, they can give more time to such work than formerly because of time saved in preparing corn. Whereas grinding corn by hand formerly took two to three hours per day for the average household, the introduction of power-driven mills (used by all Indian households in 1964) has eliminated two of the three hand grinding operations; the time saved amounts to practically a day per week. Moreover, the expansion into service occupations has been overwhelmingly dominated by men, and while in some households the loss of males to service occupations has increased the responsibility of women and children for farming the family's land, in the majority of recent unions wives' roles are solely domestic.

TABLE 10
Influence of Wealth Upon Selection of Spouses

Places in Wealth Order	Unions	
Separating Households	1936-41	1955-64
1-33, 1936 1-70, 1964	13	36
34-66, 1936 71-140, 1964	14	15
67-99, 1936 141-210, 1964	6	13
100-133, 1936 211-280, 1964	3	2

Note: The 1936 figures are taken from Sol Tax, *Penny Capitalism*, p. 202. The intervals shown for 1964 are larger simply because of the increase in population.

As a consequence of this altered role of wives in household production, marriages are less often contracted with the end in mind of gaining an additional worker in the household. More often formerly than at present, the landowners encouraged their children to select spouses from poorer households to insure the establishment of residence in the wealthier household. Since men usually initiate the marriage proceedings, this resulted in a tendency toward patrilocal residence, with husbands usually wealthier than wives, and daughters of the wealthiest families frequently marrying late in life or not at all. In 22 of the 36 unions from 1936 to 1941, the man was wealthier than his wife. This tendency now has disappeared, and 36 of the 66 wives married since 1954 were wealthier than their husbands. Patrilocal residence for at least a few years after marriage continues to predominate, although neolocal residence is increasing and matrilocal residence is not uncommon. Neolocal residence is often possible earlier than formerly because of the economic independence young men can attain through service employment. Of those 63 recent unions for which data on residence after marriage were obtained, 36 lived patrilocally, 13 lived matrilocally, and 14 established neolocal residence.

Not only do Panajacheleños show an increasing concern to marry persons of comparable wealth, but this tendency is particularly strong among the wealthy. Of the 36 unions involving spouses within 70 points in the wealth order (hence roughly within the same quartile), all but 7 united persons in the upper half of the wealth order.

These data indicate that marriage contributes less to scrambling wealth within the community than formerly. When this is combined with the reduced effectiveness of *cofradía* service and alcohol consumption in liquidating wealth surpluses, it is not surprising that the wealthiest quarter of the population controls a measurably greater share of the community's resources than previously. While there is no evidence that Panajacheleños are as yet any more conscious of a wealthy class than before, it seems likely that this consciousness will grow with respect to at least the Protestant sector of the population. Because they have the lion's share of especially the construction business and are exempt from expenditures for *cofradía* service and liquor, they tend on the average to be wealthier than other Panajacheleños. The median wealth for Catholic households (natives) in 1964 was $850; the average was $1,300. For native Protestant households the median was $1,000 and the average $1,525. Of the 49 Protestant households (including foreign Protestants), 20 were among the wealthiest 25 percent of the population. Given the disproportionate wealth of Protestants and their marked tendency to marry fellow Protestants, their wealth is expected to increase disproportionately to the wealth of the Catholic sector of the community.

With greater wealth security, conspicuous consumption will in all likelihood continue to increase the visibility of wealth differences among Catholics as well as Protestants. Data on ownership of bicycles and radios suggest this trend: of 39 Indian-owned bicycles in 1964, 19 were owned by persons in the wealthiest quartile and all but 9 by persons in the upper half of the wealth order. Of 43 radios, 25 were owned by the wealthiest quartile. Protestants already manifest fewer restraints on conspicuous consumption than Catholics, and accordingly their more rapid economic advancement can be expected to produce a consciousness of at least a wealthy Protestant elite within the community.

° 4 °

Bases of Security

I A M concerned with two sets of attitudes at this point: attitudes toward employment by Ladinos and in occupations serving Ladinos, and attitudes toward allocation of resources. The latter domain involves attitudes toward community service and bases of identity and security alluded to in the previous chapter.

Despite the considerable range in wealth among Panajacheleños in 1936, only a small minority had sufficient resources to withstand prolonged illness, crop failure, or unemployment from a drinking spree without economic hardship or the threat of economic disaster. There were many households so poor that the hope of financial security was too remote to warrant the planning and saving such security would entail. Fatalism, characteristic of most Panajacheleños to a greater or lesser degree, encouraged reliance upon the saints or destiny for protection from illness, crop failure, and undeserved vicissitudes. The care of those saints not housed permanently in the church or privately owned rotated tradition-ally among households at one-to two-year intervals, each *cofradía* having a staff of one *cofrade* and two or three ranked *mayordomos.* Service was by appointment through the elders, obligatory through community pressure, and unremunerated. In fact, considerable expense was involved, and the higher offices commonly exhausted the savings of several years. This service (five to seven times over approximately twenty years) together with civil offices in intervening years, functioned effectively to integrate all households into a status hierarchy. A degree of psychological or social security was thereby derived from membership in a community where the socially approved goal of production, beyond basic household needs, was conspicuous consumption on behalf of the community. Wealth inequalities indeed there have always been, but their visibility was low, and the collective image was maintained of a brotherhood of the poor.

Acceptance of this image and the demands upon one's time and savings which it involved can be assumed always to have varied among individuals, depending on wealth and individual hierarchies of values. Money has alternative uses, some more legitimate than others, even in closed, cor-porate communities, and thus a latent conflict of values exists where resources are insufficient to satisfy both communal demands and individual priorities. The latter may be merely a new home or clothing or may include purchase of additional land or tools for a new occupational venture. For those wealthy enough to do both there is no conflict; for those too poor to dream dreams, it remains latent; but for those who see the possibility of insuring financial security by putting their savings to work, the conflict becomes manifest.

In Panajachel the traditional norms were challenged in the 1940s, beginning with two men, Francisco Calel and Pedro Queché, who successfully refused to accept *cofradía* offices when asked by the elders to take their turn. They were thirty-eighth and ninety-ninth in the 1936 wealth order, both within the middle half of the scale. The precedent established, six more refused in 1945, going to Solola to plead their cases with state officials. The law legally exempted from community service (civil offices) those who volunteered for military training in Guatemala City or Quezaltenango. Since civil and religious offices were not as clearly distinguished in the minds of Panajacheleños, those with military training claimed legal exemption from *cofradía* service as well. *Cofradía* service never had been mandatory under the law, and in reiterating this, state officials supported the men in their resistance to the local elders.

Protestantism also provided exemption from care of the Catholic saints, although not from civil offices in the hierarchy of community service. The first Indian family to convert had other than strictly economic motives,[1] but the history of Protestantism in Panajachel since 1940 makes it clear that economic motives have figured centrally in the interest many families have shown in the new religious affiliations. Like the first two men to refuse *cofradía* service, the first six families to accept Protestantism were in the middle half of the wealth range: four were in the second quartile and two, in the third.

The expansion of culturally acceptable employment possibilities further accelerated the shift in values, providing ready sources of cash income and new uses for savings. The history of these developments makes clear, however, that the traditional norms had been challenged even before the occupational base had altered. Indeed, they were challenged initially by persons who did not find recourse to military training or Protestantism necessary to withstand the negative sanctions of the community.

The subsequent twenty years have witnessed so extensive a shift in values that by 1964 *cofradía* service no longer was a norm in Panajachel, even among Catholics. The Catholic Action movement was partially responsible. The *cofradías* still existed, and the number of households unaffiliated with Catholic Action or Protestantism was as large in 1964 as was the population in 1936. Yet the *cofradías* were staffed with difficulty; even most Catholics were unwilling to accept the offices, and in some cases those accepting did so with the understanding that expenses would be shared by the body of elders.[2] The attitudes toward community service have altered, much as Tax anticipated they would. His diary of 1941 reads:

It may be concluded (tentatively) that it is the military that makes feasible the conversion of Indians without great complications or interference with the local *costumbres*. But since more and more young men seem to prefer military service to local ones, even when no question of religion is involved, it may be supposed that military service itself will account for considerable weakening of the cult of the saints in the near future. I shall not be surprised if in ten years the political services will have been separated from the religious, and that the saints will be taken care of purely voluntarily. If that happens, I shall expect to find many Indians no longer involved at all with the cofradía organization, and the remainder growing *less* secular in respect to it. What I mean is that there will be a selection of religious-minded people who will participate in the religion of the community as religiously-inspired devotees, and their religious attachments will tend to increase. [1950: 2, 123]

The shift in attitudes and values is broader than concern with *cofradía* service, or even with autonomy in allocation of resources in general. It involves a wider range of stances toward Ladinos, with whom some Indians associate more informally than previously in occupational, educational, and religious contexts. The new contexts and altered bases of interaction with Ladinos have in turn influenced world view, or belief patterns and bases of identity. This is particularly true of Protestants and those Indians remaining through six grades of elementary school. In both contexts, Indians adopt the more informal bases of interaction characteristic of Ladino associations. The shifts in belief patterns and bases of identity have not been highly visible; indeed, they have been rather incidental by-products of accommodations to Ladino society for which the economic rationale was highly visible. More significantly, the economic rationale reflected entrepreneurial values basic to Panajachel culture. Perhaps because of this, the marked changes in dress patterns, bilingualism, occupational involvement, curing practices, religious affiliations, and even the demise of the *cofradías* have not symbolized to many Panajacheleños the disintegration or basic cultural change they suggest to the casual observer. If factionalism and psychological disorganization have been precipitated by the altered hierarchy of values less in Panajachel than reported elsewhere in Guatemala (and this is my conclusion), then it may be due to the greater individualism, entrepreneurial bent, and secularism of Panajachel culture. The heavy involvement in cash crops and reliance upon the market possibly place Panajacheleños further along the folk-urban continuum in these respects than even other Indians of the lake region. If so, it is fortuitous that Panajachel should have become the focus of tourism and Ladino recreation in the region, providing such a laboratory for viewing the adjustive potential of the "penny capitalists" par excellence.

Attitudes Toward Employment

Prior to 1940, Panajacheleños were reluctant to work for Ladinos, sell land to Ladinos, or interact with Ladinos any more than necessary. It was unheard of for a Ladino to work for an Indian. Foreign Indians were not subject to the same restraints, and indeed a number had come to Panajachel to take advantage of the hotel employment available as early as 1930. No Panajacheleño sought hotel employment prior to 1950, and yet by 1964 there were thirty-six men so employed. This number constituted two-thirds of the Indians hired by Panajachel hotels. Foreign Indians also set the precedent for selling native fabrics to tourists, importing fabrics from Totonicapán and Chichicastenango, and purchasing small quantities from Indian women around the lake. One of the first such entrepreneurs was Juan Cutillo, a Maxeño house employee of the Taxes in Chichicastenango who accompanied the Taxes to Panajachel and subsequently established his own weaving business there. Panajacheleños are cognizant of the lucrative nature of such businesses, and yet not a single Panajacheleño has experimented with this endeavor. Nor were any Panajachel women weaving fabrics to sell to tourists on the beaches as neighboring Catarinecas (Santa Catarina) were doing in Panajachel in 1964. Pan-

A Panajacheleño-owned textile shop established in 1974.

ajacheleñas questioned about this said they would be embarrassed to be seen selling to tourists, just as some men expressed an unwillingness to play the servant role in hotel work.

While the range of culturally acceptable employment had broadened considerably by 1964, obviously sanctions or preferences still limited Panajacheleños' choice of occupation and made some jobs more acceptable than others. In order to measure attitudes toward and preferences among the wider range of occupations available in 1964, I discussed this history of occupational diversification with thirty-eight informants selected for comparing belief patterns. During the initial interview I asked each informant to order in terms of his preferences eleven drawings depicting Panajacheleños involved in: (1) farming; (2) marketing; (3) conducting divinatory *costumbre* (ritual) as a *zahorín* (shaman); (4) fishing; (5) road maintenance; (6) construction work; (7) store-tavern management; (8) selling native fabrics to tourists on the beach; (9) working the pumps in a gas station; (10) caring for a chalet; and (11) waiting on tables in a hotel.[3] The first six were engaged in to some extent by Panajacheleños in 1936, although fishing was a virtual monopoly of the neighboring Catarinecos and road maintenance was unpaid obligatory duty of each household for two weeks out of each year. It was a salaried job in 1964. There were seven Panajachel *zahorines* in 1936, but only three still living in 1964. Most informants were amused that I included this as one of the options because of the questionable status *zahorines* have in the minds of many Panajacheleños. Even persons standing in respect and awe of shamans realize that a living cannot easily be made in this manner; therefore no one placed this calling high on his list of preferences.

Assuming that there would be a predisposition to order the occupation cards in terms of present skills and available financial resources, I encouraged ordering on the basis of the "good life," assuming the opportunities and capital needed were available for any of the occupations. For female informants or older men who found it difficult to think of themselves engaging in some of these pursuits, I suggested that choices be made with a husband or growing son in mind. Discussion of reasons for the ordering then followed, and I regret that I did not make more systematic notations (or tape recordings) of these remarks to permit a more exhaustive summary of the reasons offered. My primary interests were in eliciting the order of preferences, reactions to the suitability of traditional Indian dress in the various contexts, awareness of gossip directed at Indians in service occupations, and correlation between preference order and the earning potential of the various occupations. Farming was a poor bet financially compared with some of the service employment, and given the traditional attachment to the soil on the one hand and entrepreneurial propinquity on the other, I was interested in assessing the effect of differential earning power upon preferences.

Concern with gossip seldom was volunteered in discussing any of the occupations, although when specifically asked about those occupations encountering the most gossip, sixteen volunteered that hotel workers were subject to criticism. Many indicated that sanctions had been stronger earlier. Five included gas station employment along with hotel work in this

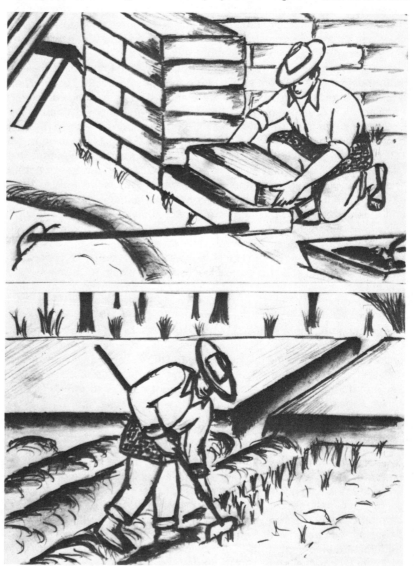

Illustrations used in study of occupational preferences, mason and farmer.

category, and two also included chalet care and construction work. Seven volunteered that store owners frequently are accused of being avaricious and of taking unfair advantage of the *gente pobre* (poor folk). One is reminded of Foster's thesis that income from services to one's fellows is resented more and presents a greater threat to the solidarity of the community than does income derived from services to outsiders (1967). Despite this reputation, store management rated high among preferences, and in Panajachel store management has continued through two genera-tions in at least two households.[4] Protestants in general played down the prevalence of gossip, and the informants from agriculturally based house-holds appeared less conscious of gossip than those actually engaged in service employment. Since no Panajacheleños are engaged to any visible extent in fishing or selling native fabrics to tourists, informants found it odd that these should have been included as options.

Frequently the opinion was expressed that each person was free to choose whatever work he pleased, in accordance with his abilities and occupational destiny. Yet no Panajacheleño expressed this attitude toward occupational destiny as strongly as did one Catarineco informant similarly questioned about occupational preferences. He balked even at the idea of speculating about what occupation would be desirable for his son, saying repeatedly that vocation is a matter of *suerte* (luck), and each individual must find the calling intended for him. I suspect Panajacheleños shared this concept of predestination in vocation, as in health, wealth, etc., more strongly before the expansion into service occupations began. In this regard I questioned most informants about the predestined roles of mid-wifery and shamanism. In 1936 the opinion was general among Tax's informants that shamans and midwives at least are born with these callings; among my informants, very few agreed to this with regard to midwives, and most denied it even with regard to shamans.

Table 11 compares the popularity of the occupations among the 38 informants. Of the 11 preferring farming above all other occupations, 6 are involved full-time in agriculture and 5 supplement farm work with other employment. To look at it another way, most who lack a land base adequate for farming prefer other occupations, in most cases occupations they are not engaged in currently. Several indicated that if farming paid better, they would prefer it above the occupations given priority in their ranking. Only 5 of the 22 listing construction work as their first or second choice are currently engaged in construction work; this is the overwhelm-ing choice of occupation for the majority of informants employed as unskilled laborers, farm hands, or business employees. The most surpris-ing finding was the lack of interest in hotel work, despite the fact that several of the informants were thus employed.

To examine the correlations among religious affiliation, education, and occupational preference, table 12 gives the order of occupational preferences for the informants as a group (the listed order) compared with the order for Protestants, Catholics, informants with less than five years of schooling, and informants who completed elementary school. The order-

TABLE 11
Occupational Preferences, 1964

	1st choice	2nd choice	3rd choice	4th choice
Construction worker	12	10	2	7
Farm worker	11	5	7	6
Chalet guardian	4	8	6	4
Store-tavern owner	5	5	4	3
Merchant	3	4	4	8
Gas station attendant	1	4	4	2
Hotel worker	—	2	4	5
Road worker	1	—	2	2
Textile vender	—	—	4	—
Fisherman	1	—	—	—
Shaman	—	—	—	—

ing in each case was determined by totaling first, second, third, and fourth choices and weighting these totals to arrive at a single ranking for the various persons of each category.

TABLE 12
Religion, Education, and Ranked Occupational Preference, 1964

	Protestants (17)a	Catholics (21)	>5 years of school (10)	<5 years of school (28)
Construction worker	1	2	1	1
Farm worker	3	1	5	2
Chalet guardian	5	3	4	3
Store-tavern owner	2	5	2	5
Merchant	7	4	7	4
Gas station attendant	4	6	3	6
Hotel worker	6	7	6	7
Road worker	9	8	9	8
Textile vender	8	9	8	9
Fisherman	10	10	10	10
Shaman	11	11	11	11

a. The numbers in parentheses indicate the number of informants within each category, whose combined preferences yield the 1-11 ranking of occupational choices.

Indians with the maximum amount of schooling available locally are presumably less hesitant to work with and for Ladinos and feel more at home with Spanish and the mathematical skills necessary for, say, operating gas pumps or managing a store. Accordingly, these latter occupations are more frequently preferred by those who had finished elementary school to less remunerative, but more traditional pursuits such as farming and marketing. Of the 22 men who had completed five or more years of school by 1964 who were not still in school, only 4 were farming, compared with 6 in hotels, 3 in gas stations, 5 in construction, and the other 4 in stores or other private businesses. Construction work and store management are particularly desirable to Protestants who, more than Catholics, gave as a reason for preferring these occupations the greater autonomy and independence they provide. These attitudes are reflected in the proportions of Protestants and Catholics so employed (table 13). For the same reasons, Protestant informants showed less interest in chalet care, while Catholics seemed less bothered by the subservience entailed. For the labor force as a whole, however, comparable percentages of Protestants and Catholics are thus employed.

TABLE 13
Occupational Distribution by Religion, 1964

	Percentage of	
	Protestant Work Force	Catholic Work Force
Self-employed farmers	12%	24%
Farm hands	5	13
Construction laborers	16	8
Finca, road laborers	8	10
Self-employed businessmen	4	2
Merchants	—	3
Carpenters, masons	16	8
Hotel employees	11	9
House servants	2	3
Business employees	11	5
Chalet guardians	16	16

To test the correspondence between occupational preferences and the incomes from the occupations, I asked each informant to order the cards according to earning power after he had ordered them in terms of preference. Or, as frequently happened, in the course of discussing the occupational preferences I asked for the average daily or monthly income from each. The correlation was determined by totaling the point discrepancy for each occupation in the two rankings, and the range was from complete one-to-one correspondence in four cases to 27 points' difference. The average discrepancy was 14 points for Protestants and only 11 points for those who had completed elementary school. By comparison, Catholics as well as all Indians with less than five years of school averaged 21 points' difference. Looking at the four whose preferences corresponded exactly with their assessment of income potential, three are Protestants and one is a Catholic. The latter has had eleven years of schooling and is the most acculturated of my informants by all criteria; the other three have had eight, six, and three years of schooling respectively.

Of course a number of alternative occupations were offered as first choices in the course of the interviewing. One informant expressed a desire to become a Protestant minister, another a teacher, another a truck driver, and one even aspires to owning a coffee *finca.* There are, in short, few occupations to which Panajacheleños do not feel free to aspire. On the other hand, cultural biases regarding the good life strongly affect attitudes concerning the most appropriate ways of making a living.

Attitudes Toward Allocation of Resources

Having described the lifting of sanctions on occupational dependency upon Ladinos, I turn to the increasing freedom enjoyed by Panajacheleños to allocate their resources as they choose. It is my thesis that Protestantism, Catholic Action, and military training owed their popularity during the 1940s and 1950s primarily to the greater autonomy they provided Panajacheleños in use of time and savings. This autonomy facilitated the effective exploitation of new employment opportunities. To document this thesis, the history of Panajacheleños' involvement in these institutions must first be reviewed.

Protestantism

Among the foreigners to establish residence in Panajachel as early as the 1920s were Protestant missionaries who used Panajachel as a base for missionary activity in various of the lake towns. Panajacheleños were slower to show interest in this new religion than Indians across the lake, and the first conversion occurred in 1938, a full decade after a foothold had been established in San Pedro la Laguna. When Tax terminated field work in 1941, there were two or three Indian households active in the one Protestant sect, Centroamericanos. In the early 1940s, the Assembly of God established a mission in Panajachel to serve the lake region, and in 1964 approximately 90 percent of the Indian Protestants were fairly evenly divided between these two sects. The others were Baptists and Jehovah's Witnesses. The latter's missionaries came first to Panajachel in the early 1950s but gained no adherents and left to return again in 1960. As of 1964 they had a small following, including two Indian families and a larger number of Ladinos. The Baptists established their center of operations in Panajachel in 1964 and as of our departure in mid-1965 had a small but active group of adherents drawn primarily from the other Protestant sects.

Determining membership was complicated by the lack of records. Regularity of attendance and observance of the moral code are the chief criteria of membership, and by the end of our stay I had an accurate accounting of those active as of mid-1965 as well as a longer list including inactive families whom non-Protestants nevertheless identified as Protestants. In addition I determined the great majority of all Panajacheleños who had at some time since 1940 identified with Protestantism; these totaled one-third of the adults living in 1964, of whom only one-half were active in 1964. These active members of the four sects represented families or individuals of 49 households, including 14 foreign households. Of the 134 active Protestant adults, 62 were born in other communities or are children of immigrants to Panajachel. Eighteen of these are married to Indians of Panajachel ancestry, leaving some 22 Protestant households where both spouses are native Panajacheleños. Somewhere between the number of active members and the number of Indians who at some time have tried Protestantism lies the number of Indians sufficiently influenced by Protestantism that they are no longer considered Catholics. On the basis of general consensus among several Catholic and Protestant informants, I included in this category a total of 81 families, or 272 persons, for the purposes of this study. Of the 81 families, 38 converted in the 1940s, 32 in the 1950s, and only 11 from 1960 to 1965. The declining rate of conversion plus the high percentage of inactive or former Protestants suggest a waning interest in Protestantism.

Catholicism

In 1936 there was no resident priest in Panajachel; indeed, there had been neither a priest nor a roof on the church since the 1903 earthquake that toppled virtually every church in the region. By 1964 there were two resident priests serving Panajachel and neighboring communities, the church had been rebuilt, and a large convent was under construction. The growing Ladino population accounts in part for these changes, although throughout the region an influx of Catholic priests and revitalization of Catholicism occurred in the early 1950s. The success of Protestantism after a slow beginning may provide a partial explanation. In the 1940s Paulino priests centered in Solola had encouraged indigenous efforts to revitalize Catholicism, and in 1952 a resident priest of the Carmelite order was again assigned to Panajachel. The Catholic Action movement, whose adherents locally became known as "Catequistas," established a local chapter which gave Indian discontents and progressives an alternative to Protestantism. Unlike some communities, where Catholic Action drew its chief support from Catholics desiring to reform "folk" Catholicism, in Panajachel many Catequistas regarded Catholic Action as a rebuttal to Protestantism and a buttress to traditionalism.

I do not have exact figures on membership within Catholic Action a decade ago, but it appears that during the last half of the 1950s both Protestantism and Catholic Action enjoyed their height of popularity. In 1964, the number of active Catequistas (that is, those attending evening classes in the catechism, masses, etc.) was sixty. As with Protestantism, interest is waning, and most of those who remain active are related by kinship ties. In Panajachel, Catholic Action, unlike Protestantism, has appealed neither to foreign Indians nor to Ladinos.

Military Training

I do not know how many Panajacheleños had volunteered for military training prior to 1940. The number was not great, for such service did not provide exemption from *cofradía* service before that date. A half-dozen elderly Panajacheleños in 1964 had experienced military training prior to 1940, and in several instances they had accepted *cofradía* posts upon their return to Panajachel. Since 1940 at least forty men have volunteered for such training, and of these not one has accepted *cofradía* service since returning.

Initially sanctions were heavy even on Protestants who did not also enter military service in lieu of *cofradía* service. All five sons of the first convert had military training, but it is noteworthy that a generation later not one of his five eligible grandsons has felt it necessary to enlist. In 1964 only one Panajachel youth was undergoing military training, and interestingly his father was head of one *cofradía* and his brother a *mayordomo* in yet another. The youth still needed the excuse of military service in breaking with strong family tradition, as had *every other* married Indian residing in Jucanyá (the predominately Indian and more conservative sector of Panajachel) who had not accepted a *cofradía* post. These latter are older married men, however, who sought military training during the period of stronger feelings ten to twenty years ago. The younger men, with very few exceptions, are neither entering military service nor expecting to serve in *cofradías*. If the sanctions were stronger they would be doing one or the other.

Their attitude is typified by one thirty-five-year-old Panajacheleño who entered the army and now feels exempt from service to the community. Like all who have served in the army, he wears western dress, speaks fluent Spanish, and gives the appearance of being quite ladinoized. When discussing the decrease in crop yields and family income over the past two decades, he attributed the change to the lack of respect shown the saints and decreasing interest in the *cofradías*. Nevertheless he will never accept a *cofradía*. He wants to buy an aluminum canoe and knows that he can never save enough money if he begins participating in the *cofradías*. The informant is not opposed to *cofradías*. He is one of an increasing number of nominal Catholics who join the Catequistas in advocating that the saints be placed in the custody of the church and the priest. It is generally agreed that this will happen in time, as it has already in San Pedro la Laguna. However, as long as there are individuals willing to staff the *cofradías,* not even the Catequistas campaign actively for the change.

To the above appraisal of attitudes of the nominally Catholic population (those for whom *cofradía* service is a possibility) must be added the impact of Protestant and to a lesser extent Catequista teachings which certainly have opposed the *cofradías* on religious as well as economic grounds. The fact that religious differences have not precipitated any pervasive faction-alism on this score, however, suggests the priority of economic motives. The objection to *cofradías* is less to their existence than to the obligatory participation by those who see a more satisfying future and status in alternative uses of their savings.

Economic Factors in Religion and Military Training

Many Panajachel Protestants would object to the implication that their only or primary motive for converting to Protestantism was to avoid *cofradía* service and associated expenses. I suspect this generalization applies more accurately to the families who affiliated briefly with Protes-tant sects and then dropped away. The active Protestants include many foreign households, for whom the cost of community service was never an issue. Moreover, the active Protestants contribute to the salary of a pastor and rental of church buildings. The cost per year does not begin to equal what *cofradía* service can involve; yet *cofradía* service is only periodic, and over the years the difference would not be great. Also, a minority of the native Protestants accepted Protestantism as a result of marrying Protes-tants; their family ties are assumed to be the primary motive for accepting the new faith. Finally, one Protestant joined after accidentally dropping and killing a baby when in a drunken stupor. In his case the moral issue of liquor was the overriding factor, and Protestantism offered support in breaking with the habit and tradition.

The tradition of alcohol consumption bears brief review, since it is abstention from liquor that Protestantism symbolizes in the minds of many Protestants and most Catholics. The Catholic ceremonial contexts in which drinking is virtually obligatory have precluded until recent years the possibility of Catholics' abstaining completely from alcohol. Excessive drinking was regretted but was not regarded as a vice. The financial, rather than the moral, cost was counted, and the good citizen was one who controlled his drinking but who nevertheless drank, out of respect for liquor itself and for the ceremonies of which alcohol was an essential part. Liquor was holy, and there was no socially acceptable excuse for not drinking in ceremonial contexts apart from ill health. In nearby San José Chacayá an Indian was observed to empty his glass of liquor into a flask at his neck through a funnel in his shirt. In this way he could participate in the ritual sharing of liquor without jeopardizing his health. Even in Protestant circles the custom persists of drinking together; soft drinks are substituted for alcohol. In funeral processions I have observed Protestants and Catho-lics together carrying the coffin. At intersections of paths where liquor traditionally was shared en route to the cemetery, the family of the deceased provided a choice of beverage. Soft drinks have replaced liquor at Protestant wakes, home prayer meetings, and visits for the purpose of asking for a bride.

Since liquor is the largest single expenditure associated with cofradía service, it seems reasonable to assume this was an expense many Panajacheleños hoped to eliminate by avoiding such service. Altering the traditional patterns of liquor use has proven difficult for Panajachel Protestants, however; most have not found the financial saving worth the sacrifice. Of the 47 converts to Protestantism known to have been moderate to heavy drinkers prior to conversion, only 20 have remained active members.[5] Eleven of the latter have given up liquor completely, but 9 still drink occasionally in private. Of the 27 who have dropped out of Protestantism, 20 have reverted to their old drinking habits; the remaining 7 have noticeably decreased their consumption from preconversion habits. When experimentation with religion became the vogue in the 1950s and cofradía service was weakening rapidly in status, the encouragement to stop drinking was appealing to many Panajacheleños. Many converted at this time, but membership was short-lived and usually terminated or was interrupted on the occasion of a large fiesta when old habits and social ties virtually forced the older segment of the population to conform to traditional definitions of religious and social responsibility. It is a fact that attendance figures fall at the time of fiestas, and it is this inconsistency among some Protestants that evokes the most criticism of Protestants from fellow Protestants and Catholics alike. I conclude that while liquor costs (in health and savings) have contributed to Protestantism's appeal, the inability of most converts to do without liquor and associated benefits explains in large measure the waning interest in Protestantism.

Liquor is a major expense of cofradía service, but it is not the only one. Food, fireworks, and musicians' fees are associated expenses. Moreover, time becomes as important an economic consideration as the cash outlay, particularly for men employed in service occupations. The number of men avoiding cofradía service through military training indicates important economic factors other than merely liquor. In this regard it is noteworthy that six young men quickly volunteered for cofradía service in 1965 when they learned this would exempt them from compulsory drill each Sunday in the local company of reservists. The ruling, handed down by departmental officials at the request of the alcalde (mayor) and Indian elders, would quickly revive the cofradías were it not for the fact that the reserve company is organized only every eight to ten years.

To support the thesis that this wider range of economic factors largely explains the interest of Panajacheleños in Protestantism and military training, I make use of the wealth ordering of households. I postulate that to the extent economic motives for entering military service and changing religious affiliations have been primary, the wealthy will have chosen these alternatives more readily than the poor. I limit the comparisons to native Panajacheleños, since foreigners were never expected to share responsibility for the *cofradías.* The average wealth in 1964 of all former *cofradía* officeholders was $1,625—$400 higher than the average of Panajacheleños who had not served but who were eligible. The sum of $1,625 suggests the level of wealth at which *cofradía* service would be assumed a legitimate expectation. The average wealth of military volunteers was $1,615, and significantly all but seven of these volunteers were in the upper 50 percent of the wealth order. The distribution of Protestant wealth was much wider. Of the twenty-eight native Protestants who independently chose Protestantism (excluding those who converted as a result of marrying into Protestant families), half were quite wealthy and half were quite poor. The wealth of the former half averaged $1,900, compared with only $425 for the poorer half. The Protestant rich and the military volunteers, had they remained eligible for *cofradía* service, would almost certainly have been asked to serve. In fact, a number of the wealthy Protestants had already begun *cofradía* service before converting. Some of these have since dropped out of Protestantism, but in only one case has *cofradía* service subsequently been accepted again. It would appear that once Panajacheleños have broken with traditionalism to experiment with Protestantism they no longer are considered eligible for *cofradía* service, even if their membership was short-lived.

The fact that half of the Protestant households were too poor to be expected to assist with care of the saints would weaken the hypothesis of conversion for economic motives if it were not for the added factor of liquor consumption. Eleven of the fourteen drank moderately to heavily prior to conversion and have since become inactive, reverting in all cases to previous drinking habits.

The available data suggest economic motives have been less important among Indians entering Catholic Action. Not only is the average wealth of Catequista households below the average of those participating in *cofradías,* it is also below the average of all nominal Catholics. Only six of the twenty-seven Catequista men are wealthy enough to have been expected to accept *cofradías,* and two of these joined only after marrying into Catequista households. Drinking habits of Catequistas prior to entering Catholic Action were not obtained, but as all but two of the twenty-seven men drink lightly as Catequistas, it is not likely that many, if any, heavy drinkers enter the movement to escape liquor. While Catholic Action encourages temperance, a Catequista is not popularly defined as a nondrinker, as is a Protestant. Nor was membership in Catholic Action considered inconsistent with *cofradía* services initially; the Indian who served as the informal leader of the movement during its first five years was relieved of his duties after then deciding to accept a *cofradía.* He continues to consider himself as devout a Catholic as the Catequistas. In at least two other cases, Catequistas accepted *cofradías* after participation, and only gradually has the community of Catequistas come to feel the two are mutually exclusive. In other communities, such as San Pedro la Laguna and Chichicastenango, a much sharper division between church and *cofradías* has been precipitated by Catholic Action.

Economic Factors in Language and Dress

Language and dress have been the most visible indicators of ladinoization in Guatemala. It will be clear from previous chapters that knowledge of Spanish in Panajachel has obvious economic benefits. While all Indians in Panajachel speak Cakchiquel, virtually all teen-agers and all men under fifty years of age speak rather fluent Spanish. By contrast with 1936-41, when Tax found only a half-dozen women with whom he could converse in Spanish, most women in 1964 could speak it adequately for market negotiations and many could speak it fluently. A few families speak Spanish in the house more than they do Cakchiquel, or speak Spanish to all members but the mother or grandmother.

The increased bilingualism results in part from the involvement in services to Ladinos and in part from formal education. The replacement of the 1936 public school with a larger school in the 1950s, the establishment in Jucanyá of a small one-room school offering two years of schooling, and the replacement of the Jucanyá school with a new structure housing additional grades in 1965[6] reflect the continuing growth among Indians and Ladinos of interest in schooling. However, a closer study of the community statistics indicates that the increased utilization of educational opportunities is very much greater among Protestants than among Catholics, especially among nominal Catholics, both in the proportions attending school and in the numbers remaining in school through sixth grade. The fact that only four nominal Catholics have finished elementary school since 1965 suggests little change in attitudes among traditionalists toward formal schooling. A comparison of percentages of nominal Catholics attending school over the decade of 1935-44 and the decade of 1955-64 bears out this conclusion: only 8 percent more of the eligible boys and 13 percent more of the girls from traditional households were enrolled during the latter decade than during the former. One-third of the eligible boys and more than two-thirds of the girls were not in school in 1964.

The differential utilization of schooling opportunities by religious groups may be attributed in part to economic factors. Protestants tend to be wealthier than Catholics and to be employed in occupations in which children of school age cannot participate as they can in agriculture. These economic considerations may be the major explanation of the tendency among Protestants to remain in school longer, although the fact that twice as high a percentage of Protestant youth go beyond third grade suggests as well a differential value placed upon education for education's sake. There can be no doubt that the chief motive for schooling within all segments of the population is to become functionally literate, and that achieving literacy in Spanish has become universally valued in Panajachel. The mood, even of nominal Catholics, is reflected in the request of one traditionally oriented teen-ager to have his photo taken with a Spanish dictionary proudly displayed at his side.

In summary, literacy has economic value and is achieved by virtually everyone who has the additional motivation of reading the Bible. It is the only objective of formal education for the majority of Indians, and as functional literacy is achieved by fourth grade, few Indians see any reason to complete elementary school.

The economic factors underlying dress preferences are less obvious, and in view of the marked changes in these preferences among Panajacheleños since 1936, it is useful to examine the correlations of dress with religious affiliations, community service, and occupations. Table 14 compares dress patterns of the three religious groups. Protestant men wear western dress, and both Protestant men and women wear shoes in much higher proportions than do Catholics. Differences in dress preferences between the nominal Catholics and the Catequistas (men) largely disappear when one takes into consideration that military volunteers very rarely go back to Indian dress.

While Protestants are more western, or Ladino, in dress, it is equally noteworthy that all combinations of dress and footwear are found among Protestants, including even one man who retains the old *rodillera* skirt in place of trousers. The lack of conformity to Ladino dress among Protestants argues against too readily concluding that Protestantism encourages western dress, and a closer examination of the data again reveals economic factors which may be more important than the religious. In discussing occupational preferences with informants, I found general agreement that hotel employees and store or business clerks or owners needed to adopt western dress, and that chalet guardians, gardeners, and men employed in construction work would more readily secure work if dressed as Ladinos. In fact, 90 percent of hotel, gas station, and private business employees, 75 percent of construction men, and 70 percent of chalet employees wear western dress, compared with just 20 percent of farmers. If one subtracts the sizable number of veterans of military training in Ladino dress who are engaged in farming, the percentage of farmers choosing Ladino dress is even lower. From table 13, the proportions of Catholics and Protestants engaged in these various occupations can be determined, revealing 40 percent of Catholics and 60 percent of Protestants in occupations necessitating or benefiting from Ladino dress. As 61 percent of the nominal Catholics and 83 percent of the Protestants (men) wear Ladino dress, the percentage difference between occupational involvement and Ladino dress is within two points of being the same for the two religious groups. In short, while these data indicate that at least 20 percent of the Indian male population wear Ladino dress for other than employment motives, this percentage is the same for Catholics as for Protestants.

TABLE 14
Religion and Dress, 1964

	Nominal Catholics	Catequistas	Native Protestants
Men			
Ladino attire and			
Shoes	16%	17%	44%
Half-shoes	20	5	20
Caites	8	3	3
Barefoot	17	22	18
Modern Panajachel attire and			
Shoes	—	—	—
Half-shoes	8	27	3
Caites	15	6	3
Barefoot	11	14	7
Traditional Panajachel attire and			
Shoes	—	—	—
Half-shoes	—	3	—
Caites	3	3	2
Barefoot	2	—	—
Women			
Ladina attire and			
Shoes	—	—	4
Plastic sandals	—	—	—
Barefoot	—	—	—
Generalized attire and			
Shoes	4	—	24
Plastic sandals	6	25	24
Barefoot	53	25	24
Traditional Panajachel attire and			
Shoes	1	—	1
Plastic sandals	3	16	3
Barefoot	33	34	20

Economic motives may likewise account in part for adoption of western dress even when occupational success is not at stake (thus accounting for some of the 20 percent in Ladino dress but not in occupations enhanced by such dress). While many of the poorest Indians retain Indian dress, a disproportionate number of those wearing western dress are in the lowest quartile of the wealth order. The great majority of these are barefoot, however, suggesting that the cheapest way to dress is in the poorer quality trousers and western shirt and barefoot. It will be recalled that footwear, more than dress, is a criterion of wealth status for those wearing Ladino clothing. Shoes are never worn by Indians retaining Indian dress, and even other forms of footgear are less reliable indicators of wealth among those in Indian costume.

While less complete data on stockings were obtained, it is my impression that shoes without stockings are functional only for persons who are unable or feel too uncomfortable to wear them regularly, for example, the school boy who takes them off as soon as he returns home each day, or the farm boy who wears them in public but kicks them off to irrigate or work in his garden beds. In any case, shoes unmistakably connote a stance toward Ladinos which traditionally oriented Indians mistrust. Their rationalization is "Jesus wore only sandals," and it is significant that not one Indian wearing Indian dress in 1964 wore shoes.

The case of one Indian youth is instructive: he completed sixth grade still wearing traditional dress and applied for a scholarship to attend prevocational school in Sololá. Upon being awarded the scholarship, he had to decide how to dress among the predominately Ladino students in Sololá; his mother, a Catholic, preferred that he retain Indian dress, but his father, a Protestant (but still in Indian dress), consented to his son's adopting Ladino clothing. The following two years he remained barefoot, although wearing shirt and trousers. At the time of our departure from Panajachel he was reapplying for a scholarship to enable him to complete the three years of prevocational school. He had decided to buy shoes if granted the scholarship again, on the expectation of at last being able to realize his dream of completing the training to become a teacher. As a teacher he would of course wear shoes, but as long as there was any chance of his having to return to farming or other forms of Indian employment in Panajachel, he preferred to remain barefoot.

In short, a barefoot Indian declares his Indianness regardless of his clothing, while shoes are not visible indicators and leave one open to suspicion of desiring acceptance as a Ladino. There is sufficient looseness in this area, however, that dress is never an adequate indicator. One of the most traditional of my informants, with no schooling, nominally Catholic and anticipating *cofradía* service, and fully accepting of the traditional world view, wears Ladino dress, shoes, and stockings. He and his father sell refreshments and possibly feel that their Ladino appearance enhances their selling. As far as I could tell, no Indians are sanctioned for changing dress when the economic motives are evident.

In view of this, it is not surprising that at least twenty men who have accepted *cofradía* positions also wear Ladino dress. Five of these were even wearing shoes in 1964. Of the twenty, all but five had either served in the army or were in occupations in which western dress was advantageous. As five were farmers, however, I can only assume that Indian dress is not a requisite for *cofradía* service, even though the great majority serving in *cofradías* do retain the old dress.

It is apparent that a changing economic base in Panajachel, away from agriculture toward dependency upon wage work and services to non-Indians, has made economically advantageous a number of acculturative adjustments. Adoption of Ladino dress and schooling and Protestantism give economic advantage. Construction men almost without exception have adopted western dress, as too obvious an Indian identification would jeopardize their securing building contracts. The same is true of hotel workers and gas station attendants, and is less true but still a consideration in seeking work as a custodian or gardener of a chalet. Protestants are known not to drink and hence are better risks as chalet or hotel employees. Facility with Spanish is a requisite for success in any of the service occupations, and most Indian boys now become functionally literate before dropping out of school. Of those Indians seeking their fortunes in Ladino circles, only the very wealthy can afford to remain visibly Indian. It is therefore noteworthy that the wealthiest Indian in Panajachel in 1964, owner of the three launches and the thriving cargo-passenger service, persisted in wearing Indian dress, despite the fact that his father had been one of the first Panajacheleños to adopt Ladino dress. He withdrew from *cofradía* and church involvement years ago, yet he was not alienated from the Indian community in so doing. Panajacheleños have permitted individualism full rein, and the result is a community of Indians many of whom appear fully acculturated, yet who—with few exceptions—are no less Indian in self-image than in 1936.

·5·

Social Relations

I N his article "World View and Social Relations in Guatemala" (1941), Tax developed the thesis that the individualism and secularism of social relations fostered by the economic organization of Panajachel insulated a world view or "mental apprehension of reality" which was in 1940 "primitive," animistic, and folk, in contrast to the "civilized" character of social relations. He postulated the kinds of influences, or changes in social relations, that could be expected to weaken the insulation of mental culture and expose premises of world view to any alternative points of view shared by non-Indians. One such influence is education: "When and if effective education is given the Indians in substantial numbers, and they learn Spanish and become literate, acculturation to the civilized world will probably go on apace; and then their world view will become of the kind that is more usually associated with the kind of social relations they have so long had" (1941:42). Another is the gradual replacement of impersonal social relations with "the kind of intimate contacts by means of which cultural items are best exchanged" (1941:33).

It will be apparent from the preceding chapter that social interaction among Indians and Ladinos in 1964 was more frequent and in some contexts more intimate and informal than in 1936. True, some of the elderly Panajacheleños have no more to do with Ladinos than formerly. Approximately one-fourth of the adults have found it possible to restrict their labor to agriculture, and among these are many who resist any alteration of the status quo, whether in curing practices, religious affiliation, or community service. A comparable minority of adults at the other extreme have actively broadened their spheres of interaction with Ladinos to exploit whatever advantages might accrue from passing as a Ladino. The remaining half have cautiously expanded their spheres of association with Ladinos, while retaining some visible symbols of Indian identity. These latter join with the most acculturated element in saying, "Now we are civilized" (to borrow the title of Charles Leslie's book [1960]). In dress, language, curing practices, and in some belief complexes associated with their forefathers, many Panajacheleños regard themselves as liberated from superstition and old-fashioned custom. Panajachel gives the impression of being a community of Ladinos to other Indians of the lake region, and Ladinos of Guatemala City regard Panajacheleños as transitional in some significant respects.

In view of this, it comes rather as a surprise to learn that the economic acculturation typical of most Panajacheleños appears to have qualitatively influenced social interaction with Ladinos and hence belief patterns hardly at all. By contrast, those Indians completing elementary school or participating actively in Protestantism have assimilated Ladino belief patterns to a considerable degree, suggesting more informality in these contexts of association. The 1936 and 1964 comparisons in belief patterns will be examined in chapter 6. In this chapter I describe the range of social relations among Indians and Ladinos in 1964. I am primarily interested in the social relations characterizing Protestantism and schooling which make possible the confrontation of ideas lacking traditionally between Indians and Ladinos and still lacking in most contexts of association, and the barriers to the spread among other Indians of this more ladinoized world view. These objectives are equally important. Changes in mental culture occur very slowly if the changes experienced by a few transitionals do not then diffuse. If each individual of the subordinate culture must individually alter his bases of social interaction with members of the superordinate culture before a confrontation in ideas occurs, world view can be expected to narrow very slowly for the subordinate culture as a whole. This, in fact, is what appears to be occurring in Panajachel.

Ladino-Indian Relations

The nature of relations among Indians and Ladinos in Guatemala has an extensive literature.[1] Social relations in the midwestern highlands have been described as impersonal and secular, both within Indian communities and between people of different communities. "There is first of all, and even in the family, a commercial spirit; but whether or not the development of commerce was historically responsible, today impersonality is manifest not only in economic but in political and religious life, and in family relations as well" (Tax 1941:33). The commercial spirit has deep historical roots but may in itself merely reflect a pervasive secularism in the culture, characterized by a dominance of institutionalized over personal, informal relationships. In any case, the commercialism contributes to individualism and impersonality, as well as to both awareness of and indifference to cultural differences. Because of the economic integration of the lake region, Panajacheleños are mobile. Tax surmised that "the average Indian could no doubt write large fragments of the ethnography of half-a-dozen towns other than his own. . . . if there were less physical contact of people of various communities, it is not unlikely that there would be more interchange of culture" (1941:31, 34). This acceptance of cultural plural-ism means that, barring the greater language difference, Indians have

hardly more incentive for developing with foreign Indians than with Ladinos "the kind of intimate contacts by means of which cultural items are
best exchanged. . . . Acculturation to Ladinos can therefore be described
largely in the same terms as acculturation of Indian communities to each
other" (1941:33, 36).

It is useful in this respect to think of the community of foreign Indians
residing in Panajachel as a buffer between native Indians and local
Ladinos. The ethnic status of some foreigners is uncertain, and even when
surnames reflect Indian identity, some foreign Indians tend to be accepted
as peripheral members of Ladino society. On the other hand, they also are
peripheral members of local Indian society. Their presence in increasing
numbers since 1936 has weakened the distinctions drawn by both Ladinos
and Panajacheleños between each other, and the precedents they have
established in association with Ladinos have accelerated native Indians'
acculturation in various respects. The role of foreign Indians in broadening the Panajacheleños' economic base has been described.

The influence of foreign Indians upon marriage patterns is another
example. The greater freedom of foreigners in choosing spouses has
made marriage between native and foreign Indians a commonplace and
marriage between native Indians and local Ladinos more permissible than
it otherwise would have been. In 1936, Juan Rosales was the only native
Panajacheleño married to or living with a Ladina in Panajachel. A sister of
Juan's had left Panajachel to live with a Ladino husband on the coast, and
one other Panajacheleña had been left by a Ladino spouse then residing in
Guatemala City. Two or three Ladino households contained foreign Indian
spouses. Since 1936 there have been twenty unions of Indians and Ladinos, thirteen involving foreign Indians and seven involving native Panajacheleños. Several of the twenty unions have been short-lived, but in all
cases the couple established residence and produced offspring, with
parentage publicly declared in the municipal birth registry. In several
additional instances, offspring of mixed parentage have been registered
without mention of the Ladino parent's name; in these cases the parents
had not lived together and their children are considered illegitimate.

Towards the end of our stay in Panajachel the *cofrade* of the *cofradía* of
San Francisco asked Ardith and me to serve as *padrinos* (godparents) at
the marriage of his daughter to a Ladino. The daughter had become
pregnant by the Ladino, who was being forced by the girl's parents and
local civil authorities to marry her and accept responsibility for the child. In
the eyes of her parents, the mixed union was a lesser evil than the
daughter's plight as an unwed mother with responsibility for the child.

In questioning informants concerning their acquaintance with other
towns and regions in Guatemala, I asked for their ranking of preferred
places to live in the unlikely event that departure from Panajachel should
become necessary to find a spouse or employment. With a number of

informants I also asked their preference (for themselves if single, or, if married, for their children) between remaining in Panajachel married to a Ladino and living in any of the adjoining *municipios* married to an Indian of that community. Since without exception informants rated the neighboring communities of Santa Catarina, Concepción, and San Jorge at the bottom of the list of desirable communities in their acquaintance, I hoped in this manner to gain some idea of attitudes toward intermarriage. Eight of the eleven I asked said they would prefer to remain in Panajachel wed to a Ladino. When pushed to choose between intermarriage and moving to the community highest on their list, five of these eight still preferred intermarriage to moving away.

The acceptance of intermarriage is reflected also in the attitudes toward offspring of such unions. Invariably such children wear Ladino dress, but the several such youths interviewed by me gave no indication of trying to live down their Indian ancestry. One of these, a girl of sixteen, had lived for a year in common-law marriage with a local Indian of foreign parentage before separating and taking up residence with a native-born Indian. Her Ladino grandfather as well as her Ladino father had wed Indian women. Another informant of mixed parentage wears no shoes, speaks Cakchiquel to his Indian relatives, and chooses friends among Indians as freely as among Ladinos. Although he was still in his teens, marriage to an Indian appeared as likely as marriage to a Ladina. In yet another case, a Ladino son-in-law of a respected, rather wealthy Indian household lived matrilocally. Nor are the mixed unions restricted to situations where Ladino men initiate relationships with Indian women; in four of the seven marriages involving Panajacheleños, the Indians were men.

In other contexts of informal association, foreign Indians have facilitated interaction between Panajacheleños and local Ladinos. The health clinic has experimented with women's clubs which attract poor Ladinas and Indians in equal numbers. Most of the Indians, however, are of foreign origin, and their presence has made easier the participation of Panajacheleñas, who have shown considerable reluctance to join.

The same role of foreign Indians is observable in the boys' club, established to promote athletic and social events in Panajachel. Although the club is dominated by Ladinos, Indians are not excluded and at least foreign Indians have always been active. Indeed, foreign Indians were instrumental in the club's establishment. I sensed more reluctance on the part of local Indians to participate actively in the club than discrimination against them by Ladinos, and this tendency to remain apart was observable in the formation of soccer squads. Several such squads existed in Panajachel in addition to the club's team, and Ladinos and foreign-born Indians dominated all squads except one, which was comprised solely of native Indians. Some of these latter Indians on occasion also played on other teams, but there was considerable enthusiasm for the maintenance of a purely Indian team despite its usual defeat at the hands of the other local teams. They usually played against predominately Indian teams of other towns, and I should add that the maintenance of such a team is attributable in part to the inability of some Indian players to afford soccer shoes and their timidity to play in bare feet in the company of shod players.

These new contexts of association rarely involve the wealthiest Ladinos. In 1936, Tax noted a distinction between wealthy, land-owning Ladinos designated in that era as *chancles* and poorer Ladinos designated as *obreros* (workers). These terms have disappeared with the influx of Ladinos and foreign acculturated Indians, but rich and poor Ladinos are still social realities. The poorer Ladinos interact much more freely with Indians than do the sophisticated Guatemalans who have made Panajachel such a thriving resort center.

The greater range of associations of Panajacheleños with at least the poor Ladinos nevertheless has reduced to some extent the visible indicators of Indians' subordinate status. The health center treats Indians and Ladinos on equal footing; the resident doctor receives patients in his home or makes house calls to Indians and Ladinos for a fee. The wealthier Ladinos never come to the clinic, but rarely have I gone to the doctor's home when Indians and Ladinos alike were not waiting on the porch on a first come, first served basis. Ladinos and Indians are not segregated in seating at masses or school functions. The wealthier Ladinos always sit toward the front, but Indians feel free to sit among them, and poorer Ladinos are scattered among Indians throughout the room.

Dances sponsored by the boys' club or by the *municipalidad* (town hall) are never restricted to Ladinos, although the most formal dances are attended by invitation and only a few foreign Indians are invited. Indians stand around and watch at even the most formal dances held in the public hall. Indian-sponsored *zarabandas* (public dances) are open to anyone, but relatively few Ladinos participate. These are rough-and-tumble affairs, which even many Indians feel it beneath their dignity (or against religious principles) to attend; the remarkable thing is that *any* Ladinos enter the fray! Of the four marimba bands in Panajachel serving hotels and private parties, one is composed only of Indians and the others have Ladinos and at least some Indians of foreign descent. Friendships cut across ethnic lines to the extent that any marriage of at least poor Ladinos will find some Indians invited. Ladinos not infrequently drink publicly with Indians. In religious and funeral processions, Ladinos and Indians intermingle, and the wake of any prominent Indian will be attended by Ladino friends.

This does not mean that Ladino-enforced indicators of ethnic superordination are not present. To my knowledge, no Ladino has ever asked Indians to be *compadres,* while Indians increasingly ask Ladinos. I know three Ladinos who have more than fifty godchildren, and we acquired ten in the eighteen months we were in Panajachel. Indians ask even the wealthiest Ladinos this favor. Such *compadre* relationships are perfuncto-ry, with economic advantage obviously the chief motivation for Indians who prefer Ladino to Indian compadres. Apart from Protestants, Indians invariably use the formal Spanish terms of address and *"don"* or *"doña"* in addressing even poor Ladinos, while Ladinos usually use the familiar *"tu"* and virtually never precede Indian names with *"don"* or *"doña."*

Indians usually refer to themselves as *"naturales"*; in formal speeches by Indians at school functions I occasionally heard *indios* or even *indígenas* used for effect, as in the following quotation: "Nosostros, los naturales de Panajachel, O mejor dicho, los indios" ("We, the natives of Panajachel, or more appropriately, the Indians"). A number of my inform-ants reserved the term *"indios"* for their ancestors, a consequence I think of exposure to textbooks in school which use *"indios"* in describing the Maya Indians encountered by Spaniards in Guatemala. Ladinos some-times refer to Indians as *"naturales,"* but *"indios"* is more common, and *"inditos"* is occasionally used in a condescending manner. I never heard Ladinos deprecate fellow Ladinos by labeling them *"indios"* or any other term denoting Indian.

Finally, customs distinguishing the ethnic groups persist. Ladinos never

Panajacheleñas selling vegetables in the Sunday market.

sell food in the marketplace, and Indian women never carry produce in baskets carried in the hand. It is not uncommon for Ladinas to carry on their heads, however, or to support babies in carrying cloths on their backs. An increasing number of Panajachel men are embarrassed to carry loads suspended from a tumpline, and of course Ladinos never carry in this manner. As for burial customs, virtually all Ladinos are interred in vaults above ground, while most Indians are interred in graves. Wealthier Indians freely choose vaults, however, and in one instance during our stay in Panajachel a poor Ladino asked to be buried in a grave. There is no segregation of burial plots in the cemetery. I referred earlier to the fact that sweat baths are less frequently used for bathing by Indians; most continue to use the sweat bath for curing and following childbirth, and I know of at least one Ladino household (in addition to a couple of mixed households) where the sweat bath is used at least for cure of illness.

In describing forms of address above, I indicated that Protestants do not observe the distinctions in forms of address characterizing other Ladinos and Indians. Ethnic distinctions appear virtually to have disappeared among "*los hermanos*" (the brethren), as Protestants refer to themselves. Intermarriage is more frequent within Protestant circles, both between Panajacheleños and foreign Indians and between Indians and Ladinos. All Protestant congregations include as many Ladinos and ladinoized foreign Indians as Panajacheleños. Religious services are held two evenings each week, and on other evenings youth, women's, and men's groups meet in the chapel. In addition, home prayer meetings can be called by any member, and frequently birthdays are occasions of home services. I attended one such service in the home of a twenty-eight-year-old Ladina informant, and informal discussion ranged from women's hair styles in the United States to the request by a Catholic that a Protestant carpenter drill holes in the household saint's ears to facilitate his hearing the family's petitions. It became apparent that ideas diffuse rapidly in such settings. Indeed, the Ladina in question became convinced of the existence of *characoteles* (people who assume animal form) from listening to a respected Protestant Indian tell of an encounter. She had learned a variety of traditional Indian ideas through such contacts with Indians in the congregation, and one gains the impression that folklore and beliefs are shared freely in a search for the "truth" as substantiated by the Bible. The Ladina was preparing to marry an Indian of the congregation, and his petitioning for her hand had followed the traditional Indian pattern. Only the liquor was absent.

Not only do Protestants interact with fellow Protestants in a greater number of voluntary contexts than did Panajacheleños traditionally, but the associations are mutually reinforcing. The same persons form the association groups. Relationships are less formal and less prescribed, and personal ties develop much more readily than is possible in traditional contexts of association.

Social Relations Among Indians

Catholics likewise have a greater range of voluntary associations than formerly, but none of these new associations, apart from schooling and occasionally employment, foster the affective ties with Ladinos charac- teristic of Protestantism. It will be recalled that Catholic Action mem- bership is limited wholly to Indians, and with one exception to native Panajacheleños. Catequistas see much of each other, but only in the formal setting of classes in catechism held in the church. They have no supportive contexts of association apart from several annual trips to visit the saints of neighboring lake towns during fiestas.

Spiritualists form a group, not unlike a religious sect, of Ladinos and Indians. The first spiritualist, a Ladina, came to Panajachel from Santiago Atitlán around 1955 and trained a local Indian (married to a Ladina) who began to hold independent séances in 1964. While Protestants draw censure for attending séances and therefore rarely do so, Catequistas are not so restricted. Séance attenders address one another as "brother," but this relationship appears to exist only during the curing sessions; asso- ciates in this context are not associates in other contexts. The behavior during séances is highly formal and prescribed, and few persons attend the curing sessions regularly.

Moreover, the contexts of social interaction between Protestants and Catholics have not noticably altered. Protestants do not attend fiestas, movies in the Catholic church, or for the most part the wakes and funerals of Catholics. Protestants work with Catholics, it is true, but on the other hand Protestants tend to hire other Protestants. Protestants cannot serve as godparents, and most have severed such ties that existed prior to conversion. Protestants attend school with Catholics, but since so few Catholic children continue beyond fourth grade, this avenue of diffusion of ideas within the community is not highly significant. Intermarriage be- tween Catholics and Protestants must be considered an important influ- ence, but until comparatively recently parents were extremely reluctant to permit such intermarriage. To a large degree, the contexts of Protes- tant-Catholic interaction since 1940 have been limited to marketing, em- ployment, community public office, and school.

 In these institutionalized contexts of association, relationships among Indians are no more informal or intimate than Tax described them to be in 1940. Choice of associates within these contexts always has been limited, and friendships established in one context seldom are strengthened through reinforcing associations in other contexts. Families tend to sit together in the marketplace, travel together to and from the Sololá market, and usually occupy the same locations in the market. Even when launder- ing clothes at the river, locations are fixed by custom, and visiting is restricted to a narrow range of neighbors. Men do not ascend the hierarchy of civil (or *cofradía*) offices together, and there is little tendency to build

upon employment or community service associations in developing affective bonds through other voluntary associations. Finally, when Indians do
have the time and inclination to associate in informal contexts, they
traditionally have found it easiest to let behavior be patterned by the norms
of interaction in the institutionalized contexts or to drink liquor to facilitate
social intercourse.

The formality of house-to-house visiting for purposes of borrowing
implements or money, or for arranging for a baptism or a marriage, has not
changed appreciably since 1936. Visiting without some such definite
purpose was virtually unknown formerly, even among close relatives.
Compadres and close relatives customarily assisted each other in times of
illness or need, but custom dictated that visiting at other than such
prescribed times was out of order. It is my impression that the introduction
of grinding mills and the decreased reliance upon agriculture have provided particularly the women more time for visiting, but traditional restraints
upon such visiting continue to keep women close to home. Teen-age
youths and men have greater liberty in use of their free time, and soccer
has become a popular spectator sport for men. Protestants feel uncomfortable in even this atmosphere, and of course these contexts of voluntary
association among Catholics do not qualitatively influence their relationships with Ladinos.

Schooling is the one notable exception. For Indians continuing beyond
fourth grade, school associations with Ladinos can become quite intimate
and at least as conducive as Protestantism to assimilation of belief patterns. This results from the shift in proportions of Indians and Ladinos in
classes from third and fourth grades to fifth and sixth. During the earlier
years classes have as many (if not more) Indians as Ladinos, and Indians
continue to associate largely with other Indians. Once literacy in Spanish is
achieved, the great majority of Indian children drop out of school, leaving
the few who continue markedly outnumbered by Ladinos. Indians usually
adopt Ladino dress at this point if they had not done so previously, and
friendships established between Indians and Ladinos are patterned by
norms of Ladino association, which tends to be more informal and group
centered.

I turn now to the influence of these new social relations among Indians
and Ladinos upon belief patterns of the Indian community.

·6·

The Panajachel World View

PANAJACHELEÑOS traditionally accorded men more respect than they accorded women, but one gains the impression from behavior and conversation that Panajachel society is becoming more egalitarian. How does the observer document such impressions? How are comparisons made between what a community believed about the status of women in 1940 and what the same community believed a quarter of a century later?

The impressions about basic belief patterns are necessarily constructs of the observer, put together from many particular comments and actions which can be referred to as the primary data of the research. The primary data suggesting subordination of women to men included: men walking ahead of their wives, or being accused of being hen-pecked if they failed to observe this custom; women washing men's clothing apart from women's clothing and advising Ardith never to place the women's garments on top of men's in the laundry basket; an informant complaining about a woman's stepping over his tools and then relating this to the comparable danger of a woman's sweeping her broom over a man's outstretched feet. It is apparent from even casual observation in Panajachel that the people believe women and women's belongings have a debilitating or weakening effect if placed ahead of or on top of men or men's belongings. Yet even this latter generalization is not articulated by many Panajacheleños, and I interviewed only one Panajacheleño who abstracted further to relate this complex of beliefs to the subordinate status of women. Such secondary data, the products of my probing and inferring, do not lend themselves readily to discussion with informants for the purpose of assessing stability of belief. The assumptions underlying primary belief data become explicitly articulated only by those who encounter alternative explanations or points of view. When people are faced with contradictions or discontinuities, they seek explanations where they had not deemed it necessary to articulate any. Accordingly it was one of the most ardent Protestants, questioning much of the traditional world view of the community, who most clearly described the status relationships of men and women. He had come to believe the subordinate position of women to be wrong.

An alternative method of assessing the relative strength of assumptions is available to the observer where visibility of assumptions is too low among informants to permit useful discussion of community reliance upon them. It is possible to measure systematically awareness and acceptance of the more specific and readily articulated primary beliefs. Then, to the extent that one succeeds in eliciting or feels justified in inferring generalizations from these primary data, it becomes possible to assess the stability of the underlying assumptions. It is in this manner that I conclude that Panajacheleños in general are more egalitarian now than in 1940.

The problems inherent in eliciting and inferring generalizations from the primary data are just as thorny as are the problems of sampling awareness and acceptance of the primary data. I deal with the latter problems in this chapter and attempt a model of the abstracted generalizations in chapter 7. More specifically, in this chapter I compare awareness and acceptance of a sample of primary belief data among forty-six Panajacheleños interviewed in 1964-65. The informants were selected on the basis of differential exposure to acculturative influences such as Protestantism, Catholic Action, military service, and formal schooling. Correlations between these latter variables and awareness and acceptance of the primary beliefs are noted, and the differences in influence of these variables on stability of belief are explained.

I make several other comparisons in an effort to measure stability of belief through two generations of Panajacheleños and pervasiveness of Panajachel primary data among Indians and Ladinos in the region. Specifically, I compare: (1) awareness of a sample of beliefs among seven informants interviewed by Tax in 1940 with awareness of the same beliefs by informants in 1964; (2) awareness of the beliefs found most widely shared by Panajacheleños with their awareness among twenty-one Indians in thirteen other towns in western Guatemala; and (3) awareness of this latter sample among Ladinos in Panajachel and neighboring lake towns.

The primary data from which the above samples were drawn consist of literally hundreds of beliefs verbalized by Panajacheleños in explaining behavior, offering advice, and relating stories. These were recorded day by day in diaries kept by Sol and Gertrude Tax, Ardith, and myself throughout the six years of field work. In chapter 7, several hundred of these beliefs are utilized to illustrate secondary generalizations. The bulk of Tax's voluminous primary data will appear in the ethnographic volume being readied for publication.

In 1938, Tax and Redfield undertook a comparison of beliefs in Panajachel, San Antonio Palopó, and Agua Escondida. San Antonio is an Indian community; Agua Escondida is Ladino. For this comparison, Tax selected some four hundred items of belief from the primary data he gathered in Panajachel. As Redfield commenced his interviewing in Agua Escondida, a sampling problem arose. Could beliefs learned by Tax in

Panajachel from one or two informants, but not known by one or two informants questioned in Agua Escondida, be attributed safely to one culture and not the other? How many persons would have to be questioned before a judgment could be confidently made on presence or absence of a belief item in the local world view? In his 1940-41 field season, Tax undertook to measure the homogeneity of Panajacheleños' awareness of the sample of four hundred beliefs.

These data were made available to me the year before I began my own field research in Panajachel. My analysis took two directions: (1) comparing awareness and acceptance among the seven informants; and (2) inferring the assumptions or premises implicit in the four hundred items of belief. The latter analysis formed the basis of the model of Panajachel belief structure presented at the end of chapter 7. The former analysis suggested the feasibility of discussing the same sample of primary data with a small group of friends early in my own research, preliminary to narrowing the sample of beliefs and broadening the sample of informants for more extensive interviewing later during our stay.

Before turning to the generational comparisons, some orientation is needed to the terms employed by Panajacheleños in categorizing beliefs. In any Panajacheleño's store of knowledge are *cosas ciertas* (truths or beliefs), *mentiras* (untruths, or lies), and *cosas que no son ciertas* (uncertainties; hypotheses open to question, validation, and rejection). Benson Saler has referred to the latter as "unbeliefs," defined as a "proposition, meaningful to an individual, about which the individual expresses uncertainty as to whether it is true or false" (1968: 32).

While Panajacheleños do not think of beliefs as constituting a system, any more than they think of kinship or language as systematized, they do employ a rudimentary classification of beliefs in terms of function. Cutting across the distinctions among "beliefs," "unbeliefs," and "disbeliefs," are four classes or categories of belief distinguished in Spanish as *pecados, secretos, remedios,* and *señas.* These are not sharply delineated categories, and they overlap considerably.

Pecado (sinful) is an adjective used frequently as a noun, as in *"es un gran pecado"* (it's a very sinful thing), and is applicable to any behavioral injunction which if unobserved brings retribution or misfortune. The bounds for its application are elastic, and for some informants any "do" or "don't," whether sanctioned or not, is *"pecado."* For most, however, minor breaches of etiquette are not *pecados* but simply are disrespectful. The function of the category *"pecado"* is to avoid negative sanctions, be they social or supernatural.

Secretos are secrets, as a literal translation implies, but in Panajachel, at least, the privacy of *secretos* is less characteristic of this class of phenomena than is the function they serve: the prevention or causation of some condition or occurrence. In a sense, *secretos* are the reverse of *pecados,* and some informants translate them with the same Cakchiquel term: *pecados* are usually things one should avoid doing, while *secretos* are what one should do to attain a given objective. There is another difference, however. *Secretos* for the most part apply to the mundane; failure to observe them is less often assumed sanctioned. And to some extent they are regarded as less than universal in either their recognition or their efficacy. That is, *secretos* in a narrow sense belong to individuals or groups, while *pecados* are universal.

Obviously not everything one does to accomplish a desired objective is a *secreto;* a distinction in kinds of instrumental knowledge or activities becomes apparent in the order in which information often is offered. For example, when asked about the procedures for growing *pepinos* (an egg-shaped vegetable), a Panajacheleño will give the technological procedures for planting, irrigating, and harvesting, which are highly standardized and common knowledge. Usually only when asked if there are *secretos* for insuring or influencing a good crop does he commence to list from one to a dozen procedures that range from never working among *pepinos* with sandals to eating eggs prior to planting. In a few instances the *secretos* were offered with no apparent distinction made between the two sets of knowledge. These *secretos* are less commonly known than the technological procedures but are group-typical of Panajacheleños.

The rationale or explanation for a *secreto* is often not known, or indeed assumed unknowable. When I probed for explanations of "why" the *secreto* works, not infrequently a sufficient answer was, "Who knows? It's a *secreto*." *Secretos* are more frequently tested pragmatically than reasoned deductively. For this reason *secretos* often are entertained as hypotheses rather than accepted unreservedly as true.

Remedios (cures), for animals and persons, are a subclass of *secretos,* which quite possibly were less common knowledge and more zealously guarded formerly in Panajachel than they are now. While some *secretos* are *remedios,* not all *remedios* are *secretos.* Pharmaceuticals are seldom labeled "*secretos,*" although herbs and cures based on sympathetic magic usually qualify.

Señas (signs) are meanings or implications of occurrences which are often referred to as *secretos* but which involve no action and over which man has little if any control. Objects or events are referred to as having or giving their *señas.* I have, somewhat arbitrarily I admit, distinguished *señas* from *secretos* on the basis of this difference in function. Signs foretell. They are explanatory rather than instrumental in achieving something, and accordingly I have included signs under a larger category of beliefs which to my knowledge Panajacheleños do not identify by any convenient label, but which I will call "identifications." This category includes identifications, explanations, and signs, none of which are behaviors, but many of which influence behavior. Hence a rainbow is *identified* by some as the breath of a large multicolored snake; when it falls into the lake it *means* rain; and it is *sinful* to point at it (punishment: a bent finger). Or, a falling star is a spirit on an errand. On observing it one should whistle *(secreto)* to avoid its having any influence over you.

I do not want to leave the impression that Panajacheleños readily group beliefs in terms of these classificatory labels or concepts; in the few instances where I experimented with asking informants to group belief items by whatever common ideas they recognized among the items, the basis for grouping almost invariably was common subject matter. Sometimes the common function was the basis for grouping, and occasionally derivation from a common premise was recognized.

Panajachel Comparisons, 1941-64.

In trying to measure stability of world view within a community over a twenty-five-year period, one must recognize the problems of comparability of data given different observers in 1941 and 1964: variations of belief awareness and acceptance among observers of different ages within any population; and the problems of sampling error. Since the data suggest a 15-20 percent reduction in awareness of primary belief data since 1941, I must give due attention to the above problems. I begin with a full description of the samples of beliefs constituting the tools of my analysis.

Tax's sample of world view material was selected for the dual purpose of measuring homogeneity of beliefs within Panajachel and pervasiveness in towns around Lake Atitlán. Tax attended more to awareness of these beliefs than to the strength of their acceptance by informants, although he preserved in writing the data available to him, permitting a rough assessment of acceptance as well among his seven informants, from five households, ranging in age from fourteen to forty. I coded responses in terms of "beliefs," "unbeliefs," and "disbeliefs," noting acceptance and rejection of ideas new to the informant whenever opinion was expressed. Percentage awareness of those beliefs discussed with each informant ranged from 57 percent to 83 percent, with the mean level for the seven informants falling at 75 percent. Percentage acceptance of beliefs known averaged 94 percent, and of beliefs not known, 64 percent.

Since awareness of some of the 400 beliefs was very low among these informants,[1] I selected for sampling in 1964 roughly half of the original beliefs, concentrating on those most adequately sampled and most widely known in 1941 (that is, known by at least 75 percent of those asked). These 250 were used as the basis for interviewing six of the more traditionally oriented persons I came to know well during the first six months of field work. In this interviewing I of course learned many new beliefs, all of which I recorded, and some of which I added to my sample to check their pervasiveness. By mid-1964, I had selected 181 beliefs for more extensive interviewing among additional Panajacheleños.[2] One hundred and eight of these beliefs were among those utilized by Tax, and another 20 were derived from Tax's sample though not directly comparable. The remainder were new beliefs (that is, they were new to me and not included in Tax's world view data).

The 1941-64 comparisons of belief awareness which are most comparable are those restricted to the 108 beliefs common to Tax's and my own samples (hereafter termed the basic sample). Awareness of the basic sample among Panajacheleños interviewed in 1941 averaged 85 percent, compared with 68 percent among Panajacheleños interviewed in 1964.

Before too readily concluding that average awareness in 1964 has dropped 17 percent below average awareness in 1941, the possibility of sampling error in arriving at the 1941 figures must be considered. The strongest test I can devise is a comparison of data on these 108 beliefs among those of Tax's informants whose children were included in my interviewing in 1964. Three parent-child sets of comparisons are available, where parent and child were within four years of the same age when interviewed. These three cases average 19 percentage points' reduction in awareness from 1941 to 1964.

The comparability of the 1941 and 1964 samples can be questioned on the basis of different age distribution. Three of Tax's seven informants were over thirty-five, while all but three of my informants were under thirty-five. If age influences belief awareness, is it possible that a similar age distribution would yield more comparable average awareness? The size of Tax's 1941 sample does not permit a conclusive answer, but table 15 does strongly suggest that at any given age from twelve to twenty-four Panajacheleños in 1964 knew 20 percent less of the basic sample than in 1941. Only above age thirty-five did the levels of awareness for the two dates come appreciably closer to each other.

TABLE 15
Age Comparisons of Belief Awareness

	12-14	15-19	20-24	25-30	31-35	Over 35
1941 (108 beliefs)	75%	88%	89%	—	—	90%
1964 (181 beliefs)	55%	69%	68%	78%	81%	84%
Difference	-20%	-19%	-21%	—	—	-6%

I cannot, of course, answer the question of whether young adults in 1964 will, on reaching their late thirties, know 84 percent of these beliefs as do Panajacheleños currently of that age. The implication of table 15, however, is that they will not acquire much more knowledge of "traditional" beliefs than they already have; their counterparts in 1941 by ages fifteen to twenty-four already had learned virtually as many beliefs as had their elders. Moreover, a comparison of not just the *average* awareness of fifteen-to twenty-four-year-olds in 1964, but of the *range* among the twenty informants reveals that not one knows more than 78 percent of the sample; this is still 10 percent less than the least knowledgeable of the 1941 informants of comparable age.

All data I can bring to bear on the subject substantiate the suggestion that Panajacheleños in 1964 were aware of 15 to 20 percent fewer of the basic sample beliefs than were Panajacheleños in 1941.

Regional Comparisons

Even if one is convinced that group-typical beliefs in 1941 were becoming less group-typical in 1964, it can still be argued that these limited data do not justify the conclusion that some postulated "traditional world view" is eroding. What justification is there for labeling "traditional" the corpus of beliefs found pervasive in 1941 and still pervasive among traditionally oriented Panajacheleños in 1964? Could it not be that discrete beliefs come and go rapidly within a community such as Panajachel, and that comparing awareness of beliefs of seventy-five and fifty years ago would have revealed comparable shifts in average awareness? I think not, on the basis of the pervasiveness of these beliefs in the wider region. A sample of the beliefs most group-typical of Panajacheleños in 1941 was used in interviewing twenty-one residents of thirteen other *municipios* across western Guatemala, and the degree to which these beliefs are shared throughout the region argues persuasively for their deep-rootedness in the Panajachel world view (see map 3).[3]

Examination of data from the three corners of this region reveals that a fifty-five-year-old man of San Pedro Necta, Huehuetenango, shared 63 percent of 100 beliefs discussed in his interview, a sixty-two-year-old woman of Comalapa knew 81 percent of 107 beliefs discussed, and a thirty-five-year-old woman of San Juan la Laguna shared 92 percent of 103 beliefs. Three informants were interviewed in San Pedro Necta, and among the three a total of 70 percent of the beliefs were known. This would suggest that at least this high a percentage of the beliefs found most group-typical of Panajacheleños could be found in any Indian community across western Guatemala.

I have little doubt but that further interviewing in the other towns ringing Lake Atitlán would locate informants sharing 90 to 95 percent of this sample. The fact that the one Juanera interviewed should know 92 percent is significant, for of the lake towns included in the survey, San Juan has the least interaction with Panajachel. In fact, the interaction between Panajacheleños and Juaneros is little, if any, greater than that between Panajacheleños and natives of San Pedro Necta. Diffusion of ideas proceeds slowly in this culture area, given the character of social relations among Indians, and the prevalence of highly discrete beliefs must be attributed to a common world view of many generations' depth. That these beliefs are less group-typical of younger Panajacheleños in 1964 would suggest, therefore, that acculturative influences have interfered with the transmission of the cultural heritage of belief. How justifiably we can speak of erosion of traditional world view assumptions, or premises, will remain to be considered. Our immediate concern is simply with discrete beliefs, but such discrete beliefs would not be expected to be

Map 3. Homogeneity of Belief in Western Guatemala, Number of Informants and Percentage of Awareness

pervasive throughout western Guatemala if the assumptions explaining and generating them were highly local to Panajachel.

Ladino Belief Patterns

With this evidence of considerable consensus among Indians in western Guatemala of beliefs group-typical of Panajacheleños, I now examine the data available on awareness among fourteen Ladinos of these same beliefs.[4] Some striking observations emerge from comparisons with Ladino data. Only 15 percent of the 120 beliefs selected for regional interviewing are group-typical of the Ladinos, if by group-typical is meant that at least three-fourths of the informants interviewed are aware of a proposition. Forty percent of the 120 beliefs were known by fewer than one-fourth of the Ladino informants.

The comparisons of Ladino and Indian awareness and acceptance of each belief are included in part II of the model at the end of chapter 7. Careful study of that model reveals that the beliefs of which Ladinos are least aware tend to be the same beliefs that are measurably less recognized by Panajacheleños in 1964 than in 1941. While relatively few propositions of belief shared by Panajacheleños and Indians of the region are not shared as well by at least one of the fourteen Ladinos interviewed, half of the belief sample is much more pervasive among Indians than among Ladinos. More intensive discussion with Ladinos would of course have produced a corpus of propositions group-typical of Ladinos but not of Indians.

Variations Among Panajacheleños in Acceptance of Traditional Beliefs

The preceding appraisal of homogeneity of belief within Panajachel over the past twenty-five years, throughout western Guatemala, and among Indians and Ladinos lays the foundation for a detailed analysis of differential acceptance and rejection of the sample of beliefs among Panajacheleños in 1964.

Judgments of acceptance of a belief are considerably more subjective than judgments of awareness. In a few cases, more acculturated informants were wary of my probing into their bases of questioning or rejecting beliefs, but as the focus on beliefs was minimal in the initial interview and only gradually became more central, I had time to familiarize myself with each informant's tolerance to probing and his typical cues of belief or disbelief. Often informants asked me for my opinions on beliefs they realized had become controversial in Panajachel; I tried to remain credulous of everything and to avoid influencing informants' rejection of beliefs known to be controversial. I am sure I influenced responses on many occasions, but I also tried to minimize the statistical effect of such feedback by a persistent reluctance to code "unbelief" unless I was certain of at least some degree of doubt in the informant's mind. "Disbelief" was easier to assess, as informants usually made their rejection of an idea obvious. The Appendix provides excerpts from transcriptions of taped interviews; inclusion of my judgments of acceptance, doubt, or rejection in each case permits the reader to evaluate my bases of judgment. Of course, facial expressions and intonations were important indicators which cannot be elicited from the transcriptions.

The following code was used in entering the data:

1   Awareness and no indication of doubt or rejection;
     usually with expressed belief (belief)
2   Awareness and some doubt expressed (unbelief)
3   Awareness but obvious rejection (disbelief)
4   Not previously aware, but inclined to reject
5   Not previously aware, but credulous
6   Not previously aware, and no basis for judging
     acceptance or rejection

Table 16 gives the average range of rejection of known as well as unknown beliefs in the sample. In short, while informants show a preference for outright disbelief over the uncertainty of unbelief, the ratio of disbeliefs to unbeliefs remains fairly stable among those informants most inclined to question traditional beliefs.

TABLE 16
Rejection of Beliefs, 1964

	Average	Range
Known beliefs questioned (unbeliefs)	8.5%	0-19%
Known beliefs rejected (disbeliefs)	10.5%	0-53%
Known beliefs questioned or rejected [a]	19.0%	1-72%
New beliefs rejected	26.5%	5-75%

a. Index of belief rejection.

I have excluded from the index of belief rejection those beliefs not familiar to the informant in which he nevertheless evidenced disbelief. These data are interesting, for they reveal marked differences in skepticism toward new ideas. However, informants knew an average of two-thirds of the beliefs in the sample, and the tendency to reject the few unknown items of belief corresponded poorly with percentage rejection of known beliefs. Nor does extent of awareness correlate with the tendency to reject traditional beliefs. This is apparent, for example, in the case of four Panajachel Ladinos, whose range of acceptance falls well within the

TABLE 17
Informant Profiles, 1964

Acceptance	Dress[a]	Service[b]	Curing[c]	Religion	School, yrs.	Age
28%	1	—	C	P	7	20
45	1	M	C	P	4	32
46	1	—	C	P	6	28
47	1	—	C	C	11	21
52	1	—	C	P	3	26
52	1	—	C	P	0	27
63	3	—	C	P	2	21
64	1	—	C	NC	6	19
66	2	—	CS	NC	8	18
69	3	M	C	P(ex)	6	26
70	1	—	C	P	6	27
71	1	C	C	NC	7	17
73	1	—	C	P	5	15
77	1	—	C	P	3	17
80	3	M	C	P(ex)	4	22
80	2	—	ZCS	C	2	17
82	2	M	ZC	NC	0	38
83	1	—	C	P	3	16
83	3	M	C	NC	5	31
84	4	—	C	C	3	34
84	2	—	C	C	0	16
85	2	—	ZC	NC	0	34
86	2	—	ZCS	NC	3	18
86	1	—	CS	NC	3	17
87	4	—	CS	NC	2	21
87	3	M	C	NC	1	32
88	1	C	ZC	NC	0	19
90	3	M	?	NC	3	34
91	3	—	CS	NC	2	17
91	3	C	ZCS	NC	0	18
91	3	—	CS	NC	2	15
92	1	M	ZC	NC	3	21
92	3	—	C	NC	3	12
93	3	—	ZCS	C	4	23
93	1	—	CS	P	4	18
94	4	M	C	C	2	34
95	3	M	ZC	NC	2	45
95	3	—	C	P	2	14
96	4	—	ZCS	C	0	24
96	3	C	ZC	NC	2	18
97	3	C	ZC	NC	3	22
97	4	C	C	NC	0	27
98	3	—	ZC	NC	3	14
98	2	—	ZC	NC	5	13
98	1	—	C	P	5	14
99	4	—	ZC	NC	0	39

a. 1=Ladino dress, shoes, stockings; 2=Ladino dress, or generalized Indian costume with sandals; 3=2, but barefoot; 4=Panajachel Indian dress.

b. M=military; C=*cofradía*. Dashes are entered for all Protestants and Catequistas, and for nominal Catholics whose fathers refused to serve in *cofradías* or who indicated they would refuse. Where informant's father served in *cofradías* and informant expects to serve, "C" is entered. "M" is entered for informants who have themselves experienced military training.

c. C=clinic consultation; Z=family use of *zahorin* in recent years; S=use of spiritualist.

d. P=active Protestant; P(ex)=reared as Protestant but inactive; C=Active Catequista; NC=nominal Catholic.

range of acceptance of all categories by Indians, while their range of awareness falls outside the range of Indian awareness in all categories except cures and "signs." It is noteworthy that Panajachel Ladinos are least aware of the "do's" and "don'ts" observed by Indians.

In table 17, the forty-six informants, in their order of percentage acceptance of known beliefs, are listed with relevant data on dress, military and community service, curing practices, religion, schooling, and age.

At the outset I postulated that age, schooling, Protestantism, Catholic Action, and military service would be the independent variables possibly influencing belief acceptance. A cursory examination of table 17 suggests that age is significant only under age fifteen, that Protestantism and schooling correlate most closely with belief acceptance, and that military service and Catholic Action correlate hardly at all. It is interesting that if one combines Protestantism and schooling, the fifteen informants questioning beliefs most consistently are all either Protestant or have had six or more years of formal schooling. The remaining thirty-one informants include no one with six years of schooling and only three Protestants, all young. Table 18 examines the age variable, and while the division of the informants on the basis of Protestantism and schooling anticipates table 19, the comparisons elucidate the relative importance of age.

TABLE 18
Age and Belief Rejection, 1964

	12-14 (6) [a]	15-19 (14)	20-25 (9)	26-30 (5)	31-25 (7)	Over 35 (3)
All informants	8%	16%	32%	7%	15%	5%
Protestants or those with 6 years' school	5	30	48	39	55	—
Catholics with less than 5 years' school	4	13	11	4	12	5
Difference between Catholics and Protestants	1	17	37	35	43	—

a. Numbers in parentheses are numbers of informants.

It is immediately obvious that religion has little bearing on belief acceptance among those under fifteen. Moreover, as two of those under fifteen have had five years of schooling, it would appear that schooling in itself is not sufficient to narrow world view measurably in the early teens. The important observation, however, is that by age twenty the questioning is as strong as it is during any age period thereafter. Traditionally oriented informants do not vary significantly in level of acceptance from age fifteen on. Schooling and religion would appear to be the significant variables, and these become significant only by the late teens.

Table 19 isolates schooling to examine whether schooling and religion are, in fact, independent variables. The number of Catequistas is small, but it is noteworthy that the five Catequistas with less than five years of schooling differ minimally from traditional Catholics in belief acceptance. Protestants with less than five years of schooling, on the other hand, average 28 percent, or three times the average Catholic rate of rejection. For informants with five years of schooling, data are limited, and since one of the two Protestants is under fifteen, the figure of 27 percent for the one remaining Protestant is assumed more diagnostic.

TABLE 19
Schooling, Religion, and Belief Rejection, 1964

Years of School	Rate of Belief Rejection			
	Protestants	Catholics	Catequistas	Combined
0	48% (1)[a]	10% (6)	10% (2)	14% (9)
1, 2	37% (1)	9% (5)	12% (2)	12% (8)
3, 4	31% 28% (6)	10% 9% (6)	12% 12% (2)	17.5% (14)
5	27% (1)	17% (1)	— (0)	22% (2)
6 or more	44% (3)	32% (2)	53% (1)	41.5% (6)

Note: Ladinos and all Indians under fifteen years of age are excluded.
a. Figures are the averages of the percentages of beliefs rejected by the number of informants shown in parentheses.

Of most significance is the minimal difference between Protestants and Catholics once six years of school have been completed. It would appear that the beliefs questioned by Protestants as a consequence of their being Protestants are largely the same beliefs that Indians who have completed elementary school question regardless of religious affiliation. All four Catholics (including one Catequista) who have completed six years of schooling question at least 30 percent of the corpus of beliefs, while no Catholic (even Catequistas) with less than six years' schooling questions more than 20 percent. Schooling therefore does result in considerable questioning of traditional views among those who remain in school through the six grades. Of the Catholics, one went on to complete eleven years of schooling, and her percentage rejection is 53, or nearly twice the rejection of the one Catholic who only attended for six years (29 percent). The two other Catholics (34 and 36 percent) have completed seven years of schooling. With these percentages in mind, the extreme skepticism of one Protestant (72 percent) is striking. He will be discussed in more detail in chapter 8. The other two Protestants with six years of school reject 30 and 31 percent respectively. If one subtracts the Catholic who completed eleven years of school and the one highly skeptical Protestant, the Protestant and Catholic figures among those finishing six years of school are virtually identical, varying only from 29 to 34 percent.

Having established that schooling has little, if any, influence upon Indian world view until the fifth or sixth grade, I must now examine more closely the suggestion of the data that Protestantism erodes traditional world view just as fully as does five or six years of formal schooling. The range of rejection among Protestants with less than five years of school is 7 to 55 percent, and four of the eight reject more beliefs than do two of the Protestants who completed elementary school. In short, Protestantism and schooling do appear to be two independent variables. Either influence is sufficient to erode measurably traditional world view, and both apparently lead to rejection of the same facets of that world view.

This raises the question of whether it is comparable instruction in the school and in Protestant circles that produces the impact upon world view, or rather the kinds of informal relationships with non-Indians fostered both by schooling in the fifth and sixth grades and by Protestantism. That the latter may, in fact, be the common variable eroding traditional beliefs is strengthened by the observation that Catholic Action and military training do not measurably influence world view. Catholic Action subjects Catequistas to teachings not significantly different from the teachings of Protestantism, and military training involves considerable schooling. The difference lies in associates: Catequistas are wholly Indian and wholly native Panajacheleños, and military volunteers training for two years in barracks in the two urban centers of Guatemala live and study almost exclusively among Indians. By contrast, as pointed out in the previous chapter, Protestant congregations in Panajachel include as many Ladinos as Indians and a large segment of highly acculturated Indians from other communities as well. Fifth and sixth grades in the local school are dominated by Ladinos, while the lower grades contain almost as many Indians as Ladinos. Indian children through the first three or four years of school develop affective ties largely with other Indians, while thereafter friendships with Ladinos increase.

On the above data I must rest my case: that experiences fostered by Protestantism erode traditional beliefs more than do experiences fostered by participation in Catholic Action; that Catequistas question these beliefs hardly more than do nominal Catholics; that schooling in the lower grades (at least through fourth grade) has no measurable influence upon world view (apart from undoubtedly expanding horizons); and that additional elementary schooling has a marked influence upon anyone subjected to it. A comment is in order on how justifiably I can generalize from my limited sample of informants to the wider population of Panajachel. Five and six years of schooling have been available to Panajacheleños only since 1945, and in these two decades only twenty-five Indian boys and seven Indian girls have taken advantage of at least five years' schooling. My sample of ten thus constitutes one-third of the number of Indians who have completed five or more grades since 1945. Only five of these thirty-two have continued beyond elementary school, and only one has gone on to vocational school. I interviewed four of these five. As for the Protestants, my sample includes thirteen Protestants from eleven of fifty Protestant households. Six of these are third-generation Protestants, four are second-generation, and three are first-generation. There are only a dozen households with third-generation Protestants, and to have sampled half of them I believe justifies generalization from my sample to the Protestant population as a whole.

Recalling that the beliefs less pervasive among Panajacheleños in 1964 than in 1941 were largely those beliefs not shared by Ladinos, it is not surprising to find that these also constitute the majority of beliefs being widely questioned and rejected by Indians in 1964. Part II of the model at the end of chapter 7 includes the percentage rejection of each belief sampled among all the Protestants as well as the three Catholics with six years of school, on the one hand, and the Catholics with less than six years of school, on the other. For convenience I refer to the former group as Protestants and the latter as traditionals.

It should be borne in mind that the traditionals numbered twenty-five and the Protestant informants numbered nineteen. Percentage rejection of each belief sampled was based only on persons knowing the belief. As the average percentage awareness of the beliefs was 67 percent, it is useful to think in terms of the rejection percentage of part II of the model as being based on sixteen traditionals (two-thirds of twenty-five) and twelve Protestants (two-thirds of nineteen) for each belief item.

Before turning to the substantive data of the following section, we would do well to compare Tax's data on belief questioning and rejection in 1941 with data on traditionals in 1964 to determine whether, in fact, traditionals are questioning any more in 1964 than they were twenty-five years earlier. In making comparisons between Tax's data and the 1964 data on belief rejection, we must bear in mind that the number of Tax's informants was limited and that he had less interest in measuring rejection than in recording awareness. From his written summaries of interviews, I coded "unbelief" and "disbelief" only when the data made this obvious; hence the summary figures for "belief rejection" in 1941 are conservative. I suspect that, despite this, my constant attention to indicators of doubt or rejection in my own interviewing resulted in data which are not wholly comparable with Tax's. Probably his informants questioned a higher percentage of beliefs than the figures in table 20 indicate. If true, this would mean only that the differential in percentage acceptance is slightly less than indicated; the difference is not likely to be any greater. Since we are measuring only the acceptance of beliefs known to the informant, it is useful to take our figures from the larger bodies of data available to us to reduce the degree of sampling error. Hence, the 1941 sample, which consisted of 397 beliefs, and the 1964 sample, which comprised 181, are compared in table 20.

TABLE 20
Belief Acceptance

	Identifi-cations	Señas	Secretos	Remedios	Pecados	Total
1941						
(7 informants)	92%	96%	96%	95%	92%	94%
1964						
(20 informants)[a]	88	97	97	92	85	91
Difference	-4%	+1%	+1 %	-3%	-7%	-3%

a. All Catholics with less than five years of schooling are included except those under fifteen years of age. All Ladinos and all Protestants are excluded.

Comparisons of parents' and children's profiles over the twenty-five year period are given in table 21.

These four profiles reveal little pattern. The first two are least useful, since the daughter and son are unusually acculturated as a result of working for Ladinos and quite possibly as a result of the influence of the Taxes upon the thought patterns of the mother, who was their neighbor for many months. The daughter was, similarly, our domestic employee for the duration of our stay in Panajachel. The two father-and-son comparisons are more useful, especially the first of these, where the ages at interviewing were identical. The figures of tables 20 and 21 suggest that traditionally oriented Panajacheleños are questioning around 5 percent more of the traditional beliefs known to them than were Panajacheleños in 1941.

TABLE 21
Parent-Child Belief Acceptance, 1941-64

		Difference in Acceptance				
	Identifi-cations	Señas	Secretos	Remedios	Pecados	Total
Mother, daughter	-14%	-10%	-13%	-17%	-30%	-17%
Mother, son	- 8	0	-17	0	-22	-12
Father, son	- 2	+ 5	0	0	- 4	- 1
Father, son	-17	0	+ 7	-19	- 5	- 7
Average	-10%	- 1%	- 6%	-19%	- 5%	- 7%

In view of the Protestant or schooled informants' average rejection of 35 percent, this minimal change of 5 percent among traditionals is striking. To this conclusion should be added the earlier observation that Panajacheleños in 1964 were aware of 15 to 20 percent fewer beliefs of identical samples than in 1941. It would appear that the Panajachel world view is narrowing among traditionals more rapidly at this point through failure of parents to transmit traditional beliefs than through any reaction among the younger generation against ancestral "superstitions." Among Protestants such a reaction is in process, although our understanding of the history of Protestantism in the lake region would lead us to conclude that the reaction was more pronounced ten to twenty years ago, when the majority of my Protestant informants were still too young to be very conscious of any contest of ideas being waged publicly or privately in the minds of their parents.

◦7◦

Structure of Belief

H A V I N G examined the variations among Panajacheleños' belief patterns in quantitative terms, I can once again pose the question of what Panajacheleños believe. The question is answered on one level in terms of the propositions Panajacheleños themselves have formulated, referred to as the primary belief data of the study. A sample of such propositions is presented in the second part of the model at the end of this chapter. However, some of what Panajacheleños believe is not readily stated by many, if any, of them. They act in accordance with this knowledge, but until someone or something calls the assumptions into question, the need to articulate such assumptions does not arise.

To a greater or lesser degree each Panajacheleño has access to (or makes use of) these assumptions in conscious ways. And, to a greater or lesser degree such assumptions motivate or influence each Panajacheleño in subconscious ways. Ever since Sol Tax began compiling the primary beliefs in 1936, he and more recently I have pondered the theoretical and methodological problems inherent in delineating such assumptions, assessing their consistency or degree of systematization, and measuring the stability of this system of cognitive orientations.

The problems are very old ones, occupying philosophers and anthropologists alike. The former address the ontological status of cultural assumptions which must be inferred by the observer when they cannot be elicited from the natives, but which need not be articulated nor indeed consciously held by natives. The anthropologist's typical concern is less with the kind of reality his inferred assumptions enjoy than with their adequacy to explain for him the behavior he observes. A philosopher, Rex Martin, and an anthropologist, Allan Hanson, writing on the subject suggest that the observer's inferred constructs be labeled "analytical rules," akin to the grammar of a language which the native speaker uses accurately despite his inability to explain them as well as the observer learning the language:

> When speakers of a language make judgments as to the grammaticality of utterances, they do so in terms of standards or rules which are part of the operative reality of the language. The rules which the linguist infers and

writes down are rule-statements: more or less accurate formulations of the objective rules. In the same way, what we have termed "real rules" of a cultural system are objective standards and conventions to which people conform when they frame and evaluate ideas or beliefs, when they decide upon a course of action, when they "automatically" follow a convention of behavior, and so on. What we have called "analytical rules" are rule-statements. *They are not thought to duplicate anything in the native mind or culture at all.* Instead, they are more or less accurate formulations, made by the anthropologist, of the real rules. [1973:203]

Paradoxically, the observer may come to understand what the insider believes, in terms of logical constructs of rules and inferences, better than the natives of the society. Yet even with this kind of understanding the observer will less often act appropriately.

The anthropologist is a novice: he is unfamiliar with native classification and concepts and so can only apply them laboriously and with the help of rules. But, the anthropologist need not remain a novice. Conceivably he can learn the kinship terminology, theory of disease, perhaps even the whole world view, so well that he can dispense with the rules. And if he is not concerned with teaching anyone else, he could easily forget the rules. There is nothing, logically, that prohibits him from going native. [Hanson and Martin 1973:205]

I make no claims to have "gone native" in Panajachel. I was aware of progress in acting appropriately and anticipating behavior, however. Beyond modest advances in this regard, my objective was to determine the levels of generalization which Panajacheleños find it convenient or necessary to articulate. I say "necessary" in that Panajacheleños are less dependent on such reasoning for their explanations than is the observer. Truly to go native would entail not only internalizing the logical constructs but relying on such reasoning among the various ways of validating knowledge no more fully than does the typical Panajacheleño.

In the course of discussing beliefs with Panajacheleños, first in 1941 and then in 1964, it has proved possible to make some assessments of the relative importance of the several epistemological instrumentalities utilized in explaining behavior and beliefs, and to construct a model of those logical constructs accessible to Panajacheleños who become concerned to explain belief patterns in terms of more abstract rules or premises. The growing awareness among the more acculturated Indians of differences between traditional Indian and Ladino belief patterns had produced considerable interest in and hence visibility of some assumptions, facilitating such inquiry. In this chapter I present the progress to date in framing and testing a model of not only the more visible assumptions articulated by perceptive informants, but the full range of assumptions inferrable from the belief samples adequate for explaining to my satisfaction the bulk of the primary belief data collected thus far.

Theoretical Considerations in Structuring Belief

I first define the terms used and clarify what aspects of world view are being analyzed. Then I describe how the data relevant to structuring belief were gathered and are assembled in the model.

By assumptions, or premises, I mean ideas which I find helpful to state as propositions of belief, but which are sufficiently abstract that they are not common subjects of conversation and hence do not enjoy the visibility and stereotyped speech-patterning characteristic of what I label as beliefs. Thus described, premises are not necessarily distinct from beliefs; they are simply less visible or accessible to natives in the society. Where visible, the premise-belief complexes form deductive sequences for the natives which the observer often comes to understand inductively. While any belief can be accepted by natives on a variety of epistemological grounds, often either explicit or implicit in a belief are one or more assumptions or premises which function logically to explain the belief to natives (or observers) seeking such explanation. For example, a belief pervasive among Indians in western Guatemala is that bats are a species of field mouse that grows wings in adulthood. While many Panajacheleños pointed to the facial resemblance of mice and bats, only one could supply a firsthand encounter with what he assumed to be a mouse in an intermediate stage of growing wings. Most informants, of course, saw no reason to doubt this knowledge, given its pervasiveness, despite the paucity of empirical confirmation. Yet a few individuals were not satisfied with the mere fact that everyone explained bats in this manner, and in the absence of empirical verification they had recourse to an underlying premise concerning the ability of spirits of people and animals to change their forms. Thus bats and mice are like frogs and tadpoles, butterflies and caterpillars, and this knowledge together with the pervasive opinion of others makes unnecessary any empirical validation.

I will leave aside for the moment the question of how useful it is to postulate that all group-typical primary beliefs can be assumed thus explicable. I should make clear at this point, however, that while I do feel it demonstrable that the primary belief data can be explained in terms of the model of assumptions I have constructed, this is not to say that there is necessarily much consensus on the explanation offered for any given belief. The data elicited strongly substantiate Benson Saler's cautious supposition that "a given belief, after all, might prove to be the ground for alternative behaviors, and, with equal plausibility, a given behavioral sequence could conceivably find support among a variety of different beliefs" (1968).

This can be illustrated with one of the belief items in the 1964 sample: the belief that a snake should be killed either with a stick or the dull side of a *machete,* not with the sharpened blade. The reasons offered were: the skin won't cut, and the blade will glance off at an angle cutting the person; the head, if severed from the body, will spring at the ill-doer and bite him; a snake cut in half evolves into two snakes; and the blade of the *machete* that has killed such an animal will in the future readily inflict cuts on its user. Implicit in one or more of these explanations are a number of assumptions inferred by me or volunteered by informants in more reflective efforts to explain this and other beliefs viewed by them as related. One is the assumption that the life essence, or spirit, is not localized but permeates the entire body. Thus, new life can evolve from a portion of the snake and, accordingly, a belt of snake skin is a risky investment, for it might evolve into a snake. Another is the pervasive premise that certain animals, including the snake, are servants of or belong to the owner of the hill, or the Devil. Killing any such animal can result in swift vengeance, but if the cause of death can be disguised, then the spirit's report to his "owner" will be less convincing. A sharp *machete* cut is unmistakably the result of a *machete* blow inflicted by a human agent. Similarly, when seeking to kill an owl, it is safer to throw a fruit rather than a stone, since fruit could fall accidentally upon the bird, while a stone's origin is obvious. Yet another assumption is that evil creatures have a persuasive influence over weapons and can make them ineffectual. The snake makes the blade of the *machete* glance off, and only by tricking the snake by using the reverse side or a stick can one succeed in killing. Similarly, it is extremely difficult to shoot a coyote, and to improve your chances you had best place salt on the bullet and make a cross on the gun before firing. Finally, implicit in the belief that a stick is safer than a *machete* is the assumption that weapons are a mixed blessing; they punish those who use them unjustly, and as the final judge of a "just" killing is not the killer, any killing may be avenged by the weapon's turning against its user. Thus a *machete* used to kill a snake is not uncommonly left at the scene, and anyone happening upon a discarded *machete* is wise to leave it alone. This has its parallels in expressed fears of carrying knives or possessing firearms which may have been used in killing or inflicting wounds.

Having said something about the relationship of premises to beliefs, I wish to clarify my statement that premises vary in their visibility or accessibility to natives. Initially I found myself thinking of premises as varying along an implicit-explicit continuum in the minds of natives. This implied a reified body of premises differentially recognized by natives but nevertheless commonly shared on some level of subconsciousness. I think this is not necessarily true. A continuum of accessibility, where the emphasis is placed on the utilization of a given premise or its explanatory load, is more useful. This terminology facilitates incorporation of Ladinos in the discussion of the Panajachel world view; to the extent that each ethnic group has some group-typical premises not shared by the other, it is more meaning-ful to discuss differential accessibility of premises than it is to speak of degrees of explicitness in natives' minds.

Just as any typical native in a society acquires knowledge of only some percentage of the total corpus of group-typical beliefs which constitute the cultural world view, so I hypothesize that group-typical explanatory and generative premises vary in their accessibility to natives. Radin was saying much the same thing in calling attention to the differences between "men of action" and "philosophers" in a society (1927), but of course the high complexity in this area is disguised by any such simple dichotomy. I do not wish to imply that the structure of belief is a rigid system which is implanted or learned by each native in the society; rather, I view it as a slowly changing body of assumptions explicating common beliefs which any given individual acquires only in part and reworks idiosyncratically. The differential accessibility of these assumptions (and hence how widely each one is employed or elaborated), the availability of non-group-typical assumptions from outside the culture, and the differential reliance on logical constructs among the several epistemological instrumentalities are factors producing a unique "inside view" of the world in the mind of each native in the society. Determining how group-typical a given individu-al's structure of belief may be would require establishing some norms for premise accessibility and epistemological patterning of explanation.

Thus, when I set out to structure Panajachel belief, I obviously could only approximate the complex reality in framing a model which attempts to delineate the structural assumptions or premises adequate and necessary for explaining as many of the discrete beliefs as I have learned. Even with this desire to be as comprehensive as possible, it is apparent from a cursory perusal of part I of the model that the premises and cognitive orientations reflect my own knowledge system. Some of what Panajache-leños believe I also believe, for the same or different reasons, and this knowledge has not been as systematically explored and analyzed within the model of belief structure as has knowledge I find unconfirmed in my own experience and unsupported by my own logical constructs. When Panajacheleños volunteer that frogs grow from tadpoles, I pay less atten-tion than when I am told that bats grow from mice. I know the former is true, and tend to attribute to Panajacheleños the same understanding of the biological processes involved that I have acquired. Only the realization that Panajacheleños recognize many more such metamorphoses than I do prompts me to examine the possible differences between the premises each of us is utilizing.

Another complex of beliefs will clarify this bias in framing the model. Among the ailments and associated remedies I discussed with the forty-six informants was bed-wetting, prompted by the presence in Tax's data of the pervasive idea that a youth so afflicted should be requested to carry one of the heavy hearthstones to the home of a neighbor. In the course of discussing this with my first informants, other remedies were volunteered, including holding the child over a hummingbird's nest which is then set afire, and placing on the child's umbilicus sap issuing from the oak wood burning on the hearth. In time informants clarified for me that the efficacy of the visit to the neighbors lay not in the stone but solely in the child's embarrassment at being mocked for wetting the bed. All women know the meaning of such a visit, and since there is no other reason for transporting hearthstones from one household to another, a child's arrival bearing such a stone invites immediate ridicule. Implicit in the remedies involving the hummingbird and oak sap is the assumption that warming the body will lessen the likelihood of urinating. Each belief assumes also that characteristics of one thing are transferable to another; that is, the heat-producing capacity of oak and the inconsequential urinating capacity of a hummingbird can be transferred to a child. Of the three assumptions underlying these several remedies for wetting the bed, I share to some extent the first two, that shaming a child and keeping the body warm may help. Only the latter is new and unacceptable to me, and being the only additional assumption needed by me or by those Panajacheleños interviewed to explain these remedies, it is the only one of the three assumptions included in the model of belief structure presented in the model.

I am made increasingly aware of the difficulties of determining what is regarded as empirically validated by natives in another culture, let alone the difficulties of the observer's undertaking to validate empirically by his own criteria of reality every proposition he encounters.[1] I do not maintain that all the data herein labeled as beliefs are necessarily nonempirical, even by my own bases of judgment. For example, cures volunteered by Panajacheleños for burns include egg white, tomato, and honey. These are "cold" substances by native classification of all foods as hot or cold and are assumed curative because of their ability to counter the heat of the burned skin. Apart from this explanation is the possibility that such substances hasten curing simply by preventing infection or by stimulating physiological processes of tissue replacement. Certainly, by Panajacheleños' bases of judging reality, the majority of beliefs are empirically validated for many Panajacheleños. Not that Panajacheleños necessarily are less reliant than I upon empirical validation of belief, although admittedly this may be the case. Rather, our differing assumptions influence our perceptions. Frequently Panajacheleños offered as validation of beliefs perceptions I would explain otherwise. If I saw something resembling a mouse with incipient wings (as one informant claimed to have seen), I would be inclined by my knowledge to assume it another animal, perhaps a species of flying squirrel; the Panajacheleño would not feel it necessary to seek such an alternative explanation, given his knowledge. To repeat, my objective is not to determine what for me or for Panajacheleños is or is not empirically validated, but rather to determine the assumptions which generate or explain group-typical beliefs, whether in support of or in the absence of empirical validation.

I readily admit that my desire for order has led me to concentrate upon logical inference in explaining Panajachel belief far in excess of any Panajacheleño's use of this epistemological tool. Where I have sought assumptions about reality to explain the "why" of belief, my informants more often than not could provide none. Their epistemological grounds for belief are much more often pragmatism and the authority of their peers and those responsible for their socialization. Repeatedly, the only explanation offered was, "People say," and as Leonard Berkowitz points out, "in the absence of more objective tests of the validity of a belief, we tend to believe the opinions shared by all or most of the people about us are probably correct" (1963:376).

I have not sampled the differential utilization of logical inference by informants; I could not afford to risk offending by constantly probing and asking "why." I found very few informants of a philosophical bent, and even these informants have access to only part of the premises implicit in belief. Moreover, I suggest that societies, like individuals, differ in their concern with systematization and explanation of belief and behavior. The kinds of social relationships existing among Panajacheleños mitigate against the codification or consensual explication of beliefs and behaviors by elders. This would be reflected in the lack of consensus in explanation of many highly pervasive beliefs and behaviors, as well as in the comparative lack of encouragement of the "philosopher role."

While it is demonstrable that Panajacheleños to varying degrees rely on inferable logical constructs to explain belief, it is not demonstrable that the assumptions have generated the beliefs they now function to explain. If by "explanation" is meant causality, I certainly do not pretend to be explaining origins of beliefs. I speak of premises deductively generating beliefs, as I assume they do, but it is assumed that the great bulk of the belief data gathered by Tax and me has its origins in a distant past. It seems highly probable that many of the premise relationships visible in beliefs are, in fact, causal, but the frequent facility with which a given belief can be explained in terms of various premises precludes any objective demonstration of its origin.

The question which the Panajachel data pose is not how beliefs evolve, but how they become and remain group-typical. Any society in as much interaction with outsiders as is Panajachel has a constant trickle of new items of belief to peruse. And, I assume, any society has residual beliefs surviving in ritual contexts that are not readily understood because of the low visibility of the supporting assumptions. How important is it that these beliefs on their way in or out of the culture find explanation within accessible logical constructs to become or remain group-typical? One test is to abstract the assumptions from primary data demonstrated to be group-typical and to measure how fully all other elicited primary data find logical explanation under the former assumptions. If supplementary belief data do in fact readily find explanation in terms of the assumptions, the importance of this epistemological instrumentality would appear demonstrated. This has been my procedure, and in this way I attempt to assess how tightly systematized Panajachel beliefs in fact are.

Just how fully systematized mental culture can be we do not know, but we do know that if one were to look for the most tightly integrated world view he would look for a society long isolated. Panajachel has not been isolated, and Panajacheleños and their ancestors have been reworking Christian and non-Christian tenets of belief and Spanish and Mayan forms of social organization for the past four hundred years. Yet sufficient time has elapsed for a synthesis to evolve into a world view which can be distinguished from a Ladino world view, and the postconquest bases of community organization and economic interaction have insulated this world view to a remarkable extent. Inconsistencies and paradoxes inherent in this syncretic world view are demonstrable, but since Michael Mendelson focused his attention upon such paradoxes in neighboring Santiago Atitlán (1956), I will not cover this ground again. I choose to look at the twentieth-century Panajachel world view, not as an amalgamation of cognitive orientations whose roots can be traced to European or Mayan cultures, but rather as a viable system of belief which is pervasive in the region, not readily altered by the new influences that have broken in upon the lives of Indians since 1940, and exerting considerable influence upon Ladino belief patterns.

Methodological Considerations in Structuring Belief

The inferring of premises from Tax's data began prior to my own field work in Panajachel, in conjunction with analyzing the 1941 data on belief awareness and acceptance among Tax's informants. The advantage of Tax's data for this undertaking lay in the various comments of the seven informants on each of the four hundred beliefs. Their clarifications and explanations facilitated my understanding of the underlying premises in many instances. Using a method which Foster has described as "triangulation,"[2] I constructed a hierarchal model of premises adequate for subsuming the great majority of the four hundred beliefs.

I took this model with me to Panajachel but put it aside during the initial months of gathering demographic data and assessing environmental changes since 1941. What I did do in the realm of world view research during this period was to elicit awareness and acceptance data for most of Tax's sample of four hundred beliefs among some of our more traditionally oriented friends, neighbors, and compadres. Some of the premises I had inferred were volunteered piecemeal, and reformulations of others emerged with clarifications of ideas I had internalized from Tax's data. However, the minimal reliance of informants upon logical constructs made it clear that eliciting and validating assumptions in any comprehensive manner would necessitate extensive interviewing to benefit from the variable accessibility of premises among informants.

This subsequent interviewing had two objectives: (1) to measure the impact of acculturative influences upon awareness and acceptance of a sample of beliefs; and (2) to elicit and confirm structural orientations. The former was my chief objective, and accordingly I sought informants under the age of thirty-five. If I had restricted my interviewing to the problem of belief structure, I would have spent more time with fewer informants and sought out "philosophers" rather than the younger, acculturated individuals.

Some belief data at this point will facilitate understanding the process of inferring, testing, and revising premises. I again use the premise described earlier: that women over men weaken the latter physically and mentally. I label this a premise in that it was only offered to explain derivative beliefs. The distinction between premise and belief is arbitrary in this instance, however, for the premise is highly explicit in the belief that a woman should never step over a man. While the latter belief is pervasive, and the explanation widely shared, informants differed greatly in their concern with tracing this premise to its logical conclusions, given another premise—the possessions of men and women contain their owners' spirits. Accordingly, the prohibition against a woman's sweeping over a boy's or man's feet with her house broom is not universally recognized as being related to the prohibition against her stepping over his feet. Most informants agreed that sweeping over feet should be avoided (so that men sometimes leave the house when women sweep), but such behavior is not infrequently explained in terms of what I call "secondary rationalizations." Such rationalizations, or explanations, are of course part of mental culture, but they are more indicative of value and motivational orientations than of cognitive orientations. A range of undesirable fates (losing a job, becoming poor, becoming ill, incurring black magic, being summoned to "court," becoming involved in a fight, marrying outside the community, or just becoming generally luckless) are frequently offered as consequences for any disapproved behavior. It is as though the culture provided a basket of "undesirables" from which one person selects one and another person selects another to rationalize the same belief.

When discussing another derivative belief, that calming or weakening an angry dog or bull can be accomplished by sweeping its back with a broom, very few informants appeared to recognize the "woman (or woman's things) over man (or man's things)" premise implicit in the action. Those who did specified that the *secreto* was effectual only if the broom used was a woman's broom, in the same way that woman's clothing or urine over the animal could accomplish the same end. Virtually everyone questioned about thus calming a dog not only knew the behavior but also believed it efficacious. Since many of these rejected the "woman over man" assumption, it became apparent that other epistemological grounds for acceptance of sweeping a dog were available. For a few, an alternative premise satisfactorily explained the action, that is, the assumption that petting and sweeping are comparable means of soothing a dog. Hence, the use of the broom was incidental, though customary, and the kind of broom (there are men's brooms for sweeping patios and women's brooms for sweeping houses) was immaterial. While I think it probable that the latter explanation is more recent than the former and represents a reassignment of premises, obviously this cannot be satisfactorily proven. In cases of multiple explanation, it is useless to attempt to determine which explanation is primary; one can only examine which is most common.

The degree to which "secondary rationalizations" or differing premises are invoked to explain a given belief is a function of visibility of premises in the belief, on the one hand (broom for calming a dog), and the accessibility or explanatory load of the premises, on the other. Accessibility is related to the amount of behavior and belief explainable by a given premise, and hence the extent to which it is talked and thought about. The premise of "women over men" is not only explicit in this particular belief, but the premise is also highly accessible to Panajacheleños since it is invoked to explain a multitude of behavioral prescriptions and beliefs learned at an early age by every child.

When the accessibility of a premise is low, the problems of isolating or establishing its existence and its explanatory load are many. Foremost is the danger of the observer's imposing his own categories of relationships upon diverse data not consistently explained by informants. For example, when first confronted in Tax's notes with belief data including (a) sweeping a dog to calm it and (b) the prohibition against sweeping over a man's feet, I inferred a relationship based upon the act of sweeping and postulated a premise to the effect that "sweeping weakens the hold or the force of one thing upon another." Under this I naively added a disparate number of beliefs including prohibitions against (c) sweeping the house fifteen days following the birth of a child or (d) sweeping the house when one's husband is on a business trip, and the belief that (e) placing a broom behind the door will hasten a visitor's departure. I reasoned that sweeping symbolized a desire to be rid of someone or thing. It did not take much interviewing to ascertain that it was the woman's affiliation with the broom that underlay (a) and (b) rather than the act of sweeping; that (c) is premised on the assumption that persons (for example, a newborn baby or anyone during the hours when spirits are most abroad) are vulnerable to evil spirits through any possessions or body wastes which might be swept out-of-doors; and that (d) and (e) are but poorly known *secretos* with no agreement as to their rationale. They are either derivatives of premises of low visibility, or if explicable in terms of more accessible premises such as those mentioned above, the connection is not readily apparent to my informants.

This raises the second problem of inferring premises. When informants cannot explain behavior on other than pragmatic grounds (for example, "one puts the broom behind the door to make a visitor leave because it works"), one runs the risk of "feedback" or influencing informant thinking by merely suggesting premises that might be implicit in the belief. This is not so serious when it is only a matter of determining the most frequently recognized derivation among several established premises; that is, it is not of much importance to me to know whether belief "x" is more pervasively or logically premised on assumption "y" than on assumption "z" so long as I am certain of both "y" and "z." What *is* important is that I not assume "y" or "z" to be part of my informant's stock of assumptions *only* because as a model inferred by me it explains behavior "x" satisfactorily to him. I emphasize *only,* because it has proven necessary to infer and postulate premises adequate to explain beliefs for which informants consistently evidenced acceptance on epistemological grounds other than logical inference. Reliance simply upon volunteered premises would produce premises adequate for explaining only the most pervasive and most commonplace behavior and beliefs, especially when one is limited in the number of informants he has time to get to know sufficiently for such interviewing. Any attempt to ferret out premises adequate for explaining consistently the diversity of behavior and belief which natives accept on a variety of epistemological grounds requires the observer to use whatever premises the data suggest in looking for regularities and pattern. Validation or reformulation of the resultant model is then sought through questioning as widely as possible about beliefs viewed by informants as related and the reasons for their relatedness.

The means of determining beliefs viewed as related are several:

(1) In open-ended discussion informants volunteer many beliefs; it is useful to note what beliefs are volunteered in what contexts.

(2) Once an assumption or premise has been made explicit in conversation, by or for an informant, the informant can occasionally volunteer beliefs which he accepts as satisfactorily explained by that premise. In a few instances I suggested premises which seemed to be meaningful, new ideas to informants, who then volunteered derivative beliefs which they indicated they had not understood before.

(3) Operating on the basis of a postulated or validated premise, occasionally I was able to anticipate beliefs or probe in productive spheres of thought. An example will serve to illustrate this as well as procedure (2) above. Tax's data included a few beliefs (for example, one should not

engage in sexual intercourse during the several days committed to ceremonial dancing) from which I inferred an assumption that for Panajacheleños sexual functions and proper fulfillment of ceremonial roles are incompatible. These beliefs were not well known among the several informants questioned in 1964. To make the assumption more relevant to the contemporary setting, I asked about sexual prohibitions in connection with church ceremonies, and one informant volunteered that no one engages in intercourse the night before attending mass. Interested to determine whether this was a common prohibition, I asked two young women who participate in Catholic Action. One, our house servant, had never heard of this but immediately concurred that such a prohibition would be only proper. The other informant had likewise never heard of it, and having studied several years in a Catholic school and being knowledgeable about Catholic teachings, she was insistent that no such prohibition existed. Then, however, on pondering the premise which I had made explicit, she brightened and added, "So that's why the girls say one shouldn't enter the church when menstruating."

Turning to means of obtaining native explanations of *why* related beliefs are related, the usual procedure was to pick up in the course of conversation casually offered explanations of individual beliefs. By combining such interpretations with data on belief groupings, I was able to confirm and reformulate premises and learn a few assumptions I had not previously inferred. These reformulations and additions occurred early in the interviewing (when I was working with a few informants over a large corpus of world view data), and when I reached the point of trying more rigorously and systematically to validate and understand premises of apparently low visibility, no additional new premises were isolated. By the end of my interviewing I felt confident that I had isolated at least the more accessible premises, since the premises available to me by then were adequate for explaining the great majority of beliefs volunteered during the course of the extensive interviewing among forty-six informants.

The model I have come up with is an abstraction from a highly complex scene. I have tried to indicate that (1) the awareness and acceptance of discrete beliefs vary markedly from informant to informant; (2) the epistemological grounds of belief acceptance vary; (3) individuals vary in their interest in logical inference; (4) the group-typical premises vary in their accessibility to individuals; and (5) the logical explanations of a given belief frequently utilize different premises. Moreover, new beliefs from outside the Indian community are being introduced in ever increasing numbers, I suspect. Some find satisfactory explanation under traditional assumptions; others are incorporated with new assumptions which to a lesser or greater degree conflict with existing premises.

The resulting model exhibits several biases which undoubtedly distort the realities of a typical Panajacheleño's world view. First, I have attempted to be as holistic as possible in delineating as many of the assumptions implicit in discrete beliefs as Panajacheleños utilize in explaining those beliefs. In so doing I have realized that a certain distortion results from treating peripheral assumptions on the same footing with more central concepts. On the other hand, too many investigators have focused upon the central concepts of a world view to the exclusion of those which are peripheral and have attempted to explain more than was warranted by these key concepts.

A second bias which has influenced my structuring of belief has been an effort to construct as coherent and integrated a model as possible. I have sought resolutions of logical inconsistencies among beliefs insofar as informants could provide such resolutions. We assume that a certain degree of internal consistency and integration in world view is essential and that individuals differ in their tolerance of logical inconsistency. We know that the human mind compartmentalizes knowledge, making it possible to hold inconsistent ideas. Since the mind does compartmentalize, disguising inconsistencies for the believer, an outsider looking in upon a world view sees more inconsistency than does a native. This is largely because the observer does not understand the contexts of beliefs, and as he becomes cognizant of the underlying assumptions and concepts which generate beliefs, the inconsistencies begin to disappear. Within a given "compartment" or context, little inconsistency is tolerated by the mind and hence the culture. As an outsider I have attempted to gain the perspective of contexts of belief association which eliminates inconsistencies, but in so doing I probably have produced more coherency and integration of world view than most Panajacheleños find necessary for successful functioning. In short, it can be argued that in my attempt to integrate a wide assortment of discrete beliefs I have paid less attention to the basic concepts of the Panajachel world view than to inferring as many assumptions as necessary for resolving paradoxes. The possibility exists that in the minds of most Panajacheleños beliefs simply form clusters around concepts and within these contexts find their explanations. The concepts, while impinging upon one another and requiring a minimal coherency and integration, may be but loosely strung together. I suspect that by restricting my attention to several such concepts or belief clusters I could have presented a more typical and certainly more vivid portrait of a Panajacheleño's view of the world. In so doing, however, I would probably have rested content with some inconsistencies in belief associations which at least some Panajacheleños resolve within the broader context of assumptions available to them. I have decided to make my objective the delineation of whatever assumptions Panajacheleños utilize in explaining the myriad beliefs group-typical of their culture, accepting the rather mechanical bias this emphasis gives the resulting structure of belief. Even this goal, of course, I have not fully achieved.

Some contextual orientation is needed to make sense of the model. An overview of the basic concepts will orient the reader until he feels sufficiently "enculturated" to follow the premise-by-premise unfolding of the belief structure. In providing this overview, I necessarily go beyond elicited statements of belief and piece together inferences which I cannot validate as realities in the mind of Panajacheleños. Another function of such an overview is to present some of the paradoxes referred to above which are more apparent to the observer than they are to Panajacheleños.

An Overview of the Panajachel World View

The terms most frequently employed in the several hundred beliefs used in structuring Panajachel belief are spirit and blood, death and illness, destiny and justice, good and evil, strength and weakness. A discussion of spirit and destiny will touch on all of these.

The spirit of man is essentially good. It comes from heaven to earth for a sojourn which usually is confined to one lifetime in corporal embodiment and never more than two. The universe of the spirit is therefore the heavens and the earth. Each domain has its owner, and the human spirit belongs to both. The spirit, by associating with the body and forming a personality, is a product of good and evil. To the extent that the earth is identified with the "owner of the hill," or the Devil, and to the extent that life on earth is perceived as an undesirable confinement of the spirit, life is not considered an end in itself.

There is thus an ambivalence about this life. It is the model upon which all existence, including that of spirits after death, is patterned, yet life necessarily involves the working out of a destiny involving compromises. Success in earthly terms necessitates strength, and strength comes from earthly as readily as from heavenly sources. One has to reconcile the two to live successfully. The weak are claimed by God at an early age, and one solution to the dilemma of life is to remain pure and place one's faith in returning to the heavenly realm in the afterlife. Death for the young can be considered a blessing. The other solution is to live life to the fullest, and this is the solution which society encourages one to seek. Upon the *zahorin* more than upon anyone else is bestowed the power and strength to capitalize upon weaknesses of others. He can turn all to his advantage in thwarting even his own destiny if he chooses to align himself with the Devil and selfishly pursue the role of *brujo* (witch) in prolonging his own life and the lives of clients who pay his price.

The ambivalence about life carries over into alternative conceptions of time and human destiny. The Christian concept of linear time, proceeding from the Creation, when all was good, to a Final Judgment occasioned by moral deterioration, is a part of every Panajacheleño's world view, I suspect, yet coexisting with this image is the awareness of nature's repetitive cycle bound up with earth as the provider of the sustenance of life. The latter concept implies no value judgments of past versus future but rather sees the future embodied in or anticipated by the past and present.

For Panajacheleños, spirit is ethereal yet embodied in the blood or life fluid of those substances possessing fluids. The human spirit is not constrained by this embodiment and can leave the body at its own discretion or under the influence of stronger spirits. Spirit is the essence of all existence, and all spirits are posited with the same feelings, drives, and social organization as spirits attached to human beings. Spirits are ordered in terms of power and authority, and soul strength is influenced by destiny and by association with sources of strength during the life of the body.

To the foregoing I expect all Panajacheleños would agree, but there are problems. Most assume the spirit in man is a single entity which when thus fated must periodically assume animal form to roam at night. Such spirits *(characoteles)* are believed by some Panajacheleños to leave the human form and temporarily enter animal form, while other informants assume the body is itself transformed. The latter interpretation is consonant with the belief that the individual has but one spirit which cannot leave the body for any length of time without death ensuing; the former interpretation is consonant with the belief of many that the individual has two spirits, one localized in the heart and the other in the back. Only the spirit of the heart leaves the body during life, and at death it dies. The other is immortal. Whether they believe in one spirit or two, most Panajacheleños assume that the spirit imparts a destiny to the self which includes the destined hour of death. Yet this destiny is subject to alteration by alignments with sources of strength, forces of good and evil, and irresponsibility. For most informants, judgment of the individual's successful realization of his destiny and utilization of the forces and resources at his disposal comes only at death. A few Panajacheleños expressed the belief, however, that the judgment and justice are carried out at the close of this life; hence the prolonged suffering of some elderly persons and the enjoyment of good health to old age by others.

Perhaps this overview of some central concepts together with perusal of part I of the model will enable the reader to feel somewhat at home when confronted with the many primary data of part II, from which the structure has been inferred.

A Model of the Structure of Panajachel Belief

Presenting the full model and supportive belief data together is unwieldy: part I is limited to the assumptions and cognitive orientations which elucidate the primary belief data used in Tax's and my own interviewing, and part II presents these data together with all new belief data which find elucidation within the model. Included in both parts is the range of premises inferred or elicited by me and judged accessible to some Panajacheleños. Where evidence of informants' utilization of premises or related concepts is available in quotations from taped interviews, this is indicated through use of quotation marks. Actually, the numbered propositions of the model frequently incorporate a number of closely related ideas which informants articulated more readily than the more integrative propositions I have termed premises. Where evidence was lacking of Panajacheleños' ability to articulate concepts I had inferred, quotation marks are lacking. The premises are grouped in part I in terms of some integrative propositions which I feel subsume the premises in economical and consistent fashion. These higher-level generalizations, while emerging inductively from the premises, are strictly my own formulations, serving primarily as a rationale for ordering the data.

In part II, the beliefs constituting my sample for the extensive interviewing are preceded by data on Ladino and Indian awareness and acceptance. Those used to measure regional awareness are preceded as well by this information. These sets of data constitute the basis for the comparisons presented in chapter 6, as well as the basis for the assessment of premise strength among Indians and Ladinos presented in part I and discussed at the close of this chapter.

Virtually all new beliefs (new to me and not recorded in Tax's data) learned in the course of my interviewing are included in part II to illustrate the premises further and test the adequacy of the premises to explain data other than those used in the initial formulation of the model. The few new beliefs which do not find satisfactory explanation under the premises are discussed below. Finally, in the few instances where premises are poorly illustrated by new beliefs or those of my sample, I have included some additional items from the sample of four hundred selected by Tax which prompted the initial formulation of the model.

Beliefs volunteered to me in the course of extensive interviewing which did not find explanation are crucial in assessing the adequacy of the assumptions to explain belief and behavior. The beliefs subsumed under the thirty-five premises number 362, half of which were volunteered after I had chosen my sample of 181. Twenty-one of these are not readily explained by the model. This means that the premises formulated on the basis of Tax's data and revised on the basis of my initial interviewing were adequate for explaining 90 percent of beliefs elicited after choosing my sample (or 95 percent of all the primary data used in interviewing). Some of the 10 percent doubtless find satisfactory explanation under postulated premises; but no explanations were offered by informants, and the relationships are too obscure for me to posit with certainty. Some suggest other premises, and in such cases I probed for evidence of informant visibility of additional premises, but without success.

For example, money and fish seem to have an ambiguous relationship. On the one hand, I was told that money on one's person would result in poor luck when fishing; on the other hand, several attested that dreaming of catching fish foretells becoming wealthy. Fish are eaten by Panajacheleños only during Easter week, and fish are said to be the "sleepy seeds" from Christ's eyes. One can thus speculate that fish are good as money is evil, but no one was willing to agree that fish are good. Rather fish, along with money and metal, have the same disagreeable odor, and fish should never be eaten before working one's crops lest the odor repel spirits. I can go no further, and no informant asked could shed any light on the rationale for the beliefs.

Similarly, the ambivalence of many phenomena is confusing (to me!). A cat in the doorway at noon keeps spirits from entering, while its presence there at night lets them in. Likewise, a broom or *machete* left beside a sleeping child or in the doorway will keep spirits away, except at night when the tools either cannot or will not afford the same protection. The ambivalence was observed in many areas: for example, the protective-dangerous quality of crosses carries over to priests, whose spirits are reported to wander about at night haunting people. Even fire, believed protective and of God by most Panajacheleños, was believed evil and of the Devil by two informants from one of the more traditionally oriented households. The same is the case with phenomena such as the rainbow. Most Panajacheleños consider it dangerous and issuing from a snake, while some claim it to be a sign from God and a blessing to be acknowledged with an offering of thanks. I am reminded of Mendelson's observation: "At all times, too, there is the fundamental ambiguity about good and evil . . . which prevents us from forcing Atiteco thought into the relatively clear-cut categories of our own system" (1957:436).

It is not that a dichotomy of good and evil is wholly lacking; it is just that the phenomena that belong exclusively to one pole or the other are few. I have tried to summarize this orientation in part I of the model. There I suggest that Panajacheleños think less in terms of moral absolutes than in terms of a contextual appraisal of behavior: everything must be judged in its context. Tax was told in 1940 that Mars is the patron saint of thieves, under whose protection robbery can take place with impunity. Moreover, one explanation offered Tax for the moon's one eye was a blow from the sun who desired that the poor be able to steal as necessary without being seen. Only one person I questioned about these beliefs or about the relativity of "crimes" such as robbery would admit to the assumption that robbery under some circumstances is justifiable. Protestantism and the presence of police and courts pledged to enforce national laws would be sufficient explanation for a change in attitudes. Still fundamental, however, is the assumption that there are few absolutes and that action must be considered in its context. While awareness of such an orientation helps explain several discrete beliefs, I do not list a premise to the effect that there is no sharp distinction between good and evil or no moral absolutes. This would simply acknowledge the absence of something present in my world view.

The remaining beliefs for which I lack adequate explanation are listed below. It will be noted that several seem to conflict with postulated or volunteered premises, as, for example, the belief that a *zahorin'*s power will be cut if he eats buzzard flesh. All other beliefs about consuming animals of the "hill" or Devil lead one to assume that considerable power and strength are thus derived. Such contradictions are surprisingly few, and probably the apparent contradiction in this belief could be resolved with more information. Usually the contradictions stem from new premises which conflict with existing assumptions, as, for example, the conflicting ideas regarding the wisdom of giving or loaning one's possessions (see premise 27). With regard to this latter premise, possibly item 18 below is explained in terms of protecting the giver's interest by repelling the gift's spirit through use of the left hand. While I suggest explanations for some (in parentheses), I am only guessing.

1. Dreaming of losing a tooth foretells the approaching death of someone in the family.

2. One can cure goiter by rubbing the growth with a sandal.

3. One can cure someone of talking in his sleep by hitting his mouth with a sandal.

4. A pot should never be covered with a pot of larger size. (See premise 16.)

5. Failure to offer food to twins one encounters will result in your clothing going to shreds.

6. A broom upside down behind the door and a cross of salt on the fire will result in a visitor's prompt departure.

7. If a wife sweeps the house while her husband is away on business, he will have poor luck in his undertaking. (Perhaps spirits encountering his spirit in the sweepings could then work ill against him?)

8. If a *zahorin* eats a buzzard, his power will be cut.

9. A woman can ward off the spirit of a *characotel* by biting her braid.

10. If a girl breaks one of the sticks of her loom she will not be able to weave well unless she drinks the droppings of ground corn from the grinding stone mixed in the water of the *nixtamal* (ground corn mixed with water).

11. A girl who plays with a banana tree stalk will have breasts of unequal size. (Possibly through metaphorical association of "like causes like"; the clumps of bananas hang at different levels and ripen at intervals.)

12. Egg white rubbed on the legs or soles of the feet assists a child in learning to walk well. (Possibly metaphorical association with chicken's ability to get around so well on two legs.)

13. Clothing on backwards protects against evil spirits at night.

14. A murderer can avoid being haunted by his victim by cutting off the latter's finger and burying it at the spot of the deed.

15. The fingernails of one's deceased father should be cut to insure that the crops produce well.

16. Water constantly boiling on the fire insures that bees will be content and remain on the premises.

17. A woman's hair combings placed at the foot of the *güisgüil (vegeta-*ble pear) plant insure that the yield will be good. (Perhaps through metaphorical associations, as the plant is a vine with tendrils resembling hair.)

18. A gift should be accepted with the left hand.

Stability of Belief

I speak reservedly of erosion of premises, fully cognizant of the danger of generalizing too readily from beliefs to supportive assumptions. The wide range of explanations offered in rationalization for not killing a snake with the blade of a *machete,* while an extreme example, illustrates well the problem involved in assessing the strength of any given premise on the basis of differential acceptance of beliefs which *some* informants explain in this manner. For those beliefs in which one or two premises are particularly visible, however, the judgment of premise strength is more justifiable. For approximately half of the premises or related concepts within the model, I have ventured such an assessment, summarizing in part I of the model the data presented in part II. Thus, even for the premises on which I do venture an assessment, the reader can readily make his own judgment by referring to the data of part II.

Indians with considerable contact with schooling or Protestantism (referred to hereafter simply as Protestants) are questioning the interpretation of dreams as the wanderings of the spirit, while continuing to accept that some spirits can assume animal form. They accept the equation of spirit with blood and the influence of physical states upon blood strength, but they are beginning to question that blood strength varies between Indians and Ladinos. Protestants do not conceive as pervasively of the spirit's permeating one's possessions and body as do traditionals. Similarly, they are less inclined to assume that characteristics and conditions are transferable through physical or emotional association, with the exception of the susceptibility of the foetus to emotional involvement of the mother.

Spiritual guardianship is less widely extended by Protestants than by traditionals, although sufficient doubt has been cast upon the sacred nature of corn to cause half of even the traditionally oriented informants to doubt the spiritual distinctiveness of the three colors of corn and the necessity of propitiating spirits of crops. The same influence of Protestant teachings is observable in traditionals' questioning of the personification and deification of the sun and moon. All Panajacheleños accept the influence of the moon upon life fluids, and the dichotomy of hot and cold (food) substances remains strong. Interestingly, Protestants and traditionals alike are more prone to accept the Devil's power over animals attributed to his domain than to personify and fear the weather phenomena and fire identified with God. Belief in the ambivalence of crosses is shared by Protestants. Protestants may be rejecting the moral dichotomy between left (evil) and right (good), but since those rejecting the significance of nervous twitching frequently explained it on just this basis I have no strong indication that the left-right dichotomy is in fact weakening. Protestant questioning of the power of women to weaken men is eroding this complex of beliefs among traditionals. Similarly, reduced concern among Protestants over the danger of imitating the dead is influencing traditionals to some extent. This is not the case, however, with the concept of strong days and hours and the vulnerability of the living to molestation by spirits at such times; one-third of the Protestant informants are questioning this complex of beliefs without any noticeable effect upon traditionals. The same is true of the traditional ban on giving away or loaning one's possessions lest the spirit be offended and leave, or of adversely influencing one's luck by undue anticipation or concern. With regard to dreams, Protestants generally are aware of culturally prescribed dream meanings, but they reject them rather consistently. Ladinos, on the other hand, know fewer of them but accept those they do know.

The concept of a predestined length of life is questioned by slightly less than half the Protestants, while universally accepted by traditionals. This is less the case with the extension of destiny to the roles of *characotel, zahorin,* and midwife. Protestant distrust of *zahorines* is causing some traditionals to question the status of *zahorines* as destined to this calling. Protestants tend to question the possibility of reincarnation and the inevitability of punishment at death. This is not to say that Protestants question the concepts of justice and judgment for one's conduct in life; they merely assume those faithful to Protestant teachings are assured immediate acceptance into heaven. Protestants are inclined to reject the logic of sympathetic magic more than traditionals, but there is considerable inconsistency among both groups in acceptance of this logic.

Beliefs questioned by more than 15 to 20 percent of the traditionally oriented informants are very few and in all but two cases are questioned by higher percentages of Protestants. Many beliefs are questioned as a direct result of school instruction, including the traditional explanation of eclipses, rainbows, stars, and comets. Only one premise is eroding markedly among traditionals: women passing over men weaken the latter physically or mentally. The reasons for its erosion appear to be various and are worth reviewing.

Informants offered the following evidence for their rejection of specific beliefs under this premise: Ladina girls step over boys' feet protruding from desks in school with no admonition from the teacher; women in the markets frequently have to step over food that men eventually eat; and women in the cities often are above men on bridges or in two-story buses. A number of informants cast doubt on the damaging influence of these new behaviors yet still asserted that the traditional behavior is proper and respectful. I suspect that many informants rejecting one or more of the specific beliefs on pragmatic or other grounds still accept the underlying assumption that men are by nature superior to women.

Support for a different orientation toward sexual status is latent in Protestant teachings of sexual equality, and indeed Protestant women find themselves in new roles on an equal footing with men. The reaction of one Protestant informant was to gloss over the contradictions and note that Protestantism also teaches that Eve was responsible for the fall of Adam. For others the reaction is to doubt the traditional assumption to the point of rejecting not only the premise as formulated in the model but the more basic orientation toward sexual status as well. A quotation from an interview with a young man is revealing in this regard. After discussing various of the beliefs of the "woman-over-man" complex, I decided to ask about the underlying explanation. I suggested that perhaps these *secretos,* or beliefs, follow from a more fundamental idea about the effect that women, or maybe women's blood, have over men. He replied:

"Yes, what I think is . . . well, I don't think it has anything to do with blood. . . It's because the responsibilities of the man are very important, being the care of the family and taking care of all the needs. The man has to keep a lot in his head. But with the woman, it's different. She works mostly in the kitchen, in work that is, in a sense, less important and inferior. For this reason, as well as for the reason that women are weaker and more fragile, people say the female sex is less important. These *secretos* result from the fear that men will be lowered to the woman's level. But at the present time this is changing, and women have become almost—in fact, sometimes women are *more* capable in their thinking and managing things than men. Women often have abilities or advantages greater than men. People may attribute this to these *secretos,* but in fact the woman doesn't make the man inferior, it's just that intellectually she may happen to be superior.

That the beliefs are eroding uniformly for only one premise among traditionals strengthens the conclusion that the majority of Panajache-leños (it should be remembered that only one-sixth of the population is Protestant and only thirty-two individuals have gone beyond fourth grade) are not questioning traditional beliefs to any noticeable extent, despite the marked questioning of many belief complexes by Protestants and those with six years of education.

Virtually every concept which Protestants accept less than traditionals is peripheral to the Ladino world view. The only exceptions are concepts of strong or dangerous days and hours and related beliefs premised upon the danger posed by spirits to the living. Ladinos tend to share these with traditionally oriented Indians, whereas Protestants appear at least less anxious if not less credulous. On the basis of his study of Indian and Ladino communities in the *municipio* of San Antonio Palopó, Redfield also compared ethnic belief patterns; his generalizations supplement in a useful manner my more piecemeal comparisons (Redfield 1945).

Acceptance by

Ladinos	Traditionals	Protestants [*]	Propositions, Premises, and Beliefs [**]

I. Reality is spiritual and unitary and is manifested in changing forms.

A. Being is essentially a spiritual, not a material, phenomenon; corporal existence is not so much a stage as a condition which comes and goes in the career of the spirit.

Ladinos	Traditionals	Protestants	
			1. Human spirits are not confined to their bodies or human form.
50-75%	>75%	<50%	"The spirit can leave whenever it wants to."
50-75	>75	>75	"Spirits can change their forms."
			2. Blood carries the strength of body and spirit.
50-75	>75	50-75	"Some people have strong blood."
			3. Blood strength and temperature change with emotional and physical states of the body.
			"The hotter the blood, the stronger it is."
			"Blood becomes stronger the longer one lives."
<50	>75	<50	*4. One's spirit is in all parts of the body and in one's personal belongings.*
			Possessions or refuse of individuals contains their spirits.
<50	>75	<50	*5. Characteristics, conditions, and illnesses are transferable through physical and emotional association.*
<50	>75	50-75	Consuming the substance of something imparts its characteristics to the consumer.

B. The conditions and processes of being are the same for all beings.

Ladinos	Traditionals	Protestants	
			6. "Everything has its spirit."
			"Dogs are like people; they have souls."
			7. Spirits have human attributes.
<50	50-75	<50	"Spirits have feelings and want respect and appreciation."
			8. Life fluids and fertility are affected by phases of the moon.
50-75	>75	>75	Substances are softer and wetter when the moon is waxing or full.
			9. Plants and animals are hot, cold, or a balance of the two.
>75	>75	>75	Some illnesses result from an imbalance of hot and cold foods, and their cures consist of applying or consuming foods of a temperature to restore the balance.

II. The forms interact within a framework of prescribed relationships.

[*]Includes all Indians who have completed 5 or more years of school.
[**]First-level propositions are printed in bold type and preceded by roman numerals; second-level propositions are lettered. Premises are marked with arabic numerals; those in quotation marks are quoted directly from taped interviews. All others are inferred.

Acceptance by

Ladinos	Traditionals	Protestants	Propositions, Premises, and Beliefs
			A. The world is controlled by owners of the earth and sky; beings belong more to the one than to the other.
			10. Many things have their owners, or saints, who look after them.
>75%	>75%	50-75%	"The Devil has animals who serve him and whom he protects; killing them is risky."
<50	>75	50-75	"God is in the fire, wind, rain, and lightning."
			"Fire doesn't like the Devil."
50-75	>75	50-75	"Fire is God's representative in the home."
<50	>75	>75	"Hearthstones represent the stability of the home."
			11. "The rich get money from the Devil."
			"Money is bad."
			12. Crosses are of the dead and of the church; they are protective, yet dangerous.
	>75	>75	"Crossroads are frequented by spirits."
>75	>75	50-75	*13. The left side of the body is affiliated with evil in man and is not trustworthy.*
			"There are two roads in life—the left and the right—and the left is evil."
			14. Animals are blessed or accursed, according to their roles in the life of Christ.
50-75	>75	>75	*15. Some foods are holy and carry protective power against evil spirits.*
			B. Relationships among beings are basically authority relationships and are as much a given as existence itself.
			16. The social relationships characteristic of man are characteristic of all spirits.
			Kinship and *compadre* ties link all spirits.
			"Younger siblings are stronger than older siblings."
			"Animals and angels have community duties, just as do people."
			17. Siblings are rivals for affection and food.
			"An older sibling sometimes 'eats' his brother."
50-75	>75	<50	*18. A woman (or her belongings) over a man (or his belongings) weakens the latter physically or mentally.*
<50	>75	>75	A woman's power can be used beneficially to weaken or calm males.
			19. Spirits and evil forces have dominion over the living, unless one is stouthearted.
			"The dead can summon the living."

Acceptance by

Ladinos	Traditionals	Protestants	Propositions, Premises, and Beliefs
			20. *Colors vary in strength and power.*
			21. *Some numbers are especially powerful.*
			III. Given his limited perspective, it is unavoidably difficult for man to know and observe prescribed relationships. He must use his knowledge as responsibly as possible.
			A. There is a capriciousness and uncertainty in life which one can never eliminate but which one can minimize by expedience.
			22. *Religious or ceremonial observances are incompatible with sexual functions.*
			23. *Quarreling or disharmony in the household adversely affects the welfare of the family.*
			24 . *To imitate the dead can result in death.*
			25. *Vulnerability to misfortune or molestation by spirits is greater at some times than at others.*
>75%	>75%	50-75%	"Spirits are out on strong days and at strong hours." "When the time changes is a dangerous time to be abroad." "The night is the daytime of the dead."
50-75	>75	50-75	Care should be taken not to expose oneself to spirits when they are abroad.
			26. *Tools or weapons that have tasted blood are more prone to continue inflicting injury.*
			27. *Giving part of something you own away, or loaning it, risks losing its spirit.*
<50	>75	<50	"Loaning cuts your luck."
50-75	>75	<50	28. *Preoccupation or undue concern often backfires and increases the cause for concern.* "If someone believes strongly enough that something will happen, it will."
50-75	>75	50-75	"Dreaming of something often means just the opposite is going to happen."
			B. The time and nature of future occurrences often are knowable in advance to those who know how to interpret the signs.
			29. *The order or time of occurrences foretells something about the future.* "How something begins determines how it ends."
			30. *The unusual or unexpected foretells future events.*

Acceptance by

Ladinos	Traditionals	Protestants	Propositions, Premises, and Beliefs
<50	>75	50-75	31. *Repetition of an occurrence can correct what was done the first time.*
		IV.	**The universe is moral. There is an ultimate justice which insures that those who accept and observe prescribed relationships are rewarded.**
		A.	Each being must sojourn on earth in responsible fulfillment of its spirit's destiny.
			32. *Destiny and luck determine one's life.*
50-75%	>75%	50-75%	"Everyone has his appointed time to die."
			33. *To live to old age is possible only with strong blood or the help of evil forces.*
		B.	There are few absolutes, and behavior must be judged in context. The final weighing or accounting comes only at death.
<50	>75	50-75	34. *"There is justice in the universe which assures that each receives his just due eventually."* "God knows what we do, and he will punish and reward."
			35. *The moral fiber of mankind is deteriorating.*

1. Pervasiveness in the Region [a]	2. Panajacheleño Awareness [b]	3. Ladino Awareness [c]	4. Acceptance by Traditionals	5. Acceptance by Protestants [d]	Premises and Supporting Beliefs
					Premise 1. Human spirits are not confined to their bodies or human form.
					"The spirit can leave whenever it wants to."
13/13	95%	70%	100%	30%	The spirit leaves the body when we sleep; dreams are wanderings of the spirit.
10/13	78	21	88	45	A buzzing sensation in the inner ear is caused by the spirit's departure or entry.
					Sleeping on one's side keeps one from dreaming.
	56	64	100	90	It is dangerous to awaken a person who is tossing and obviously dreaming, lest his spirit not have time to return.
					A child can have his soul dislodged when badly frightened; beating the ground where the spirit was lost reunites it with the body.
					"Spirits can change their forms."
13/13	100	70	100	86	Some persons (*characoteles*) have spirits capable of changing into or entering animal form.
					There is a Panajacheleña who changes her sex each month.
11/13	93	64	100	86	One species of mouse changes into a bat.
	97		100	100	Lizards hatch from eggs laid by snakes.
					Premise 2. Blood carries the strength of body and spirit.
					"Some people have strong blood."
	65	70	88	50	Indians have stronger blood than Ladinos.
6/12	60	12	85	70	*Zahorines* have strong blood, enabling them to live long lives.
6/12	37	50	100	70	Midwives have strong blood and live long lives.

a. Number of towns in which at least one informant knew the belief/number of towns where belief was sampled. 11/13 means that the belief was known by at least one informant in each of 11 of the 13 towns where the belief was sampled.
b. Based on the number of informants questioned for each belief.
c. Percentages of Ladinos knowing and also accepting the beliefs.
d. "Protestants" includes Indians who have completed 5 or more years of school.

1.	2.	3.	4.	5.	Premises and Supporting Beliefs
6/12	55%	30%	100%	73%	*Characoteles* have strong blood and live long lives.
		90			Men have stronger blood than women.
					Premise 3. Blood strength and temperature change with emotional and physical states of the body.
					"The hotter the blood, the stronger it is."
	77		100	100	A baby can receive *ojo* (illness) or become *ojeado* (ill or weak) if gazed upon by a menstruating or pregnant woman, a drunk man, or anyone hot and sweaty.
					The blood of someone intoxicated is dangerous to give in blood transfusions.
					Blood is strongest and hottest at noon.
					One should not engage in intercourse when one has an open wound, lest the blood become too hot for the body to contain.
					One should not engage in intercourse in the sweat bath or near the fire.
9/13	60	7	82	82	A rabid dog can be cured by cutting his ears and tail to bleed him.
6/11	70	7	100	92	A rabid dog can be cured by bathing him in cold water (to reduce the temperature of his overheated blood).
					"Blood becomes stronger the longer one lives."
					It is dangerous to sweep the house until a baby is at least two weeks old. Its spirit, present in waste around the house, is weak and easily harmed or stolen by spirits out-of-doors.
					Premise 4. One's spirit is in all parts of the body and in one's personal belongings.
					Possessions or refuse of individuals contains their spirits.
					One's spirit is present in his name; second names are useful, especially at night, to avoid losing your spirit through someone's use of your right name.
					A belt of snake skin is a risky investment, as the skin contains the spirit, and a new snake might evolve.
					Dry limbs of fruit trees should not be cut or burned, lest the fruit be spoiled.

1.	2.	3.	4.	5.	Premises and Supporting Beliefs
9/13	87%	57%	96%	75%	Toys or clothing of children should not be left outdoors overnight lest spirits play with them and affect the child's spirit.
11/13	92	35	88	44	Hair combings should be kept throughout one's life since at death the spirit must take all its possessions with it. If they are not readily recovered, the spirit remains to haunt.
	60	0	100	22	The same is true of nail trimmings.
	90	25	95	56	The same is true of teeth (Ladinos and some Indians throw milk teeth into the roof straw to insure strong replacements; the above rationale is lacking).
					Premise 5. Characteristics, conditions, and illnesses, are transferable through physical or emotional association.
					A child shouldn't occupy a chair recently used by an elderly or infirm person; the illness or rapid aging can afflict the child.
					Sadness leaves with the throwing into the river of a bouquet of flowers one has gathered.
					If a face afflicted with pinkeye is comically painted, the amused observer receives the ailment.
					Counting warts on another person's body transmits them to the counter.
5/8	15		80	?	Fever can be passed from one's body to that of a chicken held against chest, back, or feet.
13/13	80	20	100	40	Fatigue can be removed by brushing one's legs with some branches and leaving them at a roadside cross.
11/13	46	57	100	67	A necklace of corncobs around a dog's neck causes passers-by to ridicule the dog and receive the dog's affliction (usually a cough).
8/11	60	43	100	100	A pregnant woman much taken by any animal (dog or monkey) risks giving the animal's appearance to the child.
3/8	80	57	94	100	A pregnant woman's emotional involvement with anyone may result in the baby's resembling the person admired, desired, or disliked.
					The *tenemaste* (hearthstone) is lazy; sitting on it brings laziness.
10/12	71	18	94	22	Eating a tortilla that has touched the hearthstone can make one lazy.

A Model of the Structure of the Panajachel World View: II (Cont.)

1.	2.	3.	4.	5.	Premises and Supporting Beliefs
					Consuming the substance of something imparts its characteristics to the consumer or another substance in which the consumer has an interest.
10/13	70%	7%	90%	23%	Eating the chicken's head or neck gives a boy weak neck muscles; he won't be able to carry.
8/13	75	8	78	40	Eating the chicken's feet gives weak legs.
9/13	88	35	92	52	Eating the chicken's wing tips makes one jealous.
5/13	52	0	60	84	Eating the chicken's heart makes one unable to drink much liquor (because chickens drink so little).
	96		100	85	Drinking a bull's blood gives one its strength.
	72		100	100	Eating white eggs before working among *pepinos* imparts egg shape and white color to the fruit.
	70		100	100	Eating *chipilín* (a "hot" plant) wilts *pepinos*.
					Eating brown beans produces strong, brown streaks on the *pepino* fruit.
					Eating double bananas can result in the birth of twins.
	25		100	?	Eating baby mice is a cure for alcoholism (because baby mice drink so little).
					Feeding a dog the leftovers from a child's dish will result in the child's eating greedily and ravenously like a dog.
					Feeding to a child the food dropped from a parrot's beak will impart the parrot's ability to speak clearly.
					Sympathetic magic: like causes like. (Note: Numerous beliefs subsumed under other premises also use reasoning based on sympathetic magic. Those listed below are not readily explained by any of the other premises.)
					Pregnant women shouldn't blow up balloons, lest they become too large with child.
					A clean white cloth used for planting corn will insure high-quality corn.
					When shelling corn, do so systematically or corn next season will be unevenly arranged on cobs.
					Keep teeth from decaying by rubbing with a tooth from the cemetery.

A Model of the Structure of the Panajachel World View: II (Cont.)

1.	2.	3.	4.	5.	Premises and Supporting Beliefs
					Stealing a hollow object results in always having an empty stomach.
					Tools appropriate to the sex are placed in the sweat bath on the newborn's first bathing to insure that he grows up with good work habits.
					A mother can increase her milk supply by eating a tortilla that expanded in bubble form which was then soaked in milk.
					Salt placed on your tongue will result in the gossiper's experiencing a dry tongue.
7/12	75%	50%	94%	21%	If you bite your collar, a gossiper will bite his tongue.
	81		96	55	Pots placed on limbs of a papaya tree affect the size of the fruit.
	67		100	100	Cutting the trunk of a papaya tree results in strong sectional creases on the fruit.
0/5	40		86	25	Goiter can be reduced by rubbing the growth with a gourd.
	100		85	70	Playing with a burning stick and making circles in the air results in encountering a snake.
	60		45	43	Warts can be removed by throwing stones over one's shoulder while dancing in the vicinity of a certain bird that has warts on its legs.
13/13	93	57	100	63	Dreaming of an attack by a bull, dog, or snake results in experiencing such an attack when awake.
7/13	30	14	100	?	Dreaming of being treated for illness in the sweat bath results in becoming ill.
	65		100	100	Entering the *pepino* garden after leaving the sweat bath imparts the heat of the bath to the plants.
	65	?	100	72	Entering the *pepino* garden with shoes or sandals results in tough skin on the fruit.
	78	67	95	72	Hummingbirds urinate very little; to cure a youth who constantly wets the bed, burn a hummingbird's nest and place the boy over the smoke.
3/7	30	75	100	100	For curing bed-wetting, place warm resin from a burning stick of firewood (oak) on the umbilicus (to warm the body).

Premise 6. "Everything has its spirit."

Money has its spirit.

Stones have their spirits.

1.	2.	3.	4.	5.	Premises and Supporting Beliefs
					Each kind of onion has its own spirit.
					Each plot of ground has its spirit (or the spirits of persons who previously lived there); permission should be asked to build a house.
13/13	90%	38%	100%	23%	Corn has its spirit.
	90		50	20	Each color of corn (black, white, yellow) has its spirit.
					"Dogs are like people; they have souls."
11/13	86	83	100	50	Dogs should not be teased, or a swelling will result on the knee of the teaser.
					Dogs which have witnessed a mass are especially peaceful.
					Watching dogs copulate is punished with a sty on your eye.
					If one throws a corncob at a dog to make it leave the house, it will defecate in the house.
					A merchant who teases a dog by holding its nose or tail will be punished with poor business.
					A dog in the patio at night knows when spirits are nearby and howls to warn the household.
					The spirits of deceased dogs go first to heaven and then return to help people ford rivers.
					Premise 7. Spirits have human attributes.
					Male spirits are abroad on Mondays; female spirits are out on Fridays.
					The large grinding stone is female; the *brazo* ("arm") is male.
13/13	95	38	58	0	The sun is male; the moon is female.
					Fruit trees have male spirits; women shouldn't climb them.
					"Spirits have feelings and want respect and appreciation."
9/11	90	38	22	10	Eclipses occur when the sun and moon quarrel.
	70	66	75	20	Spirits are repelled by strong smelling substances such as garlic, chile, or *cal* (lime).
7/13	15	0	100	?	Corn resents coffee; tortillas shouldn't be dipped in coffee.

1.	2.	3.	4.	5.	Premises and Supporting Beliefs
8/13	70%	21%	88%	50%	Reheating tortillas makes the corn suffer unnecessarily.
11/12	67	21	80	70	Leaving the *comal* (griddle) on the fire longer than necessary is disrespectful.
					If a papaya tree drops its fruit before fully ripened, or a fruit tree drops its blossoms, tie a woman's skirt around the trunk to embarrass the tree.
					When felling a tree, cover the trunk lest it be embarrassed among its fellows.
					If you must leave the kitchen while food is on the fire cooking, beat the pots with your belt (of cloth), admonishing them to keep busy while you're away.
					If a grinding stone breaks, it should be properly buried.
					Trees are always happier when girls are born, since boys grow up to cut them down for firewood.
					No animal should be killed unnecessarily.
12/13	92	14	100	79	Placing one's feet or sitting on a hearthstone or grinding stone is disrespectful. (Many say dirtiness is the only reason for this.)
12/13	90	70	45	15	Incense and thanksgiving ritual should be offered to the spirit of corn at harvest.
					Premise 8. Life fluids and fertility are affected by phases of the moon.
					Substances are softer and wetter when the moon is waxing or full.
					Hermaphrodites change sex with each full moon.
					Women conceive more readily when the moon is full.
					Pregnant women shouldn't be out during lunar eclipses, lest they or the children be affected.
13/13	78	64	100	93	Lumber for construction should be cut when the moon is waning or new, to reduce rotting from excessive moisture.
12/13	55	38	93	80	Corn, or other crops to be stored, should be harvested when the moon is new or waning to reduce spoilage.
					Plants (roses) should be grafted in a waxing moon to insure rapid fusion.

1.	2.	3.	4.	5.	Premises and Supporting Beliefs
	83%		100%	100%	Any operation, such as hog castration, should be done when the moon is new or waning to reduce blood loss.
	42		100	90	Stomach worms are most effectively treated when the moon is full; at this time they consume any medicine most readily.
					Premise 9. Plants and animals are hot, cold, or a balance of the two.
					Some illnesses result from an imbalance of hot and cold foods, and their cures consist of applying or consuming foods of a temperature to restore the balance.
					Eating fruit (cold) at night can give indigestion.
					Throwing fruit peels (cold) into the lake or river (cold) causes indigestion.
6/11	55	10	100	88	Cures for burns are achieved by applying cold foods such as egg whites.
6/10	90	100	100	100	Cures for burns are achieved by applying cold foods such as tomato.
4/8	75		100	100	Cures for burns are achieved by applying cold foods such as lard.
6/10	50	25	100	100	Cures for burns are achieved by applying cold foods such as honey.
	40		100	?	Fever can be lowered by applying lard to the feet.
					Fever can be lowered by applying mustard to the feet.
4/6	85		100	89	Pinkeye can be cured by applying lemon juice.
10/11	97	83	100	95	Headache is alleviated by placing lemon slices around the head with a cloth.
					Premise 10. Many things have their owners, or saints, who look after them.
					Drunks have their saint (in the form of a dog) who protects them.
					The sweat bath has its owner, the patron saint of midwives, Santa Ana.
					Indians and Ladinos have their respective guardian saints.
					The Devil is owner of the earth; any blood spilled on the ground is drunk by him.

1.	2.	3.	4.	5.	Premises and Supporting Beliefs
					The lake has its owner; anyone urinating in the lake is punished with stomach inflammation.
	66%		88%	30%	If you throw fruit peels in the lake or river, you will receive a stomachache.
3/12	45	7%	55	20	The rainbow is the breath of a multicolored snake.
12/13	97	28	60	17	Pointing at the rainbow is punished by a bent finger or arm.
					"The Devil has animals who serve him and whom he protects; killing them is risky."
13/13	96	70	93	85	Cats' quarreling in the patio or on the house roof foretells illness.
9/13	77	21	100	67	Bats are sent to investigate illness in the home; it is best to kill any bat that enters the house lest it report illness to the Devil.
13/13	97	76	100	67	Owls are sent to announce the death of someone found ill by the bat; hooting near the house means someone will die.
					If you try to kill an owl, throw fruit rather than stones in case you succeed only in wounding it; the Devil will think it an accident.
					If a snake enters the house, someone will die.
					Use the back side of a *machete* to kill a snake (so that the cause of its death won't be so obvious to the Devil?).
					A buzzard perched on the house or entering the room means someone will die.
					If a buzzard should defecate upon you when passing overhead, you will become ill.
					God is in the fire, wind, rain, and lightning.
8/12	77	25	100	53	It is sinful to complain of the rain; if you do, it will pour at your funeral.
9/13	90	43	100	59	It is sinful to complain of the wind; if you do, your mouth will become twisted.
7/9	90	33	100	88	The lightning seeks out trees harboring snakes or other such evil animals.
9/12	67	36	100	82	The lightning seeks out people harboring evil thoughts.

1.	2.	3.	4.	5.	Premises and Supporting Beliefs
12/13	100%	100%	100%	100%	To be out-of-doors during a storm with anything of metal (scissors, tools, watch, etc.) or pointed is dangerous. (It is especially bad to have on one's person a ring or some remembrance of a loved one other than one's wife.)
					"Fire doesn't like the Devil."
					The fire complains by crackling when it is fed wood over which a snake has passed.
					Smoke won't leave the house if a bat is fluttering around the door.
					"Fire is God's representative in the home."
13/13	95	36	46	0	The sun is God.
6/12	60	60	94	55	Fire is God (or the Holy Spirit).
					When carrying fire from the house, it should be covered so that the sun doesn't see you are removing it.
					Taking fire out at night when the moon is out (and can see it) results in gray hair. It is best to wait until there is no moon.
					The ashes should be cleaned out only at night.
10/13	67	57	83	42	It is disrespectful to step over the fire.
					Fire should not be loaned, especially at night.
12/13	86	60	95	53	Crackling fire is a warning of an impending quarrel.
7/10	66	73	100	84	Crackling fire means a visitor will call soon.
					A promise can be sealed by spitting in the fire (in any other circumstance, spitting in the fire is sinful).
					A cross made of ashes or of pitch pine (used to start fires) is especially effective against spirits.
					"Hearthstones represent the stability of the home."
4/11	52	0	94	67	If you move the eldest (largest) of the hearthstones, you will constantly be moving your home.
3/12	18	14	88	?	If the stone breaks, some misfortune will befall the household.
7/12	72	0	100	90	Animal hairs placed under the hearthstone will keep a newly acquired animal at home.
5/12	71	0	100	90	A tortilla passed three times over the stones and fed to an animal will keep it at home.

1.	2.	3.	4.	5.	Premises and Supporting Beliefs
12/13	92%	28%	100%	79%	Sitting on the hearthstone is disrespectful, often punished by hemorrhoids.

Premise 11. "The rich get money from the Devil."

The wealthy sometimes get their money through pacts with the Devil; sometimes they sell him their children.

One who kills a buzzard will have poor luck in business.

Possession of a bat's wing brings good luck in business.

Possession of an owl's foot brings good luck when playing *taba* (a game of chance).

Keeping a black cat in a store attracts business.

A snake encountered in a dream or on a path may leave money for you if you place your sombrero over the snake.

"Money is bad."

Your luck will be cut if you exchange money over the fire or place money near the fire (its spirit is repelled by the fire).

Money in one's possession when fishing results in no catch.

Premise 12. Crosses are of the dead and of the church; they are protective, yet dangerous.

Doves' feet make the sign of the cross; they are blessed by God, but having too many around is dangerous.

A cross made with the left hand may be effective against spirits, but it is risky.

Scissors (in the form of a cross) above one's bed keep out thieves and spirits.

| 13/13 | 100 | 84 | 70 | 40 | A cross of any strong substance (pitch pine, *cal*) on a door will keep out spirits. |

"Crossroads are frequented by spirits."

| | 83 | | 95 | 94 | *Characoteles* make their transformations at crosses or at crossroads. (One informant suggested they choose crosses in order to ask forgiveness for their deeds as *characoteles*.) |

A Model of the Structure of the Panajachel World View: II (Cont.)

1.	2.	3.	4.	5.	Premises and Supporting Beliefs
5/13	75%	38%	88%	86%	Playing or resting at crossroads is risky.
					To injure an enemy, bury a black chicken at a crossroads for nine days, then dig it up and throw it in the person's yard.
					Premise 13. The left side of the body is affiliated with evil in man and is not trustworthy.
					"There are two roads in life—the left and the right—and the left is evil."
6/11	62	86	94	93	Left-handed persons are unusually strong and often quarrelsome.
10/12	61	71	100	65	A twitching left arm, leg, or eye is a sign of impending misfortune; on the right side, it is good luck.
11/13	92	86	100	67	A burning left ear lobe means someone is speaking ill of you; a burning right ear lobe means the comments are flattering.
					The left thumb tells the Devil or spirits the thoughts of the body's spirit as told to it by the right thumb when one sleeps with hands together.
					The left toe consorts with spirits if left uncovered at night.
					A cross made with the left hand wards off evil spirits, but it is risky to do.
					Important transactions should be made with the right hand.
					Premise 14. Animals are blessed or accursed, according to their roles in the life of Christ.
					Horses and mules are bad animals.
					Sheep and cattle are good animals.
					If a horse bites off ends of corn tassels, it stunts the corn's growth; but if a person breaks off the end, there is no such effect.
9/11	84	28	100	67	To dream of a horse entering the patio is a sign of impending death.
					Bees and doves will remain only among peaceable families.
					Premise 15. Some foods are holy and carry protective power against evil spirits.
					Salt on a bullet insures hitting a coyote.

1.	2.	3.	4.	5.	Premises and Supporting Beliefs
					A cross made of salt on the hearth (with a broom behind the door) results in a guest's speedy departure.
					Salt rubbed on a *characotel* while it is still in animal form will keep it from returning to human form.
					To cure fright, drink warm water with salt and ashes mixed in.
					A burned tortilla, eaten before going out at night, fortifies one against evil spirits.
					Liquor is holy; tobacco is holy.
8/11	35%	16%	88%	100%	Liquor poured over a snake makes it harmless (also explained in terms of making it drunk).
10/13	90	50	100	93	Tobacco juice or a cigarette on a snake makes it harmless.
					Tobacco juice in one's mouth provides a protective film against the snake's poison when sucking the poison from a bite.
					Water sprinkled around the walls or placed in the doorway keeps spirits out.
					Honey is a holy food, useful in many cures.
					A bees's sting is curative or punitive: if you are ill, the sting serves as an injection of penicillin; but if you have sinned in some way, it is a punishment.

Premise 16. The social relationships characteristic of man are characteristic of all spirits.

Kinship and *compadre* ties link all spirits.

Similar animals are relatives: goat and deer; domestic and wild cats; dog and coyote.

The lakes of Guatemala are siblings of the ocean.

The volcanos are brothers.

The three hearthstones are sisters.

The three colors of corn are sisters.

Death and sleep are sisters.

Grinding stones are husband and wife; if the husband (the *brazo*) breaks, the owner's husband will die.

1.	2.	3.	4.	5.	Premises and Supporting Beliefs
					Pot and jug are husband and wife (care should be taken not to place some containers on top of others; perhaps because a female pot should not be placed over a male jug?).
					Stealing an odd number of ears of corn or giving away an odd number of tortillas is bad, because one won't have a mate.
					Compadre relationships exist between some animals: buzzard and frog.
					"Younger siblings are stronger than older siblings."
					Lake Atitlán is a younger brother of the ocean but is stronger and more violent.
					Sleep is younger than death, but stronger.
					Domestic cats are younger than wild cats but always win in fights between the two.
					Animals and angels have community duties, just as do people.
					Angels have their annual responsibilities; 12 are appointed each year to be rainmakers, and occasionally an elder fills one of these roles while still living.
					The Devil selects a new slate of *alguaciles* (bats), *mayores* (buzzards), and *regidores* (owls) each January 1.
					Animals have their duties: frogs grind corn for the Devil; buzzards eat all decaying flesh.
11/13	45%	7%	50%	25%	It is sinful to bury dogs or animals that die; they belong to the buzzards.
					Premise 17. Siblings are rivals for affection and food.
					"An older sibling sometimes 'eats' his brother."
					If babies continually die, it is a sign that an older sibling is "eating them"; to satisfy his hunger, make him eat an entire chicken.
					The next oldest sibling carries the newborn infant into the *temazcal* (sweat bath) for the latter's first bath. Afterwards he shares a ritual meal with the midwife.

1.	2.	3.	4.	5.	Premises and Supporting Beliefs
					Premise 18. *A woman (or her belongings) over a man (or his belongings) weakens the latter physically or mentally.*
13/13	88%	50%	60%	33%	A woman's stepping over a man will make him useless.
12/13	94	57	75	30	Sweeping over a man's feet is sinful.
11/13	92	83	67	43	If a woman climbs fruit trees to harvest the fruit, it affects the fruit or the tree adversely.
12/13	88	35	85	52	A woman's stepping over a man's tools weakens them, and they soon break.
11/13	84	28	82	33	Women should avoid stepping over food intended for a man; if this happens, the woman should eat it all herself.
					A woman's stepping over root crops cracks them.
12/13	82	35	67	44	Woman's clothing over man's clothing in a laundry basket is as bad as a woman stepping over a man.
					A woman's urinating under a fruit tree hurts the fruit as surely as her climbing the tree.
					It is worse for a woman to step over the fire (saint of the fire is masculine) than for a man.
					Women's mats or baskets should never be placed over the heads of boys.
					A woman's power can be used beneficially to weaken or calm males.
	15		100	?	A woman's skirt (but it must be a new one) placed over a man's face will cure his snoring.
2/12	73	0	100	89	A woman's broom brushed over an excited or angry dog calms him.
		0			A woman's clothing or urine over a bull's head calms him.
5/10	60	31	100	89	A woman's urine over a snake immobilizes it.
					Premise 19. *Spirits and evil forces have dominion over the living, unless one is stouthearted.*
					Spirits encountered in human form can give one a bad fright unless you stand up to them bravely; if you succeed, they often leave you money.
					A flashlight won't work when you encounter a spirit unless you quickly make a cross over it.
	45		73	66	When bitten by a snake, grab the snake, bite it, and it will die instead of you.

1.	2.	3.	4.	5.	Premises and Supporting Beliefs
	62%		70%	57%	If you whistle on sighting a shooting star (spirit of a *zahorin*), you won't be frightened or harmed.
					If you whistle on feeling an earth tremor, your children will not be harmed (the spirit of the tremor will not try to steal spirits of members of the household).
					"The dead can summon the living."
10/13	74	86%	95	93	Pregnant women should remain indoors during eclipses; the moon, near death, wants to take her children with her.
					A father can summon his son, who serves as his father's walking stick in heaven.
					The owner of a pet dog can summon it to accompany him to heaven.
					Premise 20. Colors vary in strength and power.
					White is a cold, weak color.
					In cures where a chicken is specified (lowering fever or curing heart attacks), black chickens are preferred.
					Red is a strong color. Crosses tied with red string are especially powerful. (Is red strong by analogy with the fire?)
					Premise 21. Some numbers are especially powerful.
					To harm an enemy, bury a black chicken at a crossroads for nine days; then throw it in his yard.
					A *characotel* makes three somersaults to change out of or back into human form.
					Three strands of garlic are as effective as a cross in keeping spirits away.
					Premise 22. Religious or ceremonial observances are incompatible with sexual functions.
					Sacristanes, when charged with care of the church, should abstain from sexual relations.
					Dancers at fiestas should abstain during the several days' involvement in dancing.
					The night before attending mass should be free from sexual involvement.
					Menstruating women should not enter the church.

1.	2.	3.	4.	5.	Premises and Supporting Beliefs
					Premise 23. Quarreling or disharmony in the household adversely affects the welfare of the family.
11/13	88%	64%	100%	100%	Bees and doves won't stay around a house where there is constant bickering.
					Crop yields are reduced by quarreling at home.
					If a woman beats her daughter, the daughter's children may die.
					A man's business will not prosper if he uses the proceeds from his crops on other women.
					Children can die from quarreling between parents.
					Premise 24. To imitate the dead can result in death.
10/11	90	21	88	37	If one sleeps with his head to the west, he will dream of the dead or never awaken (the dead are buried with their heads to the west).
					It is risky to measure someone, since corpses are measured in determining the size of the coffin.
					Tying a rope around someone's waist in play is dangerous; the dead have such a *cordon* tied around them.
					It is best not to sleep on one's back or you will have bad dreams (the dead lie face up).
					Premise 25. Vulnerability to misfortune or molestation by spirits is greater at some times than at others.
					"Spirits are out on strong days and at strong hours."
9/13	96	71	96	74	The strong hours are noon and midnight.
12/13	98	78	95	60	The strong days are Monday, Wednesday, and Friday.
6/13	45	45	100	67	One is most likely to dream on the nights of strong days (one's spirit is most inclined to leave at such times).
					Night is the daytime of the dead.
					Zahorines usually prefer to do *costumbres* at noon or midnight on strong days.
					Spiritualists prefer strong nights for conducting séances.
					The *ronda* (making the rounds, a security check) of spirits still takes place at noon, just as formerly the *alguaciles* (constables) made their rounds at noon.

1.	2.	3.	4.	5.	Premises and Supporting Beliefs
					"When the time changes is a dangerous time to be abroad."
					January 1 is the day the Devil rounds up his slate of servants; anyone out in the *monte* (hills) may be seized and forced to serve.
					The most dangerous time to dream is Sunday night.
					At midnight all stops still; a boat on the lake won't continue on its course until you drop something in the water.
					"The night is the daytime of the dead."
9/13	82%	35%	75%	58%	Women shouldn't comb their hair after dusk as this is when the dead awaken and comb theirs.
5/11	81		95	80	Women shouldn't sweep the house after dusk.
					Care should be taken not to expose oneself to spirits when they are abroad.
9/13	87	57	96	75	Toys and clothing shouldn't be left out at night.
					Fire shouldn't be taken from the house at night.
					One shouldn't initiate a business undertaking on a strong day.
					Blankets or trash baskets shouldn't be shaken out or emptied at noon.
					Hair shouldn't be washed at noon.
					One shouldn't bathe in the sweat bath at noon or on strong days.
					Hair shouldn't be cut at night.
					Women shouldn't comb their hair at noon.
					The house shouldn't be swept after dusk.
7/13	87	73	89	87	The house shouldn't be swept at noon.
9/13	58	35	93	36	Fire should never be loaned at noon.
					Premise 26. Tools or weapons that have tasted blood are more prone to continue inflicting injury.
	40		100	50	If a *machete* is used to kill a snake, the *machete* should be abandoned.
	90		100	100	It is best to use the back side of the *machete* or a stick to kill a snake.

1.	2.	3.	4.	5.	Premises and Supporting Beliefs
					A gun that has killed someone should not be kept around.

Premise 27. Giving part of something you own away, or loaning it, risks losing its spirit. (Note: This premise conflicts with a prevalent assumption [especially among Protestants] that generosity always calls for sharing and loaning anything you have.)

"Loaning cuts your luck."

It is risky to loan or give away salt, pepper, corn, or any food.

If cures you know are shared with others, they may not work for you any longer.

1.	2.	3.	4.	5.	Premises and Supporting Beliefs
6/13	52%	31%	82%	0%	One should never sell or give away the first part of the crop to be harvested.
9/13	58	35	93	36	Fire shouldn't be loaned at noon.
					Money shouldn't be exchanged at noon.

Premise 28. Preoccupation or undue concern often backfires and increases the cause for concern.

"If someone believes strongly enough that something will happen, it will."

If one counts warts, they multiply.

If one tries to combat mice in the fields by traps or poisoning, they multiply; if one forgets about them, they stay under control.

If one worries about encountering spirits, one is more apt to do so.

1.	2.	3.	4.	5.	Premises and Supporting Beliefs
8/11	75	38	85	30	To measure a child in hopes of detecting growth can stunt his growth.
9/12	83	70	100	45	Eating the first tortilla that is made may result in never getting full (overanxiousness).

Eating a second tortilla before finishing your first one results in never getting full.

Measuring a *machete,* or anything, by comparing it with another will weaken it.

"Dreaming of something often means just the opposite is going to happen."

If one worries or thinks about a dream, it is more apt to come true.

1.	2.	3.	4.	5.	Premises and Supporting Beliefs
11/13	77%	57%	100%	55%	To dream of eating well means one will become poor or ill.
11/12	50	60	100	57	To dream of dancing, or enjoying a *fiesta,* means someone in the family will die.

Premise 29. The order or time of occurrences foretells something about the future.

Dreaming soon after retiring foretells what will happen in the distant future; dreaming just before awakening foretells events soon to take place.

An eclipse early in the night means the death of an older child; late at night, it means the death of a younger child.

A child conceived during the day will resemble the father; one conceived during the night will resemble the mother.

"How something begins determines how it ends."

The weather of the first twelve days of the year anticipates the kinds of weather to follow in the twelve months.

Giving credit early in the morning (by a storekeeper) results in being asked for credit all day long.

Changing large bills in the morning will mean one will be giving money away all day long.

Premise 30. The unusual or unexpected foretells future events.

An itching palm means a debtor will repay soon.

Sparks dancing beneath a kettle mean a debtor will repay soon.

A glass or utensil breaking means misfortune.

A cracked mirror is a sign of a quarrel.

| | 12 | | ? | ? | A broken pot signifies misfortune. |

A sneeze means someone is thinking of you.

A fly landing on your face means someone is thinking of you.

Premise 31. Repetition of an occurrence can correct what was done the first time.

| 3/9 | 75 | 25 | 94 | 56 | To cure a burn, place the burned finger in or near the fire again. |

1.	2.	3.	4.	5.	Premises and Supporting Beliefs
3/5	46%		100%	100%	To cure one with chills, surprise him with a dunking of cold water.
2/4	30		100	85	To cure one who has received a fright, give him another scare.
					If bitten by a snake, prick yourself again with the fangs of a dead snake to cure.
					If you accidentally step between two persons, you will "cut their luck" unless you reverse your direction and pass back through them again.
					*Premise 32. Destiny and luck (*suerte, fate) *determine one's life.*
					Catarinecos fish because only they are given the luck of catching fish; they are destined to be fishermen.
	92		85	60	One is a *characotel,* midwife, or *zahorin* by destiny, with no choice but to assume this role. (Specifically asked about the role of *zahorin*.)
					Spiritualists and teachers are destined to this work.
					A flame above the ground designates buried money; only the person who sees the flame can recover the money, and if he tells anyone about it, none will be found.
					A snake encountered on a path (or in a dream) that lets you place over it your sombrero has money for you which he will leave under the sombrero.
					"Everyone has his appointed time to die."
10/12	93	84%	95	58	A noticeable surplus of earth after burial means the deceased went before his time had come (killed by sorcery).
	92	54	100	59	Persons who die unnatural deaths (murdered, drowned, etc.) haunt the place of death until their rightful hour to die arrives.
					For burials in cement vaults, the sign of a premature death is the caving in of the newly formed cement.
					Premise 33. To live to old age is possible only with strong blood or the help of evil forces.
					Characoteles live long lives through an ability to capture souls of victims and gain additional years.

1.	2.	3.	4.	5.	Premises and Supporting Beliefs
					Brujos can kill another by the same name when summoned to judgment and hence live beyond their appointed hour.
					Midwives live long lives, but they are always poor regardless of how long and hard they work (and hence freed from suspicion of collusion with the Devil or of ''buying time''?).
					The good die young.
					Eating animals of the hill (opossums, skunks, etc.) makes one strong and able to withstand sorcery; but it makes one smell offensive so that he can't enter heaven.
					The dead burn in hell the number of years they have lived.
					The rich live long lives because they can hire *zahorines* to ward off sorcery. They usually get their money from the Devil.
					Premise 34. There is justice in the universe which assures that each receives his just due eventually.
					''God knows what we do, and he will punish and reward.''
	40%		100%	67%	Everyone burns in hell for some length of time in accordance with his record as kept by God.
6/12	68	0%	96	45	The innocent dead before their time are given a second chance.
					Brujos become hearthstones at death and burn forever.
					Those living a second life live in reversed circumstances from their first life; if poor, then rich, etc.
					There will be a final judgment when present roles are reversed; roosters will lay eggs, hens will crow; flowering trees will no longer flower, flowerless trees will, etc.
					Prolonged illness before dying is a punishment for one's sins.
					Those who complain of the rain will be punished by a downpour at their funeral.
6/11	70	20	100	62	Those killed through sorcery await the death of the *brujo* responsible to insure that justice is meted out at the heavenly tribunal.

1.	2.	3.	4.	5.	Premises and Supporting Beliefs
					Premise 35. The moral fiber of mankind is deteriorating.
					Crops used to produce better when people were more reverent and faithful in supporting *cofradías* and serving saints.
					People used to live longer when their diet was more akin to that of Christ's.
					People shouldn't wear shoes, eat at tables, or cut hair short (women), because Christ didn't do these things.
	97%		100%	65%	Excrement (falling stars) of God used to be coins which Indians picked up each morning in their fields; with man's falling away from righteousness, only mounds of worms are found.

◦ 8 ◦

Bases of Identity

I N 1941, Tax surmised that an Indian was first of all a Panajacheleño, second an Indian, and only third (if at all) a Guatemalan in self-identity. It is apparent that the more highly educated Protestants and Catequistas are less narrowly Panajacheleños in identity than were their forefathers who, in occupation, dress, and care of local saints, were Panajacheleños in a way that they could never be Catarinecos, Sololatecos, or Pedranos. For them, identity is now more national and more ethnic (Indian versus Ladino) than it is local. This probably is an inevitable consequence of economic ladinoization with what this implies in reliance upon service occupations, investing savings in business rather than in *cofradía* service, and in mobility. This sector of the population is no longer as distinctively Panajacheleño in world view. Rather, their world view corresponds closely to that typical of local Ladinos. These Panajacheleños have adopted a stance toward new knowledge that makes relatively easy the replacement or assimilation of beliefs, and were the divergence in Indian-Ladino belief patterns greater at the outset, the gulf between the emerging syncretic patterns and the world view of their grandparents would be more of a barrier to identifying with this past. As it is, only in a few cases has world view so radically altered as to make continued identification with an Indian past untenable. Where this has occurred, the impetus has been schooling under the direction of sophisticated Ladinos whose world view differs from that of rural Ladinos more than the beliefs of the latter differ from those of Indians.

The term "ladinoization" doubles in Guatemalan ethnographic literature for both acculturative accommodations and the occasional shift in ethnic identity. The danger of such usage is the tendency to assume that the discarding of visible indicators of Indian identity by individuals or communities reflects a change in status wherein Indian identity is less strong. The acculturative stance toward Ladino society I have labeled economic ladinoization, defining this as (1) the broadening of culturally acceptable occupations to include any characteristically Ladino occupations and (2) the ascendancy of acquisitive and entrepreneurial values at the expense of communal conspicuous consumption. It will be apparent from the early chapters of this book that many Panajacheleños have ladinoized economically to a remarkable degree.

The instances of ladinoization among Panajacheleños in the sense of shifting identity are very few, however, and among my forty-six informants only three evidenced ethnic ladinoization. Two of these three, María Chopén and Lorenzo Lopez (not their real names), have Panajachel Indian ancestry back at least two generations and are fully acculturated by any visible criteria I can muster. The third is of foreign Indian parentage, only sixteen years of age, and less well known by me than the other two. María and Lorenzo represented the extremes in belief awareness and acceptance, she knowing a smaller proportion of the belief sample than any other Indian informant, and he rejecting a larger proportion than any of the others. They illustrate the extent to which a traditional world view can narrow through selective transmission over two generations, on the one hand, and through skeptical analysis, on the other.

María Chopén has a Ladina wardrobe (including shoes and stockings) and with her brother manages one of two stores owned by her father, a Panajacheleño of several generations' descent. She is unique among Panajacheleños in having enjoyed eleven years of formal schooling. She was twenty-one years old when interviewed and had recently returned from five years of schooling in Catholic prevocational and vocational schools in Quezaltenango and Antigua. I taught her English over many weeks and thus established the rapport requisite for interviewing. Although she is Catholic, her schooling has placed her below the average of Protestants in awareness and acceptance of traditional beliefs. Protestants average 60 percent awareness and 65 percent acceptance of beliefs known; María knows 53 percent and accepts 47 percent of those beliefs. The Panajachel Ladinos interviewed averaged 47 percent awareness, and María falls within the range of Ladinos' awareness in all categories except *secretos*. If we assume from table 15 that Panajacheleños have learned about as much of the traditional world view by age fifteen as they will ever learn, we can assume that María's low awareness did not result from her being away at school from ages fifteen to twenty. While I did not interview others in María's immediate family, I did interview her paternal uncle (our *compadre)* of almost the same age as her father and a first cousin (male) of nineteen. Her uncle is aware of 83 percent of the beliefs (compared with her 53 percent), and his son knows 80 percent. It seems a fair assumption that her father knows as many of these concepts as her uncle, and the difference between her own awareness and that of her cousin can reasonably be attributed to differential interest on the part of their parents in transmitting traditional beliefs to their children. She evidenced genuine interest in learning as many of the "old beliefs" as I could provide her, and numerous times she checked with her parents about ideas she had never heard. Some of these are ideas basic to the traditional world view, as for example the identification of the sun as God. This she had never heard! I go into this much detail to demonstrate, with an extreme example, the extent to which awareness, quite apart from acceptance, of ideas can change in a situation where at least some members of Panajachel society are consciously dissociating themselves from an "Indian world view" to the extent that it is recognized as distinctively Indian and not shared by the Ladinos around them. María's father is perhaps more aware of this distinctiveness of world view than any other Indian, having many years ago moved into the Ladino business district to establish a store. He is now one of the wealthiest family heads and with his resources has undertaken to provide his daughter with as hearty a boost into Ladino circles as he can provide.

Lorenzo Lopez rejects traditional beliefs more consistently than any other informant, questioning or rejecting 72 percent of all beliefs known by him in the sample of 181. Moreover, he rejects many of the beliefs which the Ladino data suggest are group-typical of the Ladino world view as well. Of the 120 beliefs for which adequate data from Ladinos are available, Ladinos largely reject or do not know 40 percent and largely accept 40 percent. The balance appear to be peripheral to the Ladino world view. Lorenzo rejects 91 percent of those not shared by Ladinos, 88 percent of those which are peripheral, and 75 percent of those widely shared by Ladinos.

Schooling appears to be responsible for this skeptical stance. Lorenzo had to drop out of school to work after completing third grade but continued studying on his own and returned to complete sixth grade at the age of nineteen. He then enrolled in prevocational school in Solola. When discussing education he could not stress its importance enough and repeatedly referred to items of knowledge acquired in school to explain his grounds of belief or disbelief. He has systematically tested those beliefs whose supportive assumptions he has come to question, and because of his skeptical stance toward traditional knowledge he provided more assistance in elucidating structural premises than any other informant. He is also a very ardent Protestant, as are his parents, and he studied for one year at the pastoral training school of the Assembly of God mission in Panajachel. He was this congregation's delegate to a national assembly in Guatemala City. Traditional beliefs which his schooling does not bring into question, his Protestant teachings do, resulting in a world view which is more "western" than it is characteristically Ladino.

Given this description of belief patterns, it is noteworthy that Lorenzo chooses to ignore his mother's surname, which is obviously Indian, and uses exclusively his father's name, which is common to Ladinos as well as Indians. This was brought to my attention by our Ladina employee, who had gone through school with Lorenzo and had been impressed by his reluctance to use his two surnames, which is the common practice among Indians. Obviously his Indian ancestry cannot be disguised in Panajachel, but it is not likely that he will long remain there. He spent one year in

Guatemala City studying welding and garage mechanics, and his ambition is to own his own service station. He is looking for a wife, but he volunteered that she will have to be "educated." The girls who qualify in Panajachel are few. Not surprisingly, the one girl in whom he had shown interest was the third informant mentioned earlier as also evidencing signs of ethnic ladinoization. She had completed five years of school. She had indicated in the course of interviewing that she would be willing to marry a Ladino, and indeed her mother rebuffed Lorenzo, commenting that her daughter would never marry an Indian! This makes it clear that regardless of his own self-identity, fellow Panajacheleños regard Lorenzo as very much Indian.

Lorenzo's case illustrates yet another observation about social relations in Panajachel. His older brother, Alberto, has had six years of school and four years of military training, and has traveled and worked in the country as widely as Lorenzo. He has married a local Indian girl and lives in very humble, Indian style. He works in a hotel but prefers to go barefoot when around home, in contrast to Lorenzo, who is never without shoes and stockings. Both are fully ladinoized economically, but Alberto appears to remain fully Indian in his self-identity. Moreover, Alberto questions only 30 percent of the beliefs he knows from my sample, less than half those questioned by Lorenzo. Alberto is no longer Protestant, which may account in part for their differences in belief profiles. That brothers only six years apart in age can differ so markedly is indicative of the degree of individualism and impersonality of social relations which characterize even the family.

Possibly there are a few other highly acculturated Panajacheleños seeking Ladino status, but their visibility in the community is too low to have made this an issue in the minds of Indians or Ladinos. Such transitionals have no designation locally, as they do in Chiapas, Mexico.[1] When I asked other Ladinos or Indians about the ethnic status of persons appearing to be ladinoized, the only descriptive terminologies offered were: he appears Ladino; he dresses as a Ladino; he is a little Indian, a little Ladino.

While my data suggest that an awareness of marked differences in world view accompanies shifting ethnic identity in Panajachel, the data also suggest that such awareness is not a sufficient cause for such a shift. Several informants question almost as high a percentage of beliefs as does María Chopén yet seem comfortably integrated into Indian society. I suspect that some correlation does exist between belief rejection and dissatisfaction with Indian status, but other factors are involved. One of the more important of these is acceptance by the Indian society of those acculturated individuals who do not feel comfortable exhibiting visible indicators of Indian ancestry or conforming to the traditional stereotype of the community-minded citizen. I was not surprised to find such acculturated individuals, but I was surprised to find that the community had experienced such pervasive acculturation without more factionalism and evidence of psychological and social disorganization.

Religion and community service have been the most divisive issues, although they appear to have polarized this community less than other towns of the region, such as San Pedro la Laguna (Rojas Lima 1968:126-52) and Chichicastenango. True, intermarriage between Protestants and Catholics can generate strong feelings. In one instance during our stay in Panajachel, a Protestant refused to attend his son's wedding to a Catholic. The marriage took place in the Catholic church, and the father had not set foot in the church since converting to Protestantism and renouncing his calling of *zahorin.* In fact, most Protestants are reluctant to enter the church; funeral processions of Catholics pass by the church where the coffin is carried before the saints, and while Protestants may serve as coffin bearers, they remain outside during this ritual. Yet the proselytizing of Protestants in the market and in the cemetery on All Souls' Day does not generate any visible signs of enmity, and I recall an occasion when Catequistas were asked by their leader to pray for a Protestant woman who died leaving no relatives to petition on her behalf.

The comparative lack of factionalism may be attributed in part to the visibility of economic motives in shifting religious affiliation. Another factor may be the lack of reinforcing distinctions particularly between the Catequistas and Protestants. In curing practices, for example, while Protestants rarely make use of *zahorines,* many Catequistas likewise rely wholly upon the clinic. Knowledge of this among nominal Catholics reduces the distinctiveness of Protestants in this regard. The rapidity of the shift away from use of *zahorines* and the associated weakening of belief in their power can be attributed in part, I feel, to the renunciation of this calling by the Protestant convert mentioned above and another *zahorin* who joined Catholic Action. To the coincidence that they did not join the same group, I attribute in part the lack of factionalism along religious lines in utilization of the health center and rejection of *zahorines.* I should add that the former *zahorin,* after becoming a Catequista, only gradually came to feel that the two were irreconcilable.

With regard to community service, Protestants continue to participate in civil offices. Although the highest office of Indian *alcalde* has been restricted to those also serving in *cofradías,* one Protestant had received the second highest office of third *regidor.* Moreover, new forms of social organization are emerging to replace or supplement the decision-making functions of the elders and local government. In Jucanyá, where *cofradía* support is strongest and visible indicators of Indian status abound, Catholics, Protestants, elders, and Ladinos succeeded in organizing and working together to introduce piped water several years prior to 1964 and to build a new school in 1965.

That the changes in the lives of Panajacheleños have not been psychologically disorganizing in many instances is suggested by comparisons of drinking patterns. Cash and liquor are more readily available than formerly, yet comparisons of adult drinking habits in 1964 and 1936 indicate that virtually identical proportions of the drinking population (that is, Catholics) drink heavily, moderately, or only in ceremonial contexts. There are a dozen men who can be described as alcoholics, drinking to excess whenever they can obtain sufficient cash or credit. Given the doubled population, however, this number is no greater proportionately than the half-dozen heavy drinkers in 1936. Several of these men in 1964 were ex-Protestants or peripheral members of Protestant sects and did evidence considerable frustration and disorganization in trying to cope with the conflicting demands placed upon them.

Comparisons of arrests over the years since 1940 for quarreling or disturbing the peace while intoxicated support the conclusion of no perceptible increase in liquor consumption. In fact, in all categories of offenses for which municipal records are kept, there has been no noticeable per capita increase since the 1930s, with the exception of fights threatening physical injury. The incidence of such quarrels has more than doubled since 1960, after showing no marked change over the previous three decades. No increase in marital infidelity has occurred since 1936, if one can accept the incidence of illegitimate births as a reliable indicator. Marriages are contracted in the same manner as formerly, although youths exercise more say in choice of spouse as a result of greater financial independence. Elopement (*robado*) has initiated 20 percent of all unions since 1955, but there is no evidence that recourse to this is increasing. In summary, there are remarkably few indications of psychological or community disorganization that can be attributed to transitional ethnic status or factionalism over religion and community service. Given the conservatism in world view among the majority of Panajacheleños, this evidence of cultural stability in social organization is not surprising.

The claim of conservatism in world view requires some clarification. Cosmological beliefs, of which I have said very little, have altered pervasively as a result of schooling. With very few exceptions among my informants, Panajacheleños no longer conceive of the earth as flat, or of the volcanos as supporting a sky of glass. It is generally known that the earth circles the sun, that stars are other suns, that eclipses are a result of the interruption of the sun's rays. I could go on, but this will suffice to make my point that these ideas can change with great rapidity without influencing the assumptions structuring man's orientation within his behavioral environment. These latter assumptions are those which I have undertaken to elucidate in chapter seven, and these are the assumptions that show considerable cohesion after three decades of acculturative accommodation to Ladino society. I anticipate that a comparable study of belief patterns twenty years hence will show relatively little further erosion of traditional beliefs among Protestants, and little if any measurable difference in belief patterns among Indians. This prediction is based on the assumptions that Protestant beliefs already correspond closely to those of the Ladinos with whom they associate, and diffusion of this more ladinoized world view will in time diffuse generally among traditionals.

One is left with the impression that the measurable changes in belief patterns, as in social organization, have been but incidental by-products of adjustments to Ladino society motivated by economic interests. Some changes have been precipitated by these adjustments which in time have altered the distribution of authority, allocation of status, and bases of community membership. In a few cases these changes have led to a shift in ethnic identity. Life in Panajachel has altered in some significant respects, but the changes have been voluntary and motivated by values basic to the culture. I have tried to provide the historical and cultural perspective which permits viewing these changes as consonant with Panajacheleños' cultural penchant for making accommodations while remaining indifferent to cultural variations.

◦ 9 ◦
Depth and Breadth of Perspective

T H E foregoing analysis of changes and continuities in Panajachel since 1941 has focused upon the impact of an expanding economic base. The expanded income base is interpreted as the independent variable influencing several cultural changes (values influencing allocation of resources, social networks, belief patterns, and bases of security and identity) which I assume would not have occurred as rapidly, if at all, without the choices made possible by the expanding economy. Measuring the interaction of these variables was facilitated by the fact that Tax initiated his study of the Panajachel economy and society prior to the advent of new employment opportunities.

And yet the ease of demonstrating some casual relationships between economic and other societal changes since 1941 should not be permitted to obscure the possibility that changes in social relations and world view were being independently affected by other, less local trends, or even the possibility that the exploitation of new sources of income was facilitated and accelerated by changes in social relations and world view produced by other developments predating Tax's arrival on the scene.

As acknowledged in the introduction, there can be no doubt that events prior to 1941 have influenced the changes in belief patterns, bases of identity, security, and interaction with Ladinos. In this respect the period from 1934-44 is important, not only because Tax's base-line descriptions of Panajachel were made during that decade, but because that period marked a transition in national policies toward Indians. The period from 1880-1934 was marked by exploitative legislation which impoverished Indians considerably by reducing their land base and forcing seasonal labor on lowland plantations. The entry of Guatemala into the international coffee and fruit markets in the late nineteenth century prompted legislation forcing Indian communities to divide communally held lands among families (from whom Ladinos could then negotiate its purchase). Land suitable for coffee rapidly passed into Ladino hands, and the *mandamientos* legislation guaranteed Ladino plantation owners the labor needed seasonally to harvest coffee and fruit. The repeal of the *mandamientos* prompted laws of debt peonage and vagrancy which, while more selective and seemingly less exploitative, insured the continued flow of Indians from highlands to lowlands from November to January, when labor demands were highest for the major cash crops.

All such legislation was repealed by 1944. After President Ubico's overthrow in 1944, reform-minded governments expanded medical and educational services, and both Catholic and Protestant clergy appeared in Indian communities in larger numbers. How this change in policies of church and state affected Indian attitudes toward Ladinos, Ladino institutions, and reliance upon traditional bases of identity and security is difficult to assess in the absence of documentation of any of these communities prior to 1935. Tax of course gathered many impressions of the effect of forced labor upon Indians, but the subsequent economic developments in Panajachel complicate an assessment of what those changes in policies of church and state alone would have meant. The effect of these latter changes upon Indian communities in Guatemala, including Panajachel, is best appraised by comparing post-1941 developments in a variety of communities. If the changes I have documented for Panajachel have occurred throughout the region irrespective of variations in community wealth and economic histories since 1940, then it will be apparent that the psychological impact of more pervasive historical developments must be assessed before too readily attributing changing values in Panajachel to expanded employment opportunities.

Regional comparisons will both test the interpretation of causal relationships I have presented for Panajachel's recent history and give the reader a more adequate basis for assessing the regional impact of social and demographic pressures whose negative consequences have been ameliorated in Panajachel by atypical expansion of resources. It will become evident that the pressure of population growth on community resources varied markedly among the lake towns as of 1965, and that where the pressure had precipitated behavioral adjustments the responses varied just as markedly. In some cases, the consensual reaction has been defensive adherence to traditional responses to a threatening, capricious environment; in others, the response has been even more united experimentation with new social networks and bases of security than Panajachel has experienced. More typically, however, the community response is divided, with more factionalism, tension, and individual disorientation than experienced in Panajachel.

Responses to pressure of people on resources, where such pressure is sufficient to prompt adjustive behavior, include both manipulation of the resource base and adjustments in the population. Where the resource base can be sufficiently increased to keep pace with population growth, or where emigration is readily accepted or encouraged, then of course there need be no pressure to change the patterning of behavior. In reality, however, few communities' resources are adequate to accommodate population growth without behavioral adjustments, and few communities are content to resolve the problem simply by encouraging the excess population to leave before prior adjustive experimentation has been undertaken. Between the parameters of expanding the occupational base and leaving the community, what adjustments have Indians tried? Are there measurable community differences in such experimentation?

The adjustments essentially are those experimented with in Panajachel, beginning with belt-tightening in consumption and more intensive farming of available land. It is safe to generalize that these adjustments have been made in all Indian communities throughout Guatemala. There are limits to such adjustments, however, so that in most instances more drastic experimentation has been undertaken. Such adjustments for which comparative data from other lake towns are available include: reductions in expenditures for ceremonial purposes and for drinking (as reflected in experimentation with alternative religious affiliation); military service; increased reliance on education for more lucrative employment; resorting to coastal migratory labor; and controlling frequency and number of births. Of these, resorting to periodic coastal employment has been largely eliminated in Panajachel, in sharp contrast to many other lake communites. Data for all the lake towns are available on all the above variables, with the exception of efforts to control frequency and number of births. Reliable comparative data on these efforts are available in three communities.

Clarification is in order of the kinds and sources of data used in the comparisons of this chapter. Tax surveyed all the towns bordering Lake Atitlán in 1935 before deciding to focus his research on Panajachel (1946). His data are largely impressionistic, dealing primarily with standards of living, income bases, and strength of traditional institutions. It is fortuitous that the data were collected just after the period of exploitative legislation. With Juan de Dios Rosales and Flavio Rojas Lima, Tax and I returned to the lake in December 1965 to repeat the survey Tax had undertaken thirty years previously. We spent a day or two in each community, filling in data charts prepared in advance. These data have been published in Spanish together with much more extensive data on the four largest lake towns gathered by Benjamin and Lois Paul in San Pedro, by Clyde Woods in San Lucas, by William Douglas in Santiago Atitlán, and by Ardith and me in Panajachel (Rojas Lima, 1968). In 1968-69 I returned to Guatemala, accompanied by Patrick Pyeatt, to collect the data used for comparing population trends since 1925 in Panajachel, Santa María Visitación, and Santa Catarina (Hinshaw et al 1972).[1] These towns, together with the others referred to on the following pages, are identified in map 1.

Regional Resources

Table 22 summarizes the data on the variables referred to above, except for spacing of children. A sample of eight of the thirteen towns is used, sufficient to cover the full range of community differences on all axes of comparison. The wealth ranking of the communities is based on the opinions of Indians questioned in each community, and supplementary data on community standards of living and resources certainly bear out the Indians' impressions that Panajachel and San Pedro Indians are the most affluent and Santa Cruz, Santa Catarina, and San Marcos Indians are the poorest. Crude death rates (see table 23) correlate roughly with Indians' perceptions of comparative wealth: the poorest communities have uniformly high mortality rates. Probably the most reliable indicator of wealth is the degree of community dependency on coastal labor, and it is noteworthy that Indian perceptions of comparative wealth correlate well with percentages of households estimated to have sent someone to the coast in 1965. I regret that our data on migratory labor are limited to the impressions of Indians, for I have come to believe that individual and community experience with such labor is a critical factor influencing attitudes toward experimentation with other strategies of adjustment to population pressure on available resources.

Since Panajacheleños had so completely emancipated themselves from coastal employment by 1963, I did not discuss the implications of migratory labor in earlier chapters as fully as they deserve. I shall do so before proceeding further. I begin with knowledge of how residents of the two communities most intimately known by me (Panajachel and Santa María Visitación) feel about coastal work. In both communities only a few families continue to rely on such employment, and the pride taken in the fact that such work no longer is necessary is considerable. Similarly, in two centers of credit cooperatives to the north of the lake (Novillero and San Andrés), participants discussing the advantages of membership are quick to point out that few members have to continue migrating to the coast. At first glance it would appear that coastal labor during the lean months in the highlands (November-January) is freely entered into by Indians, providing a symbiotic relationship between coastal and highland economies. In fact, however, a large proportion of the Indians migrating during these months are forced to do so by virtue of debts contracted with representatives of coastal plantations. Such representatives, scattered throughout the highlands, make cash loans readily available throughout the year. The only stipulation is that the debt must be met through labor on the coast. It is for this reason that members of cooperatives manage to reduce their reliance upon such employment: the availability of alternative sources of loan funds, or of credit, precludes the necessity of resorting to plantation representatives. To these impressions can be added the dislike of coastal work, stemming from climate, poor housing and working conditions, disease, the necessity of being away from one's family, and meager savings. Conditions and earnings have been described by various authors (Hurtado 1970; Schmid 1967).

Because of the undesirability of the work and the coercion resulting

TABLE 22
Strength of Traditional and New Institutions, 1965

	Poorest			Middle			Wealthiest	
	Santa Cruz	Santa Catarina	San Marcos	San Antonio	San Pablo	Santa María Visitación	Pana-jachel	San Pedro
Households migrating annually	85%	50%+	50%+	15%	25%	10%	2%	0-5%
Military service	None	None	2	15	30	None	50	25+
Schooling 6 years	None	None	None	None	None	15	25	25+
Prevocational	None	None	None	None	None	6	6	10+
Cofradía service required	Yes	Yes	Yes	Yes	No	No cofradías	No	No
Catholic Action	Weak	Weak	Strong	Mod. Strong	Mod. Strong	Strong	Strong	Strong
Protestant households	None	None	None	5-10%	30-40%	None	15-20%	30-40%
Reliance on shamans	Strong	Strong	Mod. Strong	Mod. Strong	Moderate	Absent	Weak	Weak

from poverty and lack of credit or loan possibilities in most communities, continued dependency upon such employment fosters many of the same attitudes of hopelessness, fatalism, and distrust characteristic of the pre-1934 era. Indians who continue to migrate annually have little, if any, more autonomy in shaping their destinies than they had a half century ago. When forces beyond their control impinge upon the community in this way, the reaction now, as previously, is to view the community as the only source of security. With this goes the traditional reliance upon local saints for protection, in return for which Indians pay homage through *cofradía* service and related ritual expenditures. Status derives from such community service, and alternative religious affiliations threaten the security of all.

I suggest that the pattern of community identity so characteristic of and deeply rooted in the region was intensified during the exploitative era of 1880-1934 and is weakening insofar as Indians perceive community boundaries and membership as less important in the total context of resources available to them for establishing some degree of security. In those few communities able to support growing populations without a continuing reliance on coastal migration, horizons have broadened and confidence in outsiders has deepened. Panajachel and San Pedro are good examples, the former community gradually reducing its reliance on coastal work through expanded occupational opportunities at home, and the latter community avoiding migration once legislation was repealed through atypically large landholdings suitable for coffee growing. To my knowledge, Santa María Visitación is the only really poor community in the region as of 1940 to achieve subsequently an economic base adequate for the expanding population without using coastal employment. That Visitecos (natives of Santa María Visitación) achieved this through community planning and initiative without an influx of Ladinos is noteworthy, and I review this history below. Indians elsewhere around the lake have lessened their dependency upon such coastal employment only minimally, if at all.

A variety of factors influence how readily communities move away from the traditional pattern of migrating annually to the coast. Where the households have alternative employment during the dry season in their home communities, they are less likely to migrate. Hence, Panajacheleños, even in the absence of new employment opportunities, might well have managed without extensive migratory labor because of the river irrigation system which permits year-round farming in the delta region. Pablanos (San Pablo) use spare time weaving twine and rope, endeavors which keep the great majority of households profitably occupied without migrating to the coast. Relatively few highland communities depend so wholly upon *milpa* farming that the men have no alternative sources of income during the dry season. In the state of Sololá, the towns with the least diversified economic bases are Santa Cruz and San Marcos on the lake and San José Chacayá and Concepción to the north of the lake. Predictably, large numbers of Indians migrate seasonally from the communities. The American Friends Service Committee volunteers stationed in San Jose Chacayá reported that all adult men left the town during November each year from 1963 to 1966.

Since community wealth is the crucial factor influencing ability to dispense with coastal employment, an examination of the factors influencing wealth is in order. Resources relative to population growth are the factors, with one set of variables affecting resources and another set affecting population growth.

Resources begin with a land base. Communities differ markedly in this respect. The legislation passed in the 1880s facilitating the division of land among households has eroded the nineteenth-century land base more in some communities than in others. In San Marcos all land is still communally held, but this is the exception. Elsewhere, buying and selling of land have altered community fortunes considerably. Much of the *municipio* of San Juan was purchased early in this century by neighboring Indians of San Pedro. Juaneros now are gradually repurchasing land they have been renting from Pedranos for years. Visitecos similarly lost much of their *municipio* to neighboring Clareños (Santa Clara), and disputed boundaries have led to several skirmishes during the past decade. In both cases, Visitecos and Juaneros lost their lands to neighboring Indians in part through efforts to maintain the nineteenth-century levels of ritual expenditures in the face of declining income during the era of the *mandamientos.* Apart from the land base, resources vary with custom and fortune. Some communities utilize lake resources more than do others, despite equal access to them by all. The *maguey,* which is used for rope, grows in San Pedro and San Juan as much as in San Pablo, but only the Pablanos use it for ropemaking. Land available for coffee is more plentiful in some *municipios* than in others.

Diversity of income sources figures importantly. Panajachel has perhaps the most diversified economic base, in terms of both variety of crops and availability of service occupations. Catarinecos, in relying so heavily upon lake resources (fish, crabs, and reeds), have been handicapped by diminishing supplies of all such resources. By contrast, Pablanos, while equally specialized, have benefited from a continuing demand and good prices for rope products. Santa Cruz, heavily dependent upon fruit, suffered a blight some years ago which hurt the community badly. Merchant buying and selling always has been a popular recourse, and Visitecos have used their strategic position on the west side of the lake (where a heavily used path drops down to the coast) to good advantage in turning to marketing in recent decades. Atitecos (Santiago Atitlán) and Luqueños (San Lucas) have done the same from the south of the lake. San Antonio, with considerable land, has managed to maintain an adequate standard of living by selling corn (in heavy demand in most lake towns the several months prior to harvest). Perhaps of all the lake towns, San Antonio has fared the best in maintaining an expanding population without heavy reliance on coastal employment, without an expanded occupational base, and with no apparent pressure to experiment with alternatives to traditional bases of association and security.

Despite measurable differences among communities in standards of living, or degree of impoverishment, the regional standard of living has been little altered and if anything slightly reduced since 1935. In Panajachel, where the 1936 base-line data are the most detailed, it is demonstrable that the cost of living has increased more than has the average daily wage for unskilled labor. Panajacheleños are less restricted to this minimum wage than are Indians elsewhere, but even in Panajachel there is no significant improvement in living standards. The lake towns, compared with Indian populations to the north and west of the state of Sololá, appear to be better off, but the picture throughout the highlands of Guatemala is one of growing impoverishment as a consequence of population growth.

Population Dynamics

This growth does not affect communities uniformly, however, Just as communities differ in their ability to accommodate population growth, so they also differ in the rates of growth. My interest at this point is in the extent to which ability to accommodate the increase in fact affects its rate.

Population trends in lake towns since 1950 (the first reliable census this century) are given in table 23. It is apparent that population growth has been rapid; at the 2.6 percent rate of increase averaged annually from 1950 to 1964, the 1950 Indian population around the lake would have doubled by 1973. The increase was due largely to a rapid decline in mortality since 1950, the consequence of medical assistance introduced beginning in 1944. It is ironic that such rapid population growth has insured lowland plantation owners a continuing flow of labor, despite the repeal of legislation forcing coastal migration.

Rates of population growth in the lake region are affected by birth and death rates primarily, and by movement in and out of communities secondarily. While movement from rural to urban areas is accelerating in Guatemala, none of the lake communities had lost significant numbers of people through emigration as of 1965. The trickle of Indians to the coast and to the two major urban centers (Guatemala City and Totonicapán) will almost certainly become a larger stream within a few years, however. Panajachel is the only lake town to be affected appreciably by immigration.

For a number of towns the movement in and out has been restricted almost entirely to atypical cross-*municipio* marriages. This stability of population in the region with respect to emigration and immigration facilitates measurement of natural population growth and isolation of the several variables affecting this increase.

TABLE 23
Average Crude Birth and Death Rates

Municipio	Total population 1964	Indian population		Births per 1,000 Indian population	Deaths per 1,000 Indian population
		1950	1964		
Santa María Visitación	640	458	630	49	20
Santa Clara	2,263	1,765	2,199	50	27
San Juan	2,351	1,623	2,305	51	23
Santiago Atitlán	12,938	9,106	12,397	53	29
Panajachel	3,268	1,585	2,023	53	24
Santa Cruz	1,350	1,071	1,341	54	35
San Marcos	709	508	702	56	34
San Antonio	3,570	2,261	3,273	56	29
San Pedro	3,713	2,583	3,629	57	28
San Pablo	1,773	1,131	1,773	60	25
Santa Catarina	879	661	865	61	35

Note: Rates and population figures are based on 1950 and 1964 national census reports, which distinguish Indians from Ladinos, but not native from foreign Indians.

Community differences in rates of population increase are of little utility in assessing community differences in autonomy afforded individuals in allocation of resources and experimentation with new social networks and bases of income and security. Community differences in rate of population increase can result simply from different mortality rates, reflecting differences in sanitation and availability of medical assistance. Substantial community differences in birth rates, however, are suggestive of the kinds of community differences in values, aspirations, and perception of risks in experimenting with innovations which my study of Panajachel leads me to hypothesize are occurring in the region. The differences would have to be substantial, however, since a reduction in infant mortality can in itself produce a reduction in birth rate by lengthening the spacing between births of nursing infants. A comparison of crude birth rates since 1950 in table 23 suggests community differences of such magnitude. The extremes for the region would appear to be Santa María Visitación and Santa Catarina; hence the choice of these two communities for intensive study and comparisons with Panajachel of the factors influencing natural increase. However, on investigation I discovered that more accurate census data reveal crude birth rates of 46 per 1,000 in Panajachel, 71 per 1,000 in Santa Catarina, and 51 per 1,000 in Santa María Visitación.[2]

Natural Increase

The rates of natural increase of population are affected principally by death rates and secondarily by changing attitudes toward spacing of children, age at marriage, and family size. The latter three variables are listed in the order of their importance as factors influencing birth rates at the present time and will be examined following consideration of the factors affecting death rates.

Death and mortality rates, especially for children under seven years of age, have declined markedly in the three communities since 1925 (table 24). The decline is due basically, of course, to government- and church-sponsored medical assistance, and since this assistance has been differentially available to the lake towns, post-1955 death and mortality rates can be explained in part by differing access to such outside aid. Prior to 1955, community differences in rates were not thus explainable, however, and the fact that Catarinecos during 1955-68 still lost children at a rate almost as high as in Panajachel during 1925-39 suggests that medical aid is only a partial explanation. Settlement pattern and sanitation appear to be major factors influencing mortality throughout the period under study. Santa Catarina's water supply is more contaminated by human wastes than are those of Santa María Visitación and Panajachel, and both of the latter populations live less compactly than do Catarinecos.

TABLE 24
Birth, Preschool Death, and Preschool Mortality Rates

	Santa Catarina		Panajachel		Santa María Visitación	
	1925-39	1955-68	1925-39	1955-68	1930-54	1955-68
Crude birth rate[a]	75	71	54	46	60	51
Preschool death rate						
0-6 years	40	28	23	11	20	13
0-1 year	20	21	12	6	10	10
Preschool mortality rate[b]						
0-6 years	540	394	426	240	333	255
0-1 year	270	296	223	131	167	198

Note: In determining population totals prior to this decade, I have had to rely on national censuses (1920, 1940, 1950) only in the case of Visitación. This community is the smallest of the three, and Pyeatt in the course of his research there was able to balance the 1920 and 1940 national census figures for the *municipio* with his own estimates based on reconstruction of family histories in establishing a 1930 base-line population. Tax's 1935 and 1937 censuses in Santa Catarina and Panajachel make possible the establishment of 1925 base-line populations.
a. Crude birth, death rates are per 1,000 population.
b. Mortality rate=death rate/birth rate.

The magnitude of the decline in death rates readily explains the natural increase in population since 1950; the increase would be appreciably greater if it were not for the accompanying decline in birth rates. Reduced mortality, followed by reduced natality, is in keeping with trends around the world, but the reduced mortality is inadequate to explain why birth rates have dropped so much more in Panajachel and Santa María Visitación than in Santa Catarina. The minimal decline in birth rate in Santa Catarina over the past forty years can be accounted for largely through the physiological effect of reduced infant mortality. Indian women throughout the Lake Atitlán region customarily nurse infants for two years, and the data indicate that where lactation is relied on heavily for this number of months after parturition, conception is prevented for twelve months on the average thereafter (Hinshaw et al. 1972:226). The more offspring who survive the first months of life, the less frequently their mothers can conceive. Table 24 reveals marked decreases in death rates of children between one and six years of age over the past forty years in all three towns, and this decrease may account for virtually all the decline in birth rate in Santa Catarina. In Panajachel and Santa María Visitación, however, other factors are needed to explain the more pronounced declines in birth rate. It is these factors which principally concern me in this chapter, for the other data available on these two communities suggest that we should expect atypically high interest in influencing population trends, given their success in strengthening community resources.

One of these factors is age at marriage, important because this directly affects the number of years of fecundity used for reproduction. From 1965 to 1968, women in Visitación averaged twenty-one years of age at the birth of their first child, compared with eighteen years in Panajachel and Santa Catarina (table 25). I surmise that Visitación is atypical of lake communities in this regard, and the explanation lies in a trend toward later marriage in Visitación prompted by altered expectations of young Visitecos about formal schooling and vocational training and by disrupted patterns of courtship, coupled with strong sanctions against premarital sexual experimentation (Hinshaw et al., 1972:229). In Panajachel the same changes in aspirations have occurred which tend to delay marriage in Visitación, but a larger, more heterogeneous community prevents effective sanctioning of premarital sex. Also, the rapidly changing economy gives young men financial independence earlier than formerly. In Panajachel, changes which have raised the age at first childbirth in Visitación are offset by changes which encourage earlier sexual experimentation and marriage. In Santa Catarina, the age at first childbirth has remained constant for the past thirty years, reflecting continuity in aspirations, sexual code, and sanctions. All that I know about Santa Catarina's history leads me to the conclusion that it remains one of the most conservative communities in the region.

Thus far, in examining changing birth rates, I have limited myself to physiological and structural factors (that is, age at first childbirth) which have not been consciously used by Indians to affect natality. Some evidence is available demonstrating such conscious efforts, however, and

TABLE 25
Secular Change in Age of Mothers at First Childbirth

	Panajachel	Santa Catarina	Santa María Visitación
1940-44	18.5 (20)	18.0 (28)	19.0 (7)
1945-49	19.5 (28)	18.0 (24)	18.0 (5)
1950-54	18.0 (20)	18.5 (30)	19.0 (16)
1955-59	18.5 (27)	18.0 (31)	19.5 (8)
1960-64	19.0 (43)	18.0 (54)	20.0 (12)
1965-68	18.0 (59)	18.0 (46)	21.0 (8)

Note: Ages are five-year medians computed over the number of births enclosed in parentheses. Ages were determined by locating each mother's birth in the municipal records and then searching the records for the first listing of a child by her. In very few instances were we forced to rely exclusively on women's memories for their ages.

while the efforts have limited effectiveness in the absence of contraceptive aids and the knowledge requisite for effective rhythm scheduling of coitus, they are important to identify. They indicate attitudinal changes and suggest where one might expect to find most ready acceptance of contraceptive and family-planning programs. The evidence is variations in spacing of births.

In all three communities, the spacing of births was, to a statistically significant degree, longer or shorter from 1948 to 1960 than from 1925 to 1937 (tables 26 and 27).[3] The extremes are Santa Catarina and Panajachel. In the former, the average spacing *decreased* by more than three months, and in the latter, the average spacing *increased* by three and one-half months. Whether the spacing is longer or shorter has depended on the level of concern with population trends. In Panajachel there is evidence of a desire for fewer births (but not necessarily for fewer children), probably resulting from recognition that fewer children die than formerly. Indeed, Panajacheleños are losing only half as many infants within the first year after birth and by seven years of age as they did from 1925 to 1939. Even in those instances where Panajachel infants die soon after birth, their parents are replacing those losses more slowly (by two months on the average) then they did formerly. All available evidence supports the conclusion that Panajacheleños are endeavoring to have children less often than before. By contrast, Catarinecos appear comparatively unconcerned about population trends. While they are spacing children closer than formerly when death does not intervene, they have lengthened the spacing following infant deaths by three months. Only in Santa María Visitación is there evidence of greater concern to replace infant losses than formerly.

TABLE 26
Generational Comparisons of Replacement and Normal Birth-Spacing
(in months)

	Santa Catarina		Panajachel		Santa María Visitación	
	1925-37	1948-60	1925-37	1948-60	1930-47	1948-60
Replacement spacing						
Median	11.6	14.6	13.0	14.0	16.7	13.0
Mean	13.3*	16.8*	15.3	17.2	18.8*	·14.4*
Normal spacing						
Median	31.0	26.0	28.5	30.0	28.5	29.0
Mean	31.2*	27.9*	29.3*	32.6*	30.6	30.9

Note: "Replacement spacing" is the interval between the death of an infant during the time when nursing helps to inhibit conception (12 months after birth) and the birth of a subsequent child. "Normal spacing" is the interval between the birth of a child who lives beyond that 12-month period and the birth of a subsequent child.
*Statistically significant trend between the two time periods (see table 27).

TABLE 27
Frequency Profiles of Birth-Spacing
(in months)

	Panajachel		Santa Catarina	
Normal	I	II	I	II
spacing interval	(1925-37)	(1948-60)	(1925-37)	(1948-60)
10-20	12	29	7	25
20-25	40	64	15	33
25-30	50	72	37	39
30-35	31	71	37	22
35-40	15	47	19	15
>40	17	50	14	13
Total	165	333	129	147
P (I=II) based on null hypothesis	<.001		<.001	

	Santa Catarina		Santa María Visitación	
Replacement	I	II	I	II
spacing interval	(1925-37)	(1948-60)	(1930-47)	(1948-60)
5-10	13	12	3	6
10-15	30	26	7	24
15-20	10	20	12	4
>20	5	23	10	6
Total	58	81	32	40
P (I=II) based on null hypothesis	<0.03		<0.01	

Note: value of P based on x^2 test for goodness of fit of period II curve on period I curve. Only comparisons yielding statistically significant values of P (<0.05) are illustrated. Period I and II comparisons between towns all yielded P(<0.05).

Infant deaths are followed by births four months sooner than in the earlier time period. When death does not occur, spacing has not altered significantly.

In at least Panajachel, the lengthened spacing between living children (compared especially with Santa Catarina) reflects a concern with maternal health which has accompanied the educational efforts of medical personnel who have resided in the community now for many years. I anticipate that this interest in spacing children further apart for the benefit of both infant and mother will more quickly lead to a reduction in the average family size in Panajachel than in Santa María Visitación. In Santa María Visitación, large families are popular as a means of competing more successfully for land and community prestige, attitudes understandable only against the background of seventy-five years of conflict and competition with adjoining Santa Clara.

Correlations of family size with household wealth in Panajachel suggest two trends.[4] Understandably, the wealthy tend to have more surviving children and more total births than do the poor, for the health of mother and children benefits from greater resources to pay for medical care. On the other hand, the families with the fewest births and surviving offspring also are among the wealthy, and I anticipate a trend has been initiated toward smaller families, in keeping with a shift in aspirations for children. Educational and occupational opportunities have increased, and cultural restraints on Indian utilization of such opportunities have diminished in Panajachel. Since no Indian family can afford to be unconcerned about resources, to have fewer children is the response of even the wealthy families who are most concerned with taking advantage of the new opportunities.

The noteworthy observation permitted by these comparisons is that spacing of children is subject to control by Indians of the region. The mechanisms are not wholly clear, but interviewing in Santa María Visitación and Panajachel suggests sexual abstinence is more important than withdrawal or rhythm in producing the generational and community differences in spacing. In Panajachel, where spacing has lengthened the most, paradoxically the age at first childbirth has, if anything, fallen. The result is a less rapid slowing of natural population increase than would occur if Panajacheleños were to marry as late as do Visitecos, or were Visitecos to lengthen spacing as much as have Panajacheleños. In terms of community interest in experimenting with contraceptives (if they were to be made available locally), I would expect Panajacheleños to be the most responsive and Visitecos more responsive than Catarinecos, despite the obvious fact that Catarinecos are the least able to accommodate the population increase that has been occurring. The evidence for this judgment is the demonstrated lack of interest among Catarinecos in slowing population growth, either through marrying later or spacing children further apart.

Experimentation with New Institutions

Thus far in this chapter I have examined the interplay of community resources and population level. This interplay has produced more pressure to experiment with adjustive behavior in some communities than in others, and where the pressure has developed the adjustments have varied considerably. I have focused thus far on the adjustment options most universally available in the region: migratory coastal labor, emigration, and family planning. The other variables with which these people can experiment consist of the institutional innovations in the region of recent decades: alternative religious affiliations, affecting expenditures; schooling, affecting earning power and mobility; and military training, also affecting mobility.

The differing and changing attitudes toward such options in Panajachel have been analyzed. Panajachel is atypical in the degree to which innovations have occurred, due to its position on the lake. While accessibility of the innovations is an important consideration, it is not a sufficient explanation for the marked community variations in response to such innovations.

With respect to accessibility: all towns have Indians commissioned to recruit volunteers for military training; Protestantism has been introduced to all lake towns at one time or another (beginning as early as the 1920s in Panajachel, San Pedro, and San Pablo); Catholic Action was introduced to all communities between 1953 and 1955; and six years of schooling became available to Pedranos and Panajacheleños in 1949 and to Visitecos around 1960. No more than three years of school are offered in the remaining towns (except for San Lucas and Santiago Atitlán, which with Panajachel have sizable Ladino populations). Theoretically, any town is eligible for additional years of schooling if the interest is demonstrated.

Protestantism and Catholic Action are the most significant of the institutional innovations, for both provide vehicles for increased autonomy in utilization of resources of time and money. Schooling and military training provide skills useful in broadening one's income base but do not in themselves call into question the traditional functions of wealth. The combination of schooling with avoidance of *cofradía* expenditures provides maximum flexibility in developing financial security. Protestantism appears to encourage such autonomy more systematically than does Catholic Action, however, for in the poorer towns where identity and security continue to be closely tied to community service, Catholic Action does not precipitate factionalism with respect to *cofradía* participation. It will be recalled that it did not initially in Panajachel, either. Where fatalism and defensiveness lessen, however, Catholic Action can function identically to Protestantism in challenging obligatory *cofradía* service, obligatory liquor consumption, and reliance on traditional forms of curing. Santa María Visitación is the most striking demonstration of this, and the history of this community's struggle against poverty is worth reviewing.

Santa María Visitación

I mentioned earlier in this chapter the impoverishment of Visitecos which occurred during the *mandamientos* when they attempted to maintain their ritual expenditures at the cost of selling and pawning land to neighboring Indians. At one point, as few as ten Visiteco families were year-round residents of the community, the majority spending most of each year working down on the coast. The community easily was among the poorest of the lake towns prior to 1940. Since then the Visitecos have made a remarkable comeback, in large part through community decisions to reduce ceremonial expenditures (for example, substituting *atol,* a drink made of cornmeal, for liquor in ceremonial contexts) and to seek assistance from governmental and religious institutions in establishing more adequate schooling, medical care, and an expanded economic base. Assistance in these endeavors was obtained in the late 1940s, when Carmelite priests established a center in Solola. Visitecos were among the first Indians in the region to solicit assistance, initially in the form of classes in catechism, and when Catholic Action began seeking adherents in Indian communities of the region in the early 1950s, the Visitecos joined almost to a man. Gradually land was repurchased, and by supplementing farming with wholesale buying and selling of fruit and produce in the region and on the coast the Visitecos have gradually reduced their reliance upon seasonal coastal employment. By the 1960s, only a dozen of the poorest families were still resorting to this.

The most dramatic changes have occurred in the last decade, triggered in part by the services of North American priests (three in all, the last two residing in Visitación) serving the northwest end of the lake. A community decision to disband the *cofradías* was made overnight in 1963, and within a few years the traditional diviners and curers had been almost completely replaced by medical services available from the priests (the present priest was joined by three nuns in 1960). The two years of schooling were gradually expanded to six, through persistent lobbying by Visitecos in Solola. By 1968 some ten young men had gone to Solola to continue their schooling beyond sixth grade, giving Visitación a higher proportion of youths completing sixth grade and going on to secondary school than any other town bordering the lake. One of the first such students, upon completion of secondary school, returned to Visitación to assume the office of municipal secretary, the only Indian occupying this role in the department. By 1968 the community was sending an assistant of the priest to Chimaltenango for weekly classes in agriculture development and medical care and was lobbying in Guatemala City for funds from Guatemalan and United States governmental agencies to harness a river flowing through the *municipio* for the purpose of providing electricity to the whole community. Several years before, Visitecos had raised the necessary funds to pipe water throughout the town to provide all houses with facilities for tying into a sewage disposal system. These developments set Visitación off from virtually all other towns around the lake, and certainly from all others of comparable size.

Accounting for Visitación's atypical response to grinding poverty is a challenge. Why did these Indians perceive the risks of experimenting with outside assistance and new bases of community organization so different-ly than did equally impoverished Indians in several other communities? I submit that an atypical basis of decision-making played a significant role in reducing the perceptions of the risks involved. The charismatic leader-ship of a few prominent men would appear to have been a factor also, but this begs the question of why potential leaders in other towns fail to come to the fore the way Visiteco innovators have felt free to do. Decision-mak-ing and leadership recruitment would appear to be the variables account-ing for Visitecos' success in encouraging autonomy in use of resources. Town meetings, at which every household is expected to be represented, are held in Santa María Visitación whenever important matters are to be dealt with. Continuity of informal leadership is thereby insured, as is a community-wide forum for airing opinions. The diffuse sanctions shack-ling would-be innovators and critics of the status quo in other towns are checked by discourse to an unusual degree in Santa María Visitación. Why such town meetings have become institutionalized here and not elsewhere may be a function in part of size, although Santa Catarina, San Marcos, and Santa Cruz are very little larger. The explanation probably lies in the long history of conflict between Santa María Visitación and Santa Clara over land resources. Visitecos, to survive, have had to mobilize for more efficient decision-making and concerted action. Leadership in such a situation becomes more critical than in most *municipios,* and accordingly leadership qualities have been rewarded more systematically than in other communities.

San Pedro la Laguna

Like Panajachel, San Pedro was relatively well off in 1936 when Tax first surveyed the lake communities, but like Santa María Visitación, it was a strictly Indian community isolated from the capital of Sololá. Unlike Santa María Visitación, San Pedro is large (see table 23) and has relied more on traditional decision-making procedures and organizational structure. This is important to emphasize, lest the difference in social organization obscure what I feel to be the more basic variable affecting change: confidence in one's ability to affect the future. Pedranos per-ceived less risk in experimenting with new resources, or at least accepted the risks, earlier than did Panajacheleños, possibly due to less effective exploitation of Pedranos by the pre-1934 legislation and their more rapid emancipation from migratory labor once the legislation was repealed. If the psychological burden of coastal labor was in fact less in San Pedro than elsewhere around the lake, the explanation would lie in the sizable landholdings of the community and its greater comparative wealth. Because they were less impoverished, Pedranos were in a position to benefit from the efforts of neighboring Juaneros and Pablanos to maintain ceremonial expenditures during the difficult pre-1934 era. The pawning or sale of land to Pedranos resulted in half of San Juan's falling into Pedranos' hands, and it was the best land that was lost.

Beginning with a strong economic base, Pedranos moved more rapidly than the members of any other lake community to exploit the opportunities which military service, Protestantism, Catholic Action, and formal education provided in freeing individuals to experiment with new sources and uses of income. Conversion to Protestant sects began a full decade earlier than in Panajachel, despite the fact the missionaries were stationed in Panajachel. The *cofradías* have not been disbanded, as in Santa María Visitación, but the associated ritual expenditures have been reduced even more than in Panajachel. Many youths have completed six years of schooling, made available at the same time six years were instituted in Panajachel, and more have commuted to Sololá to pursue secondary education in the capital school. Catholic Action has been important here since it was introduced to the lake region, and it is my impression that factionalism between Protestants and Catholics has been more pervasive. Pedranos have even engaged actively in the national political parties, something Panajacheleños have left almost entirely to Ladinos. In general, changes in San Pedro appear to have been more rapid, with less continuity maintained than in Panajachel. This has been reflected in more drastic change in courtship patterns than in Panajachel (Paul and Paul 1963), more openness to experimentation with contraceptives, [5] and, I suspect, more extensive erosion of traditional belief patterns. It is noteworthy in this latter respect that the one Indian interviewed in San Pedro during the investigation of regional belief patterns rejected as high a percentage of known beliefs as did the most skeptical of my Panajachel informants. Both informants were Protestants.

Santa Catarina

In contrast to Panajachel, Santa María Visitación, and San Pedro, Santa Catarina has resisted efforts of outsiders to assist in the amelioration of their poverty and has sanctioned effectively the efforts of Catarinecos to experiment with new associations. Birth and death rates are the highest on the lake, reliance on traditional forms of diagnosing and curing illness remains strong, and there appears to be little interest in experimenting with more autonomous allocation of the limited resources available to members of the community. Protestant missionaries tried unsuccessfully to gain a foothold in the 1950s, and while Catholic Action has gained a small following in the community, adherence to this movement is not yet seen as inconsistent with continuing support of the *cofradías*. *Cofradía* service and commitment of time and money to this form of conspicuous consumption on behalf of the community still constitute the major source of prestige and are viewed as the best protection against private and communal misfortune. The two years of public schooling (one Ladino teacher) available in the 1930s have not been expanded, and while a few children journey daily to Panajachel to continue their schooling beyond second grade, no Catarineco has yet gone beyond sixth grade. Nor by 1965 had any Catarineco experienced military training through voluntary service in Guatemala City or Quezaltenango. The community has never (at least not in this century) had the services of a resident priest. Perhaps in part for lack of encouragement to experiment with alternative uses of savings, Catarinecos have experienced very little change in values or expectations from life since Tax first described the community as it was in 1935 (Tax 1946).

The description of Santa Catarina comes last because the rigidity and defensiveness encountered there are more characteristic of the other small Indian communities bordering the lake than are the responses described for Panajachel, Santa María Visitación, and San Pedro. Santa Catarina may lie at the other extreme, given the community's specialized reliance on lake resources (fish, crabs, and reeds), which have diminished in quantity in recent decades. Had the new service occupations been introduced in Santa Catarina as they have in Panajachel, no doubt Catarinecos would have responded much as have Panajacheleños, although I expect more slowly and cautiously. Panajacheleños, in turn, responded more slowly and cautiously than I assume would have Pedranos, had the latter's community experienced the influx of new occupations instead of Panajachel.

The point to be made is that communities by 1935 already differed in their openness to new alternatives, and their subsequent histories reflect those differences in stances toward the social environment as well as accessibility of assistance from outside the communities. Stances toward the social environment have been influenced by the degree of impoverishment during and occasioned by exploitation from 1880 to 1934, as well as by economic fortunes since 1934.

Conclusions

At the outset of this chapter I alluded to the impact of forced seasonal labor on the coast on Indian psychological orientations. Of course individuals vary in the degree of defensiveness and fatalism produced by this imposition, just as communities have differed in the degree to which their membership was forced to migrate during *mandamientos* and since. But the general impact of the 1880-1935 exploitation must have been pro-

found. Is it possible that the insulation of Indians and the strong community bases of identity and security characterizing what Wolf has called the
"closed, corporate" Indian community (1955) resulted more from the
exploitation of Indians by Ladinos since 1880 than from cultural traditions
more deeply rooted in postconquest history? Attributing the defensiveness to these relatively recent developments, which affected Indian communities to varying degrees, facilitates explaining post-1935 community
differences in the perception of risks involved in experimenting with
institutional innovations.

In most general terms, the variations in such experimentation have
resulted from community differences in the encouragement individuals
receive to exercise autonomy in utilization of whatever resources they
possess or to which they have access, whether these be time, cash savings,
school opportunities, new employment possibilities, or alternative religious affiliations. While the same *range* of attitudes (from fatalistic acceptance of the status quo to active manipulation of one's environment) can
be assumed to be present in each community, the degree of autonomy
encouraged and hence exercised in the lake communities has varied
markedly. The degree of autonomy exercised depends on the risks per-
ceived in relinquishing the security of custom, and this perception is
influenced by attitudes of others. Because of the nature of social interaction, attitudes seldom find a forum for frank community-wide airing.
Responsibility for community service and decision-making in most communities does not fall to the innovative and progressive more readily than
to the cautious and conservative. A history of rotating responsibility for
civil and religious service has encouraged adherence to established custom and has discouraged innovation and change. Leadership abilities are
not rewarded, and there is no provision for continuity in leadership. Given
this state of affairs, it is not surprising that in most communities the risks of
initiating change individually or advocating change collectively are per-
ceived to be high in terms of one's reputation and hence one's security.

The following are the conclusions I have reached from intensive analysis
of the history of Panajachel and comparisons with data from around the
lake:

(1) The policies of church and state since 1944 and the earlier repeal of
exploitative legislation have not in themselves altered very significantly the
psychological stance of Indians toward non-Indians and toward traditional
bases of security and identity. This is largely due, in my opinion, to the
effect of population pressure on limited resources, forcing continuing
reliance on migratory labor.

(2) The most characteristic response of communities experiencing
pressure on a nonexpandable income base is fatalistic reliance on traditional responses to exploitation and a hostile environment, forcing emigration of any who seek alternative responses.

(3) An occasional community permits leadership and cooperation requisite for improving resources and making more effective use of those which do exist.

(4) Panajachel is atypical in the degree to which expanded income resources accompanied (or even preceded) population growth and forestalled the pressure of people on resources which most other communities had experienced by 1965.

(5) Panajachel, in the absence of an expanded income base, would probably not have experienced as much acculturation in social relations and bases of security, or at least would not have experienced these changes without more pervasive factionalism and individual disorientation. Had the acculturation not occurred in social relations, the world view would have altered less; had the acculturation occurred more rapidly, precipitating more factionalism, the belief patterns probably would have eroded more pervasively than they have.

Epilogue

O N T W O occasions in 1974 I visited Panajachel, for a total of two weeks. Sol and Gertrude Tax accompanied me on the second of the trips, in November. Our impressions of how the community has fared over the past decade lack the support of detailed information in most areas, yet they benefit from the impressions of numerous friends and informants.

The most visible changes of the past ten years are in construction of additional hotels (six), a new market arena, many new stores, restaurants, and tourist shops, and the continued spread of chalets over land formerly owned and farmed by Panajacheleños. These changes appear to occasion no more resentment among the Indians with whom we visited than did the growth in Ladino and tourist presence the previous two decades.

Of much more concern to the Panajachel Indians and Ladinos alike is the emigration from the United States since 1970 of approximately two hundred young adults who have adopted Panajachel as their temporary, and in some cases permanent, home. They are referred to locally as hippies. Their adoption of Panajachel extends to Indian housing and dress in many instances, as well as a level of subsistence living comparable to that of many Indians. The attractiveness of some aspects of Indian culture to these North Americans only accentuates in the minds of Panajacheleños the lack of adoption of Indian values in other domains.

Particularly difficult for Indians to understand and appreciate is the North Americans' lack of interest in or apparent need to earn a livelihood. The Indian youth are particularly aware of this, and their parents feel uncomfortable with the examples these new residents set in use of time. The examples are the more worrisome to Panajacheleños because the North Americans live among the Indian households and largely in Jucanyá, where Indians heretofore have enjoyed considerable privacy. The North Americans' mores with respect to communal living, shifting sexual alliances, and drug use fly in the face of traditional Panajachel values and prompt a host of rumors. Despite Panajacheleños' history of adjusting to newcomers, I find their apparent tolerance for this latest intrusion remarkable! Of course, the North Americans represent additional income for the community and continue to push upward the value of land. One Indian family in November was negotiating the sale of one-half *cuerda* of land (less than one-tenth of an acre) near the lake to a young North American for the handsome sum of $2,000.

Land values of $1,500 per half-*cuerda* ($3,000 per *cuerda*) are more common for property desirable for chalet construction, while land suitable only for farming is still available for $300-500 per *cuerda*. The lack of any appreciable inflation in the value of farm land may reflect the lower productivity of the land, attributed by some informants to overfertilization with commercial fertilizers. Panajacheleños have not had readily available professional counsel on use of fertilizer; and because they reason that if a little is good more should be better, some of the soil, at least temporarily, is less productive than formerly. Strawberries have been particularly adversely affected.

To make matters worse for those attempting to hold and live off their land, the Guatemalan government recently reclassified all of the Panajachel delta from rural to urban for purposes of land taxation. It will be recalled that land taxation had been initiated in 1964. Where initially very few Indians had holdings of sufficient size and value to produce a tax assessment, now many do by virtue of the reclassification. Adding insult to injury, the reclassification was made retroactive to 1964. Two families with whom I talked were being charged several hundred dollars, and one family was reputed to have been assessed $1,000. Obviously sale of parcels of land is the only way of meeting this exigency for some families. It is a mixed blessing that this forced sale of land occurs at a time when young North Americans are eager to obtain the land.

My earlier prediction that the shift in land use would continue from truck gardening to coffee cultivation appears to be correct. Less satisfactory yields of truck crops provide part of the explanation, but the availability and increasing acceptability of service occupations are, I suspect, the more important factors. Jobs are readily available for women as well as men in hotels and chalets, and Panajachel women are now competing with Catarinecas in marketing their handwoven fabrics. Some seven households now rely heavily on the sale of fish to restaurants and hotels. The fishing is done with harpoon guns by swimmers equipped with snorkel and fins. Tourists supplied the example, and the large bass at $.50 per pound make this a profitable enterprise. Several families have invested in small motor boats for rental to tourists, and two large yachts were under construction to take advantage of the growing tourist demand.

It is my impression that Panajacheleños are dominating the new employment opportunities more aggressively than before. Relatively few additional foreign Indian families have immigrated to Panajachel. Because of the increasing availability and acceptability of service employment, emigration to Guatemala City has not increased as rapidly as I had predicted. Those young people who have left Panajachel appear to have done so less because of economic necessity than because of a feeling that skills acquired in Panajachel can be marketed elsewhere to greater advantage.

In religious affiliations and schooling the situation has changed minimally except that secondary schooling is now available in Panajachel. Estimates offered of ten Panajacheleños enrolled at the secondary level last year cannot be far off. Catholic Action appears to have waned in influence, while the Protestant sects have, if anything, grown slightly. An active chapter of Alcoholics Anonymous provides Indians an alternative to leaving Catholicism in the quest for relief from the burden of drinking. The same persons engaged as *zahorines,* midwives, and spiritualists in 1965 were so engaged in 1974. The cofradías were still staffed, but with increasing difficulty.

National elections were held in Guatemala in March 1974. From all I could gather when in Panajachel in February, Panajacheleños participated no more actively in the election campaigning than they had the previous decade.

The public health clinic has continued to do a heroic job of serving not only the native, North American, and tourist populations of Panajachel but those of numerous other lake towns as well. A more dedicated, compassionate, and patient public health physician than Dr. Hernandez I have not met! The clinic added family planning staff and services around 1970, and information on these services, including contraceptive aids, is made available in most towns around the lake. As anticipated, Catarinecas have shown no interest whatsoever, while several dozen Panajacheleñas have come for counsel, examinations, and pills or IUDs. The region served by the clinic does not extend to Santa María Visitación.

Relationships between native Indians, foreign Indians, and Ladinos are increasingly fluid, with intermarriage more common than a decade ago. That intermarriage is more acceptable as well is suggested by the fact that both Indian and Ladino informants were slow to enumerate the half dozen unions which have occurred since 1965. I would not be surprised to learn that more Indian-owned businesses hire Ladinos or even that wealthy Indians are occasionally asked by poorer Ladinos to serve as *compadres.*

Economic ladinoization will increase rapidly, I predict, especially in employment. Indian informants estimated community income from agriculture to be less than 25% of all income in 1974; if correct, this would represent a very rapid decline in reliance on farming since 1965. The families with no members employed in service occupations, and thus relying fully on agriculture, must be rapidly diminishing in number. And yet at the same time I expect the number of families continuing to rely partially on agriculture is diminishing very slowly. The prospect is for a community of Indians relying on service employment for cash needs and on small gardens and fruit trees for basic food needs.

In 1974, a road was completed connecting Panajachel and Santa Catarina, and at least thirty chalets now dot the lake shore from Panajachel beyond Santa Catarina to San Antonio Palopó and San Lucas Tolimán. Panajacheleños have dominated the building of these chalets and no doubt will initiate the first stores and related enterprises catering to tourists in Santa Catarina. I will be interested in whether the rapid economic ladinoization of Panajacheleños within the view and memory of Catarinecos will produce more or less tolerance of the experimentation with new economic opportunities which some Catarinecos inevitably will undertake. It will not surprise me if Santa Catarina experiences considerable factionalism and disorganization over the next decade, expelling to Panajachel or beyond those Catarinecos who try to emulate the economic ladinoization of Panajacheleños. If these tensions do mount rapidly in Santa Catarina, this will result as much from observing the success of neighboring San Antonio in maintaining traditional values and economic base as from observing Panajachel. It is truly remarkable how different the recent histories have been, and how different the foreseeable futures likely will be, of three small communities spanning only five miles of the shore of Lake Atitlán.

One of the six new hotels constructed since 1965.

Transcriptions of Recorded Interviews

E X C E R P T S from interviews with three informants are offered to provide the reader some of the data on which assessments of awareness and rejection of beliefs were made. Using the belief response code on page 82, I indicate in parentheses my evaluations of responses for those beliefs included in the sample of 181 belief items. I enclose also in parentheses all summarized conversation, place in quotation marks the verbatim comments of the informants, and italicize my remarks.

Informant: Alberto Raxtun

(On the subject of remedies): *"What is used here to cure a child who is the victim of the 'evil eye'?"*

"Oh, well, for a child with *ojo* ["evil eye"] egg is good, but raw egg. And, well, what is used, also, is *ocote* [pitchpine]. A cross is made of two pieces of *ocote* and it is passed all over the body." (1)

"And the egg?"

"It is put inside the child's clothing, also. Then you get a pan of water and put the *ocote* in it . . . with two peppers. The peppers have to be passed over the body, too, in the form of a cross. These things are put in the water, and then the egg is broken into the water."

"Oh, this is for curing the child, not for determining if he has the illness?"

"Of course; for determining if he has *ojo* you look at the eyes that turn upwards, and the baby cries a lot and is colicky."

"I see. Then this is for curing him. And do you then throw out this pan of water?"

"Yes, and if you look at the broken egg you can see the *ojo*. Inside the egg there are the two little eyes, like little candles."

"And they tell me that this illness is often caused by a drunk, or a sweaty person."

"Yes. Sometimes if someone comes in all hot from working in the sun, or a man comes in with one woman but has another woman in some other place, it's this that causes *ojo*. It's because some people, but not all, have especially strong blood." (1)

(We then talked about strong blood; he volunteered that the quantity of blood influences its strength, and that vegetables produce blood. For this reason, Indians have hotter, stronger blood than Ladinos.) (1)

(Then I turned to the subject of curing goiter. He volunteered rubbing it with lard, or saliva, noting that since the swelling in the neck region might be mumps it is best to first treat for mumps.)

"Have you heard of rubbing or hitting the swelling with a sandal?"

"No, I haven't heard of that." (6)

"And my neighbor told me that rubbing the swelling with a gourd is helpful."

"A gourd, well, yes; but this isn't a very sure cure." (2)

"I don't understand how it helps. But you have heard of this?"

"Yes, I have heard of trying that. But what folks sometimes do for this goiter illness is to cover the swelling with a red cloth."

"But why red?"

"Well, to take away the bad."

"You mean the color red takes away the bad?"

"Yes, red takes away the bad."

"Then do people say the color red is good?"

"No, it's bad; it takes away the bad. After a little while you throw the cloth in the path, and if the color wins, then after a little while someone picks up the cloth and the goiter leaves you and enters the other person." (He laughs heartily.)

"I know something similar for ridding oneself of warts. They say that if you count warts and put a similar number of grains of corn in a cloth and throw it on a path, whoever picks it up will receive the warts."

"Yes, that's the same." (5)

"Have you heard of doing this?"

"No, not that. What I know for getting rid of warts is to cut out the biggest one, the first that appeared, and then burn it. The other smaller ones that appeared later will then disappear."

"What causes the others to go?"

"Well, since the one you cut out was the first to appear and caused the others, when you get rid of it, they go, too."

"Tell me what you know about another illness that bothers a lot of people in the United States: are there people here who sometimes walk around when they are sleeping?"

"Yes, there are."

"And how are they treated?"

"With a sandal, like you told me earlier for curing goiter. You hit the person all over with a sandal until he awakens." (1)

"But if the purpose is just to awaken him, why is a sandal necessary? Can't you just use your hand?"

"Well, it's a *secreto*." (Pauses.) "One doesn't know why it's so . . . it's a *secreto*."

"Another thing: are there remedies here for children who wet the bed a lot?"

"Oh, that's easy to cure. You take the nest of this bird, the hummingbird, burn it, and hold the child over the smoke." (1)

"But why this particular bird? Does it have to be a hummingbird?"

"Yes, well, again, it's a *secreto*. They say this bird doesn't urinate often, since it's so small. Another thing that helps is to put warm cloths on the stomach, to warm the body."

"Oh, yes, I've heard something similar; it helps to put on the umbilicus some sap from a piece of oak in the fire."

"Sure, but sometimes that isn't as certain a cure as the hot cloths or the hummingbird nest." (2)

"The only other cure I know is asking the child to carry one of the hearthstones [at this point he didn't seem to recognize the Spanish term, *tenemaste,* so I substituted the Cakchiquel term] *to the home of a neighbor. Do you know if this helps?"*

"No, that doesn't help. What has the effect is what happens when he *arrives* at the neighbor's, for she begins to ask him, 'why do you wet the bed?' " (1)

"Ah, I understand; then he is embarrassed, and this is the cure."

"Yes." (Laughs.) "It's not the stone, but just that the women know this *secreto* and when he arrives the woman asks him in for some coffee and then asks him why he always wets the bed. He becomes ashamed, and doesn't even drink the coffee but runs home."

"*I have a question about the hearthstones. I've heard it is the custom never to move them, except for one.*"

"Yes, only one. If you want a larger fire you can move two of them, but one is never moved." (1)

"*Why is this?*"

"Well, because, it always stays put; because if you move it, you may move your home. If one changes it [the stationary stone] all the time, then you constantly are changing house locations."

"*Then, it's sinful* [pecado] *to move it?*"

"No, it isn't sinful; just isn't the custom. It's the biggest one that is never moved."

"*What happens if one sits on a hearthstone?*"

"Nothing happens."

"*But some say that is sinful.*"

"They say so, maybe, because that's where food is prepared, and it would get dirty. But it isn't sinful." (3)

"*Then how about using the grinding stone for a chair?*"

"That's sinful!" (1)

"*The same reason as for the hearthstone?*"

"Yes, same reason; gets it dirty. But this is sinful."

"*What meaning does a broken grinding stone have here?*"

"Well, it means someone in the house will die." (3)

"*And is it true?*"

"No, I don't think so. Like I told you, it's one of the old beliefs. Maybe for those who believe it, something will happen; but if you don't, then nothing happens."

"*Or if the hearthstone breaks?*"

"Same thing. They say someone in the family is going to die." (3)

"*But it isn't certain?*"

"No, unless again maybe if you believe it. It's just another of these superstitions [creencias]."

"And what about loaning grinding stones to a neighbor who asks for them, or maybe it's just the loaning of one without the other that folks say is bad?"

"Well, that's because the neighbor might be careless and break it, and like I told you, if it breaks they say someone will die." (3)

"Ah, that's the reason, and therefore it is uncommon to lend them."

"Yes, and also, they say it's bad to loan fire. At times you don't have matches and need to borrow a match or a burning stick, so you go to a neighbor and ask for fire. But then they say they don't have any, and it's the same if you want food, or even a penny."

"Oh, they won't lend?"

"No, they won't lend, but not everyone. Many lend; like us, we lend and borrow fire or whatever."

"Are there some hours of the day when folks say it is more risky to lend things like fire than others? For example, in my country many say it is risky to loan things at noon."

"Yes, at noon here too. It's best then to buy matches or wait." (3)

'And what do you think, does it matter if you loan fire at noon?"

"No, not if you don't think so it doesn't matter. They say it's best not to loan salt either, because if you loan salt they say you will become poor. Your crops won't produce well, you won't have work . . . the same if you loan fire, or money, or such things. They say it is because you have loaned things if you are poor." (Laughs.)

"I have several questions concerning the fire. Many say it has its spirit. What do Protestants say about this?"

"Well, Protestants don't say anything about it. Many believe it is God, and has a spirit, but I don't believe this." (3)

"What about the things you were taught by your parents when a boy: for example, did you learn it is bad to step or jump over the hearth?"

"Stepping over, no, but we were told not to spit in it, because, well, because it is fire." (4)

"Or playing with the fire?"

"Yes, that's sinful." (1)

"And what do folks here say when the fire hisses?"

"Oh, when it makes a noise, for example, when you put a piece of cane in the fire?"

"Yes."

"They say it means there will be a quarrel. But what causes the noise is that sometimes the wood is green, or there is an insect or something in the cane or wood." (3)

"Then it doesn't necessarily mean there will be a quarrel?"

"No, but many say this."

"In my country, and maybe it's the same here, a sign of a quarrel or of someone speaking ill of you is a burning ear lobe."

"Oh, yes, when you feel something in your ear. It means someone is talking about you somewhere. Sometimes that's a sure sign." (1)

"And have you heard of biting your collar so that the person will be punished for his gossiping by biting his tongue?" (He ponders, but seems not to understand, so I demonstrate and repeat.) "Have you heard of this custom?"

"No, I've never heard of that." (6)

"What do folks say it means when you hear a buzzing inside your ear?"

"Oh, you mean like a little bell. Well, folks say when it happens at night that it's a sign your spirit is leaving. But it's just air, and you can sometimes stop it by putting your hand over your ear. Folks say it's the spirit, but it's just a belief. Right?" (3)

"How could it be that the spirit would leave? Wouldn't you die?"

(He laughs.) "Yes, you would die. It doesn't leave. I know many say that especially during dreams the spirit leaves, but I've thought about it and I say it doesn't leave." (3)

Informant: Julio Lopez

"Do folks here eat all colors of corn; are there preferences?"

"What folks say is that the white is good, but one has to eat a lot to get full. The yellow produces the most and fills one up most quickly. Folks don't much care for the black, because well, they don't like it as much because it's black."

"Is it sinful to eat the black? Does your family eat all three colors?"

"No, not sinful. We eat all colors. It's just that the yellow fills one up most quickly."

"I've heard it said that each color has its spirit. My neighbor, E.S., told me that for a long time he planted all three colors, but then one year failed to plant black corn. One night he dreamed that the three sisters, the spirits of the three colors, were quarreling, and the black spirit was asking why it had to be she who didn't get planted."

(He laughs.) "Each according to his own belief!" (4)

"Then folks don't talk of the three spirits of corn?"

"No, not like they used to. Formerly people talked about each color, or rather each crop, having its spirit, but not so much anymore."

"Oh, just the one spirit for all crops?"

"Yes, just for all crops." (Pauses.) "Well, it's changed. They *used* to talk of this." (He is obviously uncomfortable with any assignment of spirits to crops.)

"What do Protestants say of this?"

"Well, Protestants say that there is just one God and only he gives us such things."

"Then there isn't a spirit of corn, or a spirit of all crops?"

"No, nothing. Only God gives us food; there aren't other gods or spirits. But then the way of knowing these things is through the Bible; if the Bible says there is a spirit of corn then we have to accept it. This business about black corn having a spirit is just a *secreto*. It can't be." (3)

(We talked about prohibitions with regard to tortillas. He knows them all except for the prohibition against dipping in coffee. He discredits them all, however, and even thinks people don't worry nowadays about throwing out leftover tortillas. Then I asked about teasing a dog with a tortilla.)

"Yes, to offer a dog a tortilla and then not give it to him is sinful. It's because, even though the dog doesn't talk, it feels and has a spirit, they say." (1)

"And I've heard a swelling results on the knee. . . .

"Yes, the face of the dog." (3)

"Really?"

"No, that some swelling results, I doubt. But what I say is that it is bad to tease, because the dog has a soul [*alma*] and has feelings. Who then would offer it food and not give it?"

(I then introduced him to the animal cards explaining my interest in comparing the significances of various animals here and in the United States. I asked him to arrange the cards in terms of good and bad animals and then asked which animal carried the most ominous meaning for people here.)

"Well, the owl they say is bad. According to beliefs it's bad because any time it hoots near the house it means someone will die." (2)

"Oh, yes, I remember hearing this. And is it a fact?"

"Well, they say it's true; we haven't experienced it at our house, but others say it's certain."

(Asked about mice, he volunteered that mice and bats are the same when I started to ask.) (1)

"Are folks afraid of mice here?"

"No, folks say it's good to have them around the house to clean up bits of food."

"And bats?"

"Well, yes, folks fear bats. It's the belief that bats are bad; when they enter the house it means that someone will become ill or something bad will happen. But as it has never happened at our house, I don't know if it is certain or not." (2)

"I have several questions about dogs. Are there cures known here for dogs with rabies?"

"This happened to a dog of ours not too long ago, and what we did was to bathe him and sweep his head with a broom."

"And this helped?"

"Well, since they say that it is the fever that causes the sickness, it helps to bathe him." (1)

"But the sweeping, how does that help to lower the fever?"

"Well, this is a *secreto,* but it helps."

"How about for a dog's cough, are there remedies?"

"Yes, with pieces of corn cobs you make a collar for the dog and put it around his neck." (Demonstrates.) "It's a *secreto* which takes away the cough." (1)

"I have seen this but didn't understand. How about for teaching a dog to stay at home? Are the secretos *for this?"*

"No, we bought a new pup recently and just tied it up for a while."

"*Yes, we do this in my country, too, but I've also heard that it helps to cut a few hairs and put them under the hearthstone.*"

"No, I haven't heard of this, but I recall now that they say it helps to feed the dog a tortilla that has been on or passed over the hearthstone." (6)

"*But you haven't tried this?*"

"No, but my father tried it and says it is certain." (1)

(I then asked about parts of the chicken which aren't eaten customarily.)

"Here in Guatemala the legs, the body, and the wings are good for men; all is good for men to eat apart from the feet. And also the head; the man doesn't eat the head."

"*Oh really, why is that?*"

"Well, I don't know, but among Ladinos as well, they say that if one climbs a tree, he won't have the strength he needs in his legs." (2)

"*And is it true?*"

"Well, they say it's true, and for this reason a child who likes to eat the feet is told not to climb trees." (Laughs.)

"*And the head?*"

"Oh, this is because men are accustomed to carry loads with the tumpline (*mecapal*), and if a boy eats the head he won't have sufficient strength for this. But I like the head and I have eaten it." (3)

"*And have you heard of the danger of becoming jealous if you eat the wing tips?*"

(He thinks a while.) "I recall my mother telling me the wing tips shouldn't be eaten by children." (3)

"*Yes, I've heard that only adults should eat them.*"

"Yes, because they already have their families and don't have reason for jealousy." (Laughs.) "But I think jealousy is a matter of temperament (*naturaleza*), and I have eaten all of the wing. I like them." (3)

Informant: Lucas Can

"*What is said about such things as the rain and the wind? Do they have spirits and saints?*"

"Yes, the rain's saint is San Miguel." (1)

"*And do folks say it is wrong to complain about the weather?*"

"Yes, as for instance when it is very cold and one complains."

"And what happens to people who complain about the rain?"

"Well, if nothing happens at the time sometimes when one dies there is a lot of rain. Perhaps it is because he complained. It is God that sends the rain, the wind, the heat, the cold, but not all of these things are gods; there is just one God who sends these things. Not like they say in Santa Catarina where they claim the rain is God, the wind is God, the lake is God, the volcano is God . . . this results in a lot of gods!" (We laugh.) (1)

"Then what is said about the rainbow?"

"Here they say that the rainbow is a snake arising from hell. They tell stories about this, but no one has actually seen such." (3)

"Is it true?"

"No, the rainbow is only a sign. When it falls to the north it is a sign of wind; when it falls into the lake near the volcano of water it is a sign of rain; and when it falls near the volcano of fire it is a sign of summer. The many colors of the rainbow are caused by the rays of the sun and the mist in the air; the mist causes the colors."

"In my country many tell stories of looking for buried money at the end of the rainbow."

"No, the rainbow is caused simply by the sun's rays and mist. You can see it sometimes when you throw out a pan of water."

"But then why do people say it is risky to point at the rainbow?"

"Oh, that. It's a bunch of lies. They say if you point at it your finger will be bent, but I've pointed at it." (3)

"Another thing; the lightning bolts. I learned that the lightning bolts seek out bad animals, like snakes."

"Yes, that's for sure. Especially those snakes with the rattles on their tails. In the summer they are around, but during the rainy season they hide from the lightning. Here nearby not long ago the lightning struck a tree, but I don't know what animal it killed." (1)

"What about people struck by lightning; is this a sign of anything?"

"People say that when a woman is outside the house, she shouldn't have on any rings or things of metal, lest she be hit by the lightning." (1)

"Yes, I've heard that metal attracts lightning."

"Once near San Andrés, there were two men out working with their tools; one with a hatchet, I believe, and the other possibly with a *machete*.

Suddenly an angel passed over them, but they didn't see her. They just heard her voice, and she told them to leave the tools. They were frightened, so did as she said, and after they had walked on a few *cuerdas,* suddenly a bolt of lightning struck the tools back behind them."

"Another question: what significance do falling stars have here? Are they dangerous to look or point at?"

"No, the only thing is that they can cut your luck; some say when they fall it's best to whistle so that nothing will happen to you." (1)

"I've heard also that formerly the falling stars turned to coins on the ground."

"Oh, yes, but a long, long time ago, when no one knew disrespectful language and people were good. At night the coins would fall and in the morning people would go outside and pick them up on their plots of land." (1)

"And it really used to be so?"

"Yes, my father told me about it. And for the poor people who didn't have land, they got to pick up the coins which fell on the paths. But the other thing is that when people learned bad language and stopped being respectful, then the falling stars turned into worms instead. You know, those piles of maggots you see sometimes on the ground."

(We talked at some length about dreams, ending with his volunteering that spirits frequent the crossroads. This permitted me to ask about *characoteles* making transformations at such places. He agreed and reminded me of the various places in Jucanyá where paths cross.)

"Another question about dreams: are there some nights when it is more common to dream than other nights?"

"When one is most likely to dream is on Monday night, or Friday night, or Wednesday night, also." (1)

"Oh, the strong days. And how about strong hours, are there some hours here when it is best not to work, or be about?"

"No."

"In my country midnight is a time when folks prefer not to be out."

"Some say the same here, but others are out at night and don't think anything about it."

"But how about hours during the day. Are there no hours, such as six o'clock, or noon, when spirits are abroad?"

"Only at noon, perhaps; that's the time when folks are resting, and it's a sacred time." (2)

"And do folks take any precautions to keep out spirits at such times? For example, pans of water in the doorways or crosses?"

"Oh, well, some put crosses of pitch pine or bunches of garlic on their doors to keep out spirits, but I don't. Some are afraid, are ignorant, but we never put anything." (3)

"We were told that it is the custom here for women not to sweep the house at noon. Is this because it is a strong hour?"

"No, just because it is a time of rest and people should put aside their work. It's best to clean and arrange the house before noon, or after, but not during the noon hour." (1)

(I then asked about sweeping in the evening or combing hair at noon or in the evening, but he had heard of none of this.)

"And what about measuring children at night?" (No response.) "Do folks say it is best not to measure a child to see if he has grown?"

"Oh, you mean to compare heights. That's true, you shouldn't put brothers back to back or the shorter one will gain at the taller one's expense. It's the same as with, say, fountain pens. If we measure two pens together, one may break as a result." (1)

(I asked about women stepping over a man's machete and other beliefs of this complex. He accepts all of these and volunteered that women should avoid stepping over root crops or climbing fruit trees. He then added that to use a limb of a fruit tree for firewood results in the fruits being wormy as a punishment.)

"Have you heard that fruit peels, if thrown into water, can punish?"

"Yes, you may get a stomachache."

"Really?"

"Well, I've never tried it to know, but people say it will happen if you throw them into the lake or into an irrigation ditch, for example." (Ponders.) "Well, maybe it isn't certain, for come to think of it I have thrown peels into the lake from the launch, and nothing happened. Perhaps only if one thinks a lot about it and worries, does he get the stomachache." (2)

Notes

Preface

1. I use the Spanish manner of designating inhabitants of towns. Thus, an Atiteco is from Santiago Atitlán, an Antoñera from San Antonio, and a Panajacheleño from Panajachel.

Introduction

1. *Underlined* Spanish terms are defined fully in a glossary on pages *195-97*.

Chapter 1. The People

1. For my eighteen months of research I gratefully acknowledge support from the National Institutes of Health (predoctoral fellowship 5-FI-MH-20,437 and research award MH 07877). Funds granted Sol Tax by the National Science Foundation (research grant GS-189) made possible Juan de Dios Rosales' participation in the data collection.

2. I have somewhat arbitrarily designated 388 Indians as foreign in 1964. These include 206 persons who were born elsewhere and have immigrated to Panajachel since 1936. Of 160 children born in Panajachel to these immigrants, 100 were still living in Panajachel in 1964. Thus approximately 300 foreigners and their children have been added to the Indian population. These, plus the surviving foreign-born persons in Panajachel in 1936, yield a total of 388. However, this number includes 56 persons who have married into Panajachel households, 20 of whom are of foreign parentage but born and raised in Panajachel. Since these 56 are not fully Panajacheleños in the minds of many, I have called them foreign. Their offspring are regarded as native.

The figures for 1936 and 1964 are restricted to those residing within the city limits. These limits have expanded slightly since 1936 but still exclude the larger *fincas* of the *municipio* and the community of Patanatíc. The total *municipio* population reported in the 1964 national census was 3,620.

3. The health center, staffed by public health nurses until Dr. Hernandez arrived in 1962, has had a marked influence upon curing practices and community health. This is reflected in the waning influence of the three remaining *zahorines* or native diviners and curers. While a few traditionally oriented elders have thus far not made any use of the health clinic's facilities for their own maladies, I know of no household that has not used these facilities for children. This has resulted in rapid reduction of infant mortality during the critical period of transition from breast-feeding to the adult diet of coffee, beans, and corn, occurring between the ages of one and three. Whereas 26 percent of the infants born between 1936 and 1950 died between the ages of one week and four years, the percentage had been reduced to 9 percent of the children born since 1958. In contrast to postnatal care, prenatal care continues largely under the direction of midwives, minimally influenced by information disseminated by the health center. Consequently, the percentage of children stillborn or dying within a week of birth has remained a constant 9 percent for the past two decades. Vigorous massaging of expectant mothers inadvertently aborts many infants. Until prenatal care is altered, it seems reasonable to assume that the

current death rate (averaging eighteen per thousand inhabitants since 1960) will not drop appreciably. This change could occur rapidly, however, since in 1964 at least two of the five midwives, including one of the three Indian midwives, had begun receiving instruction from the physician, Dr. Hernandez.

4. In 1936, native Indian households averaged 5.1 persons and foreign Indian households averaged 4.0 persons. In 1964, these averages were 6.0 and 5.6, respectively.

5. In 1936, 32 percent of the females and 35 percent of the males were under 14; in 1964 these percentages were 41.5 and 42.5.

6. Patanatíc is a settlement of foreign Indians whose ancestors came to the area in the nineteenth century from the *municipio* of Totonicipán to the northwest. The community is located in the hills north of Panajachel and remains socially and economically distinct from Panajachel Indian society.

7. The accuracy of the 1921 census can be questioned; Tax was of the opinion in 1936 that the figure was high. On the other hand, lake villages were hard hit by epidemics in the 1920s, and a decline from 1,150 to 780 between 1921 and 1936 would easily have been possible.

8. Correlations between innovation and household wealth are discussed in chapter 3.

Chapter 2. Economic Comparisons

1. I can give only my own and various informants' impressions of the proportions of truck lands planted in the various vegetable and fruit crops. Onions dominated the truck crops at least as much as in 1936, when 36 percent of the truck land was so planted. A larger, foreign variety of onion introduced in the interim has virtually supplanted the variety common in 1936, however. Garlic, the second most important truck crop in 1936, accounted for less of the agricultural income in 1964 but had not declined in importance as much as *pepinos. Pepinos* were the principal risk crop in 1964, producing the most profit when yielding well, but apparently yielding well even less consistently than before. The greater risk involved in growing *pepinos* is reflected in the wider range of "garden magic" associated with care of *pepinos* than with any other crop. Rich soil is necessary for *pepinos,* yet for some reason the right blend of commercial fertilizer has not been hit upon. Consequently, with the loss of the more productive lands bordering the lake, fewer plots of land owned by Panajacheleños were considered worth the risk.

Possibly another reason for the decreasing interest in *pepinos* is the growing market for strawberries. Strawberries grow best in the kind of soil needed for *pepinos,* and with a good market locally as well as in Guatemala City and Quezaltenango they have become a better risk. Strawberries had been but recently introduced in 1936, yet they had become possibly the second most important truck crop in 1964.

Other vegetables, including beans, tomatoes, carrots, peas, cabbages, cauliflower, cucumbers, and radishes, are grown in larger proportions, I suspect, than in 1936, because of the expanding local Ladino market for such foods.

Factors influencing the choice of crops include not only soil type, risk, and maximum return, but also the preservability of the harvest. Thus, while garlic prices had not kept pace with market values of onions, *pepinos,* beans, and strawberries, most farmers planted some garlic to provide a cushion during the lean months of the year.

2. Because of the nature of the census (for taxation purposes) and because it was the first such census instituted in Guatemala, there were considerable misunderstandings and apprehension. On the one hand, it was not widely understood that only landholdings above a certain size (larger than the holdings of probably any Indian landowner in Panajachel) were taxable, and consequently some Indians failed to report all their plots or reported the plots as smaller than their actual size. On the other hand, there was an unrealistic fear of legal sanctions for misrepresentation or for failure to register as a landowner, even when the plot owned was a fraction of a *cuerda*. The location of each plot was designated, as well as its use (house site, coffee, *milpa,* other truck crops). These voluminous data were checked with several informants, and at least the grosser inaccuracies were rectified for my own records.

3. Since the introduction of commercial fertilizers in 1959, virtually all farmers have adopted

them, at least for onions. Experimentation with different blends of nitrogen, potassium, and sulphate was still going on, however, and these differences, plus the varieties and occasional use of newly introduced insecticides, contributed to the wide range in yields. Moreover, two and even three crops of onions grown from seedlings can be harvested from a given plot of land in a year, and with fluctuations in market prices through the course of any given year, the determination of average profits in 1964 was further complicated.

4. Sol Tax, *Penny Capitalism*, pp. 163-67, describes the diet in detail.

5. Catholic Action *(Acción Católica)* is a reform movement within Roman Catholicism, whose influence in Panajachel is discussed on pages 53 and 54.

Chapter 3. Wealth and Innovation

1. Of these criteria, accumulated savings was the most difficult to measure, and yet some estimate of savings was necessary for households with minimal landholdings but considerable earning power. Rather arbitrarily, I tripled the difference between earnings and expenditures in 1964, reasoning that this would approximate the accumulated savings of those households with considerable earning capacity. Of course, I adjusted the saving capacity of households according to whatever knowledge I had of property investment or improvement of recent years, history of community service, drinking patterns, prolonged illness, death, and any other vicissitudes within the past three years. Accumulated savings became a factor in the estimation of household wealth, therefore, only for those families with obviously more earning capacity than annual expenditures; these households totaled 89, or 23 of the 175 households worth less than $1,000, and 66 of the 116 households worth more than $1,000. In this way I made some provision for the landless families with comparatively high incomes from service occupations and yet continued to make land base the principal wealth indicator. With the value of land as high as it was, it was assured that this would weigh heavily; a family with just one *cuerda* of good land and no saving capacity was equivalent in wealth, by the formula used, to a family with no property and annual savings of $100 (a considerable saving capacity).

I have described above the data contributing to the calculation of household earnings. The calculation of household expenditures necessitated estimating food and clothing costs for persons of different ages and for households at different economic levels. In other words, an obviously well-to-do family was assumed to spend proportionately more per individual for food and clothing than a family living from hand to mouth. On the basis of detailed data on several families representing the poorest, the richest, and average sectors of the community (impressionistically determined prior to determining the wealth order of households), the per individual costs were estimated. In fact, the differences between the rich and the poor in expenditures are not great, but on the basis of the slight differences found I hoped more nearly to approximate the actual expenditures per household in arriving at an estimate of savings during 1964.

Determination of property wealth involved estimating value of buildings as well as land. Value of buildings depends upon type of construction, size, and age, all of which were recorded in the course of making the household census. Household furnishings were not evaluated, but luxury consumer goods such as bicycles (a motorcycle in one case), radios, horses, launches and canoes, and tools of consequence (limited to masons and carpenters) were taken into account.

2. Foster (1967) has analyzed the function of treasure tales in Tzintzuntzán in explaining comparable fluctuations in household wealth.

Chapter 4. Bases of Security

1. Juan Castro and Bonifacio Cululen were the first converts. Bonifacio's first wife was sister to Juan, and the two households were converted largely by Juan's Protestant brother, who was living on the coast. Bonifacio's family was the more active, and in his diary of 1940 Tax observed the following of Bonifacio:

> I spent a very interesting hour listening to Bonifacio on religion. There is no doubt at all that he is a good convert, and I doubt seriously if there is more to the matter than sincere conviction. True, even before he became a convert, he objected to the impoverishment caused by the cofradías; and that was before he had any contact (that I know of) with missionaries. But now his life and mind have certainly been changed. [1950:2077]

2. Of recent years, an alternative to *cofradía* sponsorship has been to accept a *cofradía en recomendado*. Housing is offered the saints, but the expenses for their care and associated fiestas are shared by the elders as well as the *cofrade* and *mayordomos*. Two of the four *cofradías* were accepted *en recomendado* in 1964.

3. In using sketches of occupational situations to elicit preference and attitudes, I followed the lead of George and Louise Spindler, whose experiment with such a tool is described in the *Southwestern Journal of Anthropology* (1965). I found no native artist, so I drew my own sketches.

4. Foster notes that no Tzintzuntzeño was a second-generation store owner (1967).

5. The procedure followed for determining drinking patterns of adult Panajacheleños in 1964 was described on page 19. Juan Rosales and his assistant, Manual Andrade, both adults at the time of Tax's initial study, compared memories of drinking patterns of Panajacheleños prior to conversion to Protestantism. These data were supplemented by my own conversations with other informants concerning the drinking patterns of more recent converts to Protestantism. The three-point scale using the criteria outlined on page 19 was the basis for judging drinking patterns as light, moderate, or heavy.

6. The new Jucanyá school, under construction when my research terminated in 1965, was a project initiated by residents of Jucanyá but realized in large part through financial assistance of the Peace Corps school construction program.

Chapter 5. Social Relations

1. The most extensive discussion of Ladino-Indian relations in a Guatemalan Indian community appears in Colby and Van den Berghe's monograph, *Ixil Country* (1969).

Chapter 6. The Panajachel World View

1. The sampling was motivated in part by an interest in determining Panajacheleños' awareness of beliefs learned by Redfield in San Antonio Palopó; many of these beliefs proved not widely known by Tax's informants.

2. The criteria for selection of the additional informants were exposure to one or more of the acculturative influences of schooling, Protestantism, military training, and Catholic Action. A list of about seventy-five desired informants was drawn up on the basis of my knowledge of household involvement in these institutions, and during the final nine months of field work I developed sufficient rapport with some twenty-five of these persons to permit interviewing. I added a half dozen other Panajacheleños not exposed to these influences, plus four Ladinos.

The interviewing was spread over three sittings for a total of eight to ten hours with each informant. We lived among Indians in the predominately Indian sector of Panajachel, making it possible for me to schedule most of the interviews in the privacy of my office. In some instances I went to an informant's home for all interviews and frequently went to his home for the initial interview. I paid most informants the going daily wage, but the level of rapport requisite for the interviewing meant that the venture was strictly a business proposition for only a few of the informants. Both Ardith and I taught English classes, and these attracted a number of the more acculturated Indians who later became valuable informants.

I taped the interviews and then went over the tape immediately following the interview, coding responses on 5" x 7" cards. I wrote nothing during the interviews and referred to no notes. To facilitate the subsequent coding, I followed a mental topical outline, but of course followed the informant's leads whenever possible to maximize the quantity of volunteered data.

3. I did five of the twenty-one interviews, Nicolas Hopkins and Christopher Day did one each in Huehuetenango, Clyde Woods did two in San Lucas Tolimán, and Peace Corps and American Friends Service Committee participants in community development did the remaining eleven. Two of the Peace Corps participants had had undergraduate training in anthropology, and all those assisting had been residents in their respective communities for eighteen months or more before undertaking the interviewing among friends of good rapport. I duplicated the questionnaires, phrasing all questions in Spanish to provide data that were as comparable as possible. Four of the interviews undertaken by others were taped for me, and responses were written out for all others. Some undertook to evaluate belief acceptance as well as awareness; for my present purposes only awareness or lack of awareness is important, and these assessments I regard as reliable. The beliefs used in the sample, with indication of the number of towns where they were acknowledged, are included in part II of the model at the end of Chapter 7.

4. Ladinos interviewed in Panajachel included two first cousins (girls), one of an Indian mother and the other of an Indian grandmother, a twenty-six-year-old woman born and reared in Chichicastenango until moving to Panajachel at the age of twenty, and a fifteen-year-old son of a Panajachel Indian mother and Ladino father. In addition, Clyde Woods interviewed ten Ladinos of San Lucas Tolimán in conjunction with his anthropological research in that community. The Panajachel Ladinos were questioned over the full corpus of 180 beliefs; Woods used the smaller sample of 120 beliefs constituting the questionnaire utilized in determining regional awareness among Indians.

Chapter 7. Structure of Belief

1. "If we take a fresh look at the ethnographic data it is quite true that the line between what *we* call objectivity-subjectivity may appear somewhat blurred. This is partly due to the fact that subjectivity-objectivity cannot be adequately conceived in simple linear terms, but only with reference to the total pattern of psychological field. The 'line' that we think should be drawn precisely 'here' may not be drawn so sharply at all, although it may appear somewhere else as a recognizable boundary. . . . It must not be forgotten that the empirical self and the empirical world of surrounding objects have both emerged out of a common process of maturation, socialization, and personal experience. An intelligible behavioral environment has been constituted for the individual that bears an intimate relation to the kind of being he knows himself to be and it is in this behavioral environment that he is motivated to act" (Hallowell 1955:85, 86).

2. "We can view the search for a cognitive view as an exercise in triangulation. Of each trait and pattern the question is asked, 'Of what implicit assumption might this behavior be a logical function?' When enough questions have been asked, the answers will be found to point in a common direction. The model emerges from the point where the lines of answers intersect. . . . In effect, we are dealing with a pyramidal structure; low level regularities and coherences relating overt behavior forms are fitted into higher-level patterns which in turn may be found to fall into place at a still higher level of integration" (Foster 1965).

Chapter 8. Bases of Identity

1. *Revestido* (redressed) and *reparado* (restored) are terms applied to acculturated Indians by Ladinos in Chiapas.

Chapter 9. Depth and Breadth of Perspective

1. Patrick Pyeatt was familiar with Indian cultures of the region, having served in Santiago Atitlán in the early 1960s as a papal volunteer. He spent eight months in Santa María Visitación in 1968-69, funded by a Ford Foundation grant kindly provided us through the University of

Kansas, where I was then employed. Our analysis of the data collected in Santa María Visitación, Panajachel, and Santa Catarina benefited greatly from the assistance of Jean-Pierre Habicht, a medical officer of the World Health Organization at the Institute of Nutrition of Central America and Panama in Guatemala.

2. These revised crude birth rates (see table 24) cover a slightly later span of years, 1955-68, than those included in table 23. The data of table 24 differ from those of table 23 also in the inclusion of foreign Indians in the data of the latter table. In the cases of Santa Catarina and Panajachel, foreign Indian populations in the *municipios* are sizable minorities and could account for some of the differences in crude rates of the two tables.

3. Accurate documentation of interbirth spacing requires accurate documentation of births and deaths (including stillbirths). This documentation was available for the towns under comparison to a degree unusual in nonliterate societies.

Guatemalan law since 1877 has required registration of all births and deaths in *municipio* registries; in the case of deaths, such reporting is necessary to obtain permission to bury in the community cemetery. The accuracy of this reporting is measurable only against memory records of family birth-death histories obtained through house-to-house censusing. Such censusing was undertaken in Visitación by Pyeatt in 1967-68, in Santa Catarina by Tax in 1935 and Stanford University researchers in 1968, and in Panajachel by Tax in 1936 and Hinshaw in 1964. Municipal records were copied and family histories were constructed of all one-wife-one-husband unions begun since 1925. These families total 162 in Panajachel, 112 in Santa Catarina, and 73 in Visitación. When these histories were compared with the census data, the greatest discrepancy was found in Santa Catarina, where municipal records did not include five percent of the births and 7.5 percent of the deaths (stillbirths largely) reported by informants for a sample of 65 families. In Visitación and Panajachel, the municipal records listed over 98 percent of the births and deaths reported in family interviews. I suspect that the explanation for the greater discrepancy in Santa Catarina lies in less thorough recording by one or more secretaries in Santa Catarina's history, rather than in any significant difference in the reporting practices of the Indians. I attribute the faithfulness of the recording of births and deaths by these Indian populations to the long-standing law and also to the settlement pattern: everyone lives within a five-minute walk of the secretary's office in Visitación and Santa Catarina, and within a fifteen-minute walk in Panajachel.

I do not know how accurately abortions have been listed in the municipal records. The law states that any foetus of five or more months should be reported, and the high proportion of stillbirths recorded in all three towns suggests that families do report at least some of the accidental or intentional abortions that occur. Probably few, if any, abortions prior to five months of pregnancy are reported. I am convinced that the incidence of intentional abortion in these communities is very low, given the cultural sanctions on abortion and lack of evidence of effective, institutionalized abortion practices. When abortions do occur late in pregnancy, I have no reason to question the faithfulness of Indians in reporting them as required by law, nor to believe such abortions are less faithfully reported by members of one community than by those of another. To this extent I assume that the spacing intervals compiled for the three communities share equally whatever bias there may be from failure to include all abortions.

4. Seventy-five completed Panajachel families were divided into wealth quartiles (chiefly on the bases of property and annual per capita income) to permit rough correlation of economic status with size of family, child-spacing and cessation of childbearing. No correlation with spacing emerged, but the age of the mother at last birth correlated consistently with wealth: poorest quartile, 37.5 years; second quartile, 38; third quartile, 38.5; and wealthiest quartile, 39 years of age.

5. Lois Paul (personal communication) estimates that twenty to thirty Pedranas have experimented with contraceptive pills, with the chief supplier being the Behrhorst Clinic in Chimaltenango. A Visiteco interning at the same clinic has whetted the curiosity of some Visitecos, but only a couple of families had begun experimenting by 1968. I doubt that more than one or two Panajacheleñas had experimented with contraceptives by 1965; indeed, only two Indians ever asked us about contraception in the course of our eighteen months there.

Glossary

Listed below are the meanings in Panajachel of the Spanish terms used in the text.

Alcalde	Mayor; a civil officer, and in Panajachel the highest annually changing civil officer in the Indian hierarchy
Alguacil	Constable; a civil officer who in a small town like Panajachel functions as messenger, laborer, janitor, and policeman
Alma	Soul
Atol	Beverage of corn meal and water
Bajareque	Wall construction of cane and mud, less permanent, but also less expensive, than adobe brick construction
Brazo	Cylindrical grinding stone used for crushing corn on a larger, oblong stone block
Brujo	Shaman believed to use his powers against others, usually for a fee
Caites	Sandals, usually made of a single sole with attached leather thongs which are passed between the first two toes and around the heel
Cal	Lime, used in cooking and in place of cement in construction
Catequista	Participant in Catholic Action; usually one who regularly attends catechism classes
Chancles	Designation for landed gentry (wealthy Ladinos) earlier this century which has dropped out of use, at least in Panajachel
Characotel	Person believed to assume animal form periodically by virtue of having a spirit with an animal affiliation
Chipilín	Wild herb used in cooking
Cofrade	The highest official of a *cofradía,* and an office in the politico-religious hierarchy
Cofradía	Confraternity; a group of men, consisting of a *cofrade* and two or three *mayordomos,* who have the stewardship of a saint for a year; also, the house of the *cofrade* where the saint is kept.
Comal	Griddle, of clay or tin
Compadre	Fictive kinship designation for two adults, one of whom has asked the other to sponsor or oversee his child in baptism, confirmation, or marriage
Cordón	Rope
Costumbre	Literally "custom," but referring locally to any traditional, especially ritualized, behavior
Creencia	Belief proposition

Cuerda	Land measure; in Panajachel usually 32 *varas* square (0.178 acre)
Finca	Plantation of coffee, cotton, or fruit
Gabán	In Panajachel, a woolen cloak worn by a few of the men
Güisgüil	Vegetable pear
Huipil	Blouse, usually without tailored sleeves
Machete	In Panajachel, a factory-made knife with a short handle and a long blade
Maguey	Plant whose leaf fibers are used for twine and rope products
Mandamientos	A system of enforced labor whereby employers sought and were given quotas of laborers
Mayor	An office in the municipal government and in the Indian hierarchy
Mayordomo	An official of a *cofradía* and of the politico-religious organization
Mecapal	Tumpline
Milpa	Cornfield, in which are grown principally corn, beans, and squash
Monte	The territory outside of town, whether wooded or not
Municipalidad	Town hall
Municipio	Township, the smallest political unit into which Guatemala is divided
Naturaleza	Character, personality traits
Nixtamal	Ground corn mixed with water
Obreros	Workers, employees
Ocote	Pitch pine, used in starting fires
Ojo	Literally "eye," but referring locally to an illness or weakened physical state produced by the gaze ("evil eye") of a person with strong blood
Padrino	Godparent, who is thereby *compadre* to his godchild's parents
Panela	Brown, noncrystallized sugar, usually sold in Panajachel in large balls; two balls form a *mancuerna;* half a ball is a *tapa*
Pepino	Literally "cucumber," but an egg-shaped, hard-skinned vegetable unrelated to the cucumber
Pueblo	Town; the smallest category—followed by *villa* and *ciudad*–of community that is the seat of government of a *municipio;* in Panajachel, applied to the whole delta portion as opposed to the *monte* districts
Pulique	A meat dish, especially a sauce with which meat or fowl is served
Quetzal	Unit of Guatemalan currency, equivalent in value to the U.S. dollar
Regidor	Councilman; an officer in the municipal government and in the Panajachel legal and extralegal hierarchy
Robado	Elopement (literally "stolen")
Rodillera	Small woolen blanket worn by men; in Panajachel, wrapped around the waist and extending to the knees
Ronda	The periodic rounds of the city made by the police or other authority figures such as members of the civil hierarchy, or by spirits
Sacristanes	Sacristans; officials of the church and of the Panajachel religious hierarchy
Suerte	Luck or fate
Taba	A bone (vertebra) used like dice in a game of chance

Temazcal	Sweat bath house, usually made of adobe blocks and located adjacent to the living quarters
Tenemaste	Hearthstone
Zahorin	Indian shaman, curer, diviner
Zarabanda	Public dance in a tavern or *cofradía*

Bibliography

Berkowitz, Leonard
    1963   Social psychological theorizing. In *Theories in contemporary psychology*, edited by Melvin H. Marx. New York, Macmillan.

Cancian, Frank
    1972   *Change and uncertainty in a peasant economy.* Stanford, Stanford University Press.

Colby, Benjamin N., and van den Berghe, Pierre L.
    1969   *Ixil country.* Berkeley, University of California Press.

Foster, George M.
    1965   Peasant society and the image of limited good. *American Anthropologist* 67:293-315.
    1967   *Tzintzuntzan.* Boston, Little Brown and Co.

Hallowell, A. Irving
    1955   *Culture and experience.* Philadelphia, University of Pennsylvania Press.

Hanson, F. Allan, and Martin, Rex
    1973   The problem of other cultures. *Philosophy of the Social Sciences* 3:191-208.

Hinshaw, Robert E., Pyeatt, Patrick, and Habicht, Jean-Pierre
    1972   Environmental effects on child-spacing and population increase in highland Guatemala. *Current Anthropology* 13:218-30.

Hurtado, Juan Jose
    1970   San Juan Sacatepequez. M.A. thesis, University of Kansas.

Huxley, Aldous
    1934   *Beyond the Mexique Bay.* New York, Harper and Brothers.

Leslie, Charles M.
    1960   *Now we are civilized.* Detroit, Wayne State University Press.

Mendelson, E. Michael
    1956   Religion and world-view in Santiago Atitlán. Ph.D. dissertation, University of Chicago.
    1957   Religion and world-view in Santiago Atitlán. Microfilm collection of manuscripts on Middle American cultural anthropology, no. 52. University of Chicago.

Nash, Manning
    1958   *Machine age Maya.* Glencoe, Ill., The Free Press.

Paul, Benjamin, and Paul, Lois
    1963   Changing marriage patterns in a highland Guatemalan community. *Southwestern Journal of Anthropology* 19:131-48.

Radin, Paul
    1927   *Primitive man as a philosopher.* New York, D. Appleton & Co.

Redfield, Robert
    1945   Ethnographic materials on Agua Escondida. Microfilm collection of manuscripts on Middle American cultural anthropology, no. 3. University of Chicago.

Reina, Ruben E.
    1968   *The law of the saints.* New York, Bobbs-Merrill.

Rojas Lima, Flavio, ed.
    1968 *Los pueblos del lago de Atitlán.* El Seminario de Integración Social Guatemalteca. Guatemala.
Saler, Benson
    1968 Beliefs, disbeliefs, and unbeliefs. *Anthropological Quarterly* 41:29-33.
Schmid, Lester
    1967 The role of migratory labor in the economic development of Guatemala. Research paper no. 22. Land Tenure Center, University of Wisconsin.
Schultz, Theodore W.
    1964 *Transforming traditional agriculture.* New Haven, Yale University Press.
Spindler, George, and Spindler, Louise
    1965 The instrumental activities inventory: a technique for the study of the psychology of acculturation. *Southwestern Journal of Anthropology* 21:1-23.
Tax, Sol
    1937 The municipios of the midwestern highlands of Guatemala. *American Anthropologist* 39:423-44.
    1941 World view and social relations in Guatemala. *American Anthropologist* 43:27-42.
    1946 The towns of Lake Atitlán. Microfilm collection of manuscripts on Middle American cultural anthropology, no. 13. University of Chicago.
    1950 Panajachel field notes. Microfilm collection of manuscripts on Middle American cultural anthropology, no. 29. University of Chicago.
    1953 *Penny capitalism: a Guatemalan Indian economy.* Smithsonian Institution. Institute of Social Anthropology, no. 16. Washington, D.C.
Tax, Sol, and Hinshaw, Robert
    1969 The Maya of the midwestern highlands. In *Handbook of Middle American Indians,* vol. 7, edited by Manning Nash. Austin, University of Texas Press.
    1970 Panajachel a generation later. In *The social anthropology of Latin America: essays in honor of Ralph Leon Beals,* edited by Walter Goldschmidt and H. Hoijer. Los Angeles, Center for Latin American Studies, University of California.
Wagley, Charles
    1949 The social and religious life of a Guatemalan village. *Memoirs of the American Anthropological Association,* no. 71.
Wolf, Eric
    1955 Types of Latin American peasantry: a preliminary discussion. *American Anthropologist* 57:452-71.

Index

Acculturation. *See* Ladinoization
Address, ethnic differences in forms of, 68, 69
Adobe construction, differential wealth and, 26-27
Age: belief acceptance and, 84; at marriage, 159
Agriculture: division of land use in, 11; income from, 12-15; preference for, 49; reliance upon, 14-15
Alcohol. *See* Drinking patterns
Assembly of God, 52
Attitudes: toward family planning, 160; toward occupations, 46-52

Bajareque, 24
Baptists, 52
Bathing, 26
Bats, beliefs concerning, 93
Bed-wetting, beliefs concerning, 95-96
Beliefs: assessment of, 73-75; awareness of, 77-79, 142-43, 144; categorization of, 75-77; consistency among, 103; differential acceptance of, 81-89; empirical validation of, 96-97; explanation of, 97-98; inferred, 91-92; Ladino, 81; ladinoization and, 146-47; methodological considerations in structuring of, 98-104; overview of, 104-05; regional comparisons of, 79-81; related, 101-02; stability of, 109-12; structural model of, 105-09, 113-39; theoretical considerations in structuring of, 93-98
Berkowitz, Leonard, 97
Birth rate, 7; community differences in, 157; factors affecting, 159-61
Boys' club, Ladino-Indian relations and, 66-67
Builders. *See* Contractors
Burial, ethnic differences in, 69
Burns, cures for, 96
Businesses, wealth and, 34-36

Cakchiquel, 58
Capital, occupational innovation and, 37
Catequistas, 53; belief acceptance among, 85; *cofradía* service and, 54, 55; number of, 53-54; social relations among, 70. *See also* Catholic Action
Catholic Action: autonomy and, 163-64; *cofradía* service and, 44; establishment of, 53; fiestas sponsored by, 18-19; motivation for entering, 57. *See also* Catequistas; Catholicism; Catholics
Catholicism: education and, 58-59; revitalization of, 53-54. *See also* Catholic Action
Catholics: attitudes toward *cofradías,* 54-55; belief acceptance among, 85-88; distribution of wealth and, 41; dress preferences of, 59-60; occupational preferences of, 51; relations with Protestants, 70. *See also* Catequistas
Centroamericanos, 52
Ceremonies, cost of, 18-19
Chalets, location of, 9-10
Chancles, 67
Chicken, in diet, 16
Class consciousness, wealth and, 37-41
Clothing, 17-18; cost of, 18; occupation and, 59-60, 62; religious affiliation and, 59-60; wealth reflected by, 24, 28-30
Coffee: income from, 12-13; proportion of land planted in, 11
Cofradías: attitudes toward service to, 44-45; Catequista service to, 58; cost of, 18-19, 56; military service and, 54-55; structure of service to, 43; wealth leveling and, 38, 39
Commercialism, social relations and, 64
Compadres, 67-68
Confrade, 43
Construction, preference for, 49
Consumption, conspicuousness of, 38-39
Contraception, 173
Contractors: skills of, 32; wealth and, 33